UNIVERSITY OF

D0275374

The Developing World and State Education

Routledge Studies in Education and Neoliberalism

EDITED BY DAVE HILL, *University of Northampton, UK*

The Developing World and State Education

Neoliberal Depredation and Egalitarian Alternatives

**Edited by Dave Hill
and Ellen Rosskam**

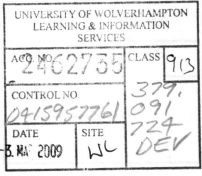

UNIVERSITY OF WOLVERHAMPTON
LEARNING & INFORMATION
SERVICES

ACC. NO. 2462735   CLASS 9(3

CONTROL NO.
0415957761   379.
                 091
DATE   SITE   724
-3. MA² 2009   WL   DEV

Routledge
Taylor & Francis Group
New York   London

First published 2009
by Routledge
270 Madison Ave, New York, NY 10016

Simultaneously published in the UK
by Routledge
2 Park Square, Milton Park, Abingdon, Oxon OX14 4RN

Routledge is an imprint of the Taylor & Francis Group, an informa business

© 2009 Taylor & Francis

Typeset in Sabon by IBT Global.
Printed and bound in the United States of America on acid-free paper by IBT Global.

All rights reserved. No part of this book may be reprinted or reproduced or utilised in any form or by any electronic, mechanical, or other means, now known or hereafter invented, including photocopying and recording, or in any information storage or retrieval system, without permission in writing from the publishers.

Trademark Notice: Product or corporate names may be trademarks or registered trademarks, and are used only for identification and explanation without intent to infringe.

Library of Congress Cataloging in Publication Data
The developing world and state education : neoliberal depredation and egalitarian
  alternatives / edited by Dave Hill and Ellen Rosskam.
    p. cm. — (Routledge studies in education and neoliberalism)
  Includes bibliographical references and index.
    1. Education—Economic aspects—Developing countries—Case studies. 2. Education
and state—Developing countries—Case studies. 3. Neoliberalism—Developing
countries—Case studies. I. Hill, Dave, 1945– II. Rosskam, Ellen, 1960–
    LC67.D44D48 2009
    379.172'4—dc22
    2008017320

ISBN10: 0-415-95776-1 (hbk)
ISBN10: 0-203-88925-8 (ebk)

ISBN13: 978-0-415-95776-2 (hbk)
ISBN13: 978-0-203-88925-1 (ebk)

Contents

Figures

Tables

Foreword

Dave Hill

At a time of the collapse of neoliberal financial systems globally and in most countries, this book critically examines neoliberal policy impacts on schooling/education in the developing world—and promotes Resistance! The contributing authors (who include left and progressive academics and labor organization/social movement activists) analyze developments in Latin America, Mexico, Argentina, Chile, Venezuela, Pakistan, India, Burkina Faso, South Africa, Mozambique, Turkey and China. A companion volume, *The Rich World and the Impoverishment of Education: Diminishing Democracy, Equity and Workers' Rights* (Hill, 2009a) has similar aims with regard to "The Rich World."

Chapters ask 'What neoliberal changes have taken place?' (E.g., privatization, vouchers, marketization, commercialization, commodification, school fees, new brutalist public managerialism, and the assault on the comprehensive/common school principles and on democratic control of schools.) And identify neoliberal 'drivers' or levers—national/transnational corporations, think tanks, pressure groups, state power, ideologies, and discourses taking place in various countries.

Chapters in this volume critically examine neoliberal impacts on equality, equal opportunities and access to schooling and education (as experienced by groups differentiated by social class, race/ethnicity/language, gender, rural/urban differentiation); impacts on democracy/democratic control of schools and education; impacts on critical thinking, and analytical skills among students; and impacts on the rights/pay and condition of education workers. In addition, and 'reforms', their bases, organizational forms, strategies, successes, failures, and prospects for the future. This examination of resistance is carried out in much greater detail in a companion volume to this book, *Contesting Neoliberal Education: Public Resistance and Collective Advance* (Hill, 2009b).

I will now examine some theoretical and academic aspects of neoliberal arguments and offer analyses of their limitations. Neoliberals such as James Tooley (2000, 2001) and neoliberal global organizations such as the World Trade Organization (WTO) (e.g., 2003, 2005) and the International Finance Corporation (IFC) of the World Bank (e.g., IFC, 2001) draw a number of unwarranted implications or conclusions about what they see as the negative role of the state in education/social provision and what neoliberals see as the positive role of the market in education/social provision. These arguments relate to the assumption that *the market/privatization is actually compatible with education.*

Education, however, is not a commodity to be bought and sold. One can buy *the means* to an education, but not the hard graft of autonomous learning itself. John McMurtry (1991, pp. 211–214), among others, has noted that education and unfettered capitalism and globalization hold opposing *goals, motivations, methods,* and *standards of excellence.* McMurtry concludes by suggesting that education and the market also have opposing *standards of freedom.*

1. *The goals of education.* McMurtry (1991: 212) notes that private profit is acquired by a structure of appropriation that excludes others from its possession. The greater its accumulation by any private corporation, the more wealth others are excluded from in this kind of possession. This is what makes such ownership "private."

As McMurtry notes,

Education, in contrast, is acquired by a structure of appropriation that is meant to *not* exclude others from its possession. On the contrary, education is furthered the more it is shared, and the more there is free and open access to its circulation. That is why learning that is not conveyed to others is deemed "lost," "wasted" or "dead." In direct opposition to market exchanges, educational changes flourish most with the unpaid gifts of others and develop the more they are *not* mediated by private possession or profit. (1991: 212)

2. *Opposing motivations.* McMurtry notes that, "the determining motivation of the market is to satisfy the wants of whoever has the money to purchase the goods that are provided. The determining motivation of education is to develop sound understanding *whether it is wanted or not*" (1991: 212) (italics added). "The market by definition can only satisfy the motivations of those who have the money to buy the product it sells." (idem)

   "The place of education, on the other hand, remains a place of education insofar as it educates those whose motivation is to learn, independent of the money-demand they exercise in their learning" (idem). In addition, "development of understanding is necessarily growth of cognitive capacity; wherein satisfaction of consumer wants involves neither, and typically impedes both." (idem)

3. *Opposing methods.* McMurtry suggests that "The method of the market is to buy or sell the goods it has to offer to anyone for whatever price one can get . . . The method of education is never to buy or sell the item

it has to offer, but to require of all who would have it that they fulfill its requirements autonomously . . . Everything that is to be had on the market is acquired by the money paid for it. In contrast, nothing that is learned in education is acquired by the money paid for it." (idem)

He continues, with respect to 4. *Opposing standards of excellence*. "The measures of excellence in the market are (1) how well the product is made to sell, and (2) how problem free the product is and remains for its buyers." (McMurtry, 1991: 113) The measures of excellence in education are (1) how disinterested and impartial its presentation/representations are, regardless of any consideration regarding commercial profit making—it is interested in truth for its own sake, and (2) "how deep and broad the problems it poses are to one who has it" (idem) . . . The first works through "one-sided sales pitches . . . which work precisely because they are *not* understood," the second "must rule out one-sided presentation, appetitive compulsion and manipulative conditioning." (idem)

McMurtry sums up this powerful critique thus: "The better the education, the more its bearers become independent to think and act on their own. The better the market, the more its agents depend on the products and services of others to perform their thinking and doing for them." (idem)

The last critical theoretical point I wish to make here in analyzing the relationship between neoliberalism and education is that the market suppresses critical thought and education itself. Clearly some aspects of the market wish to promote learning—in particular the learning of skills considered appropriate to different strata in the labor market. The point here is that capital seeks to repress those aspects of critical thought, such as those embodied in critical pedagogy, in Marxist and socialist analysis and ideology, which are inimical to its own continuation.

Thus there is the suppression and compression of critical space in education today (Rikowski, 2003). On the one hand, capital requires educated and flexible workers, but on the other hand, capital cannot countenance/ accept that workers should be thinking *fundamental critique* for themselves—or coming across in schools, vocational education or universities. As such, free thinking and oppositional thinking, have been chopped, curtailed, and circumscribed.

Critical space for critical education studies and research is being compressed in many countries through curriculum control, through the remaking of human personality and through a gamut of ideological and in some cases repressive state apparatuses. This is especially so for any fundamental critique. Rikowski describes 'fundamental critique' as "how the core processes and phenomena of capitalist society (value, capital, labour, labour-power, value-creation and capital accumulation and so on) generate contradictions and tensions in everyday life—for individuals, groups, classes, societies and on an international scale." (Rikowski, 2003)

Part of this repression is *The Naturalisation of Capital and the Denaturalisation of Dissent* (Hill, 2004). As Peter McLaren (2000) notes, one of its greatest achievements is that capital presents itself as natural, free, and democratic,

> as if it has now replaced the natural environment. It announces itself through its business leaders and politicians as coterminous with freedom, and indispensable to democracy such that any attack on capitalism as exploitative or hypocritical becomes an attack on world freedom and democracy itself. (p.32)

In analyzing the relationship between education and the market, McMurtry (1991: 213) concludes: "this fundamental contradiction in standards of excellence leads, in turn, to *opposite standards of freedom*. Freedom in the market is the enjoyment of whatever one is able to buy from others with no questions asked, and profit from whatever one is able to sell to others with no requirement to answer to anyone else. Freedom in the place of education, on the other hand, is precisely the freedom to question, and to seek answers, whether it offends people's self-gratification or not."

McMurtry adds (pp. 213–214):

> What is the best policy for buying a product—to assert the customer's claim is always right—is the worst possible policy for a learner. What is the best policy for selling a product—to offend no one and no vested interest—may be the worst possible policy for an educator. The principles of freedom are contradictory.

He proceeds to succinctly (1991) relate his arguments to the "systematic reduction of the historically hard won social institution of education to a commodity for private purchase and sale." (p. 216) "The commodification of education rules out the very critical freedom and academic rigor which education requires to be more than indoctrination." (p. 215)

Much of my own work (e.g. Hill, 1991, 2007; Hill and Boxley, 2007; Macrine, Hill and McLaren, 2009), that of the Hillcole Group of Radical Left Educators in England (Hillcole Group, 1991, 1997) and that of critical pedagogues working within Freirean and Gramscian and other radical and socialist traditions, such as Henry Giroux, Ira Shor, Peter McLaren, Joe Kincheloe, Donaldo Macedo, Peter Mayo, Paula Allman, calls for critical education and for the development of teachers as critical transformative intellectuals. Big business and their government agents now call most of the shots in university research—hence the potential importance of independent think tanks and research units. And of individual oppositional voices. Important, too, are the collective efforts of egalitarian, socialist, social democratically oriented, liberal political organizations and their publications and demonstrations—their fight back against exploitation and oppression.[1]

RESTRAINING AND RESISTING NEOLIBERALISM

There are three major restraining forces on the activities of neoliberalism: infrastructural, consumer related regulation, and legitimation.

Infrastructural Restraints

The first is the need for an educational, social, transport, welfare, housing, etc. infrastructure to enable workers to get to work, to be trained for different levels of the workforce, to be relatively fit and healthy. This restraint, though, is *minimal*—it can cope with, co-exist with, extreme poverty and the existence of billions of humans at the margins of existence. It is a basic needs provision that says nothing. It has no implications at all for equality or equity in society or in education. Indeed, as Pilger (2002) points out, and as is pointed out in a further companion volume to this book, *Global Neoliberalism and its Consequences* (Hill and Kumar, 2009), it has no implications even for the maintenance of human lives. In effect, the depredations of neoliberal globalizing capital condemns millions—in particular those in the Third World displaced by the collapse of national agricultural industries that are of no use as either producers or consumers—to death.

Regulating Capital

The second restraint on capitalism is consumer dissatisfaction and consumer protection in the form of regulations. These, and inspectors of various sorts are criticized by neoliberal and conservative/nonconservative critics as "red tape" and as "bureaucrats." Yet due to a lack of regulation and enforcement in Britain, BSE (bovine spongiform encephalopathy, or "mad cow disease") and foot-and-mouth disease flourished and were exported to continental Europe, and, in the aftermath of the privatization of Railtrack (the railway line network) in Britain, with its subsequent reduction of maintenance workforce and monitoring of safety, the number of dead in rail accidents has shot up.

State regulation operates against the freedom of capitalism to do totally as it pleases. Hence, in Britain or in India or other countries, the state policy on schools and universities is to deregulate them, to "set them free," to allow them to charge what they want and run their own affairs (see Sadgopal, 2006 for the Indian context). These state policies are similar to the "anti-bureaucracy" policies of the Republican Party in the USA and its demands for privatized "public sector" education and for education vouchers.

The "regulatory" model can be weak or strong, though the state is far from neutral with respect to capital, seeking to maximize the profits and profitability of national capital.[2] It can demand only basic standards (perhaps failing to inspect regularly, and frequently open to corruption) or it can demand strong controls, including controls over profits, as, rarely, during some periods of social democratic rule by the Labour Party in Britain.

It is interesting that in a number of rich states such as Britain and the USA, some of the most vigorously enforced current standards are those in state/public education, as noted with respect to the USA by Hursh (2001, 2008), Lipman (2004), Mathison and Ross (2002), Ross and Gibson (2007)—testimony perhaps to the crucial nature of the state apparatus of schooling, as noted above by Rikowski (2001a). While governments may well wish to privatize education, they feel they need to retain control of its content, its mechanisms and monitoring of ideological reproduction and the production/reproduction of labor power.

Resistance to and Delegitimation of Capital

The third, and most powerful, restraint is that capital (and the political parties it funds and influences) needs to persuade the people that neoliberalism—competition, privatization, poorer standards of public services, greater inequalities between rich and poor—is legitimate. If not, there would be a delegitimation crisis where government and the existing system would be widely seen as grossly unfair and inhumane. The government and existing system, nationally and globally, may also be seen as in the pocket of the international and/or national ruling classes, impoverishing millions while CEOs and the superrich executives and their politicians consume the surplus value produced by sweat shop deregulated workers—indeed the working classes *per se,* throughout the world.

To stop delegitimation and to ensure that the majority of the population consider that the government and the economic system of private monopoly ownership is legitimate, the state uses the ideological apparatuses such as schools and universities to "naturalize" capitalism—to make the existing status quo seem "only natural," to hegemonize its "common sense" (e.g., Mathison & Ross, 2002) so that populations are 'interpellated' or 'hailed' (Althusser, 1971; Cole, 2008) by the 'common sense' nostrums and beliefs and slogans of neoliberal capitalism.

Chapters such as this one are written to contest the legitimacy of government policy and its subordination to and participation in the neoliberal project of global capital, a project encompassing social experimentation and what Harvey (2005) calls "the class war from above" (see also Dumenil and Levy, 2004)—the diversion and appropriation of welfare funding and wages into the pockets of a small minority of the superrich. (A perfect example is President George Bush's "trillion dollar tax cuts" that benefited mainly the superrich). The current crisis of capital accumulation, as predicted by Marx & Engels (1977 [1847]), has led to the intensification of the extraction of surplus value, the progressing global immiseration of workers, and the intensification of control of populations by the ideological and repressive state apparatuses indentified and analysed by Althusser (Althusser, 1971; see also Hill, 1989, 2001, 2005, 2007; Greaves, Hill and Maisuria, 2007).

Clearly for the European and North American eco-warriors Rikowski described in *The Battle of Seattle* (2001) and for various groups of, trade unionists, social movements, greens, and groups such as the World Development Movement, Attac, and Globalise Resistance, the current system is not legitimate. Nor for socialist and Marxist groups, partiers and organisations. And the current system also lacks legitimacy for many in academe and many in the population at large, those who see that material conditions of their existence are demeaned and degaraded by neoliberal capitalism—or, indeed, by the capitalist system itself. Nonetheless, at the current time, a lack of effective widespread social mobilization for positive change has left the current system, the status quo for the most part intact. In many countries, such as the UK and the USA, and in some countries in the Developing World, all main parties, all parties supported by pro-capitalist mass media, support neoliberal policies to one degree or the other. However, currently, in late 2008, the antineoliberal tide is sweeping throug the electorates and govenrments of Latin America, indeed, in a socialist direction in Venezuela and Bolivia, for example and the current downturn in the profitability of capital, and the downward pressure on real wages and on "the social wage" (of welfare and social benefits) are seeing growth in support for anticapitalist movement and mobilizations throughout the Rich, Poor and Developing Worlds (see for example, the reports in *International Viewpoint*, e.g. 2008; and in *Radical Notes*, e.g. 2008).

In middle income countries in particular, a rapid growth of the middle class often promulgates widespread support for neoliberal reforms, with little consideration for the life opportunities of the poorest segments of society. In developing countries, the small percentage of people at the top rung of the socioeconomic ladder remains fairly steady in relation to the overall population of those countries.

We should recognize the opposition to neoliberalism, privatization, and land takeovers that does exist in huge and small social mobilizations, trade unions and peasant organization actions, for example. A companion volume in this series, *Contesting Neoliberal Education: Public Resistance and Collective Advance* (Hill, 2008) details examples of resistance across rich, middle income and low income countries.

The current system also lacks legitimacy for groups of workers and others throughout the world who see their governments bowing before the might of international capital, who see their national government elites and accompanying military cavalries and riot police seeking to ensure that all spheres of social life are incorporated within the orbit of global capital. Educators are implicated in the process like everyone else. The school or university and other areas of cultural and ideological reproduction (such as newsrooms and film studios) are no hiding places.

Increasingly, across the globe, educational debate is turning in the economically rich world from debates about "standards" and "school effectiveness" to wider questions such as "what is education for"? In the economically poorer world, the debate is turning to questions of free access to schooling and higher education—and why they do not have it anymore where once it existed.

The current global questioning of neoliberal fiscal and economic policies may or may not extend to questioning key and typical aspects of neoliberal policies in education—such as privatisation, decentralisation, driving down of education workers' rights, conditions and salaries, and the imposition of new public managerialist techniques of running schools and colleges/universities. We hope that the data and arguments and experiences and resistances expressed in this book will empower and promote resistance to neoliberal capitalist policies and their anti-egalitarian, anti-democratic, anti-collegiate/collective, and their anti-critique effects. It is my hope that this book, and this series, might even work towards the replacement of capitalist education per se, and the promotion of an egalitarian, democratic, collegiate, collective, and critical education globally—for all.

NOTES

1. Independent Marxist and left radical think tanks and research and campaigning groups include the Institute for Education Policy Studies (http://www.ieps.org.uk) and radical groups such as, in Britain, the Hillcole Group of Radical Left Educators (see http://www.ieps.org.uk), and the Campaign for the Future of Higher Education (http://www.cfhe.org.uk). In the USA, see the Rethinking Schools collective and publishers/activists (http://www.rethinkingschools.org), and The Rouge Forum (http://www.rougeforum.org).

2. The state is not neutral with respect to capital—but some state regulation is, to a greater or lesser extent, in the interests of national capital. In some respects national capital needs to regulate individual firms and enterprises, "rogue" capitalist operations in the interests of national capital as a whole. Clearly much of this regulation is voluntary (as with the Stock Exchange in Britain and with the Press Complaints Commission in Britain), and clearly this regulation is often not only weak, but also ineffective (as, for example in the Enron scandal, or, indeed, globally, the Chernobyl, Bhopal, and other toxic/nuclear escape disasters).The interests of capital are clearly contradictory—for example, capital requires an efficient and cheap transport system for transporting labor and goods. This interest is in contradiction to its desire not to pay for it through taxation on profits. How this works out historically and in different national settings relates to the balance of class forces and their political expression. Similarly, while politically usually acting in concert against the forces and interests of the working classes, there are different interests between different fractions of capital, for example finance capital and manufacturing capital, and between national and international/transnational capital.

REFERENCES

Althusser, L. (1971) Ideology and State Apparatuses, in L. Althusser, *Lenin and Philosophy and Other Essays*. London: New Left Books.

Cole, M. (2008) *Marxism and Educational Theory: Origins and Issues*. London: Routledge.

Dumenil, G. & Levy, D. (2004) *Capital resurgent: Roots of the neoliberal revolution*. London: Harvard University Press.

Greaves, N., Hill, D. and Maisuria, A. (2007) Embourgeoisment, Immiseration, Commodification—Marxism Revisited: a Critique of Education in Capitalist Systems. Journal for Critical Education Policy Studies, 5(1). Online at http://www.jceps.com/index.php?pageID=article&articleID=83

Harvey, D. (2005) *A brief history of neoliberalism*. Oxford : Oxford University Press.

Hill, D. (1989) *Charge of the Right Brigade: the radical right's attack on teacher education*. Brighton, UK: Institute for Education Policy Studies. Available at: http://www.ieps.org.uk.cwc.net/hill1989.pdf

———. (1991) *What's left in teacher education?* London: Tufnell Press.

———. (2001) State Theory and the Neoliberal Reconstruction of Schooling and Teacher Education: a structuralist neo-Marxist critique of postmodernist, quasi-postmodernist, and culturalist neo-Marxist theory, *British Journal of Sociology of Education*, 22(1), pp. 137–157.

———. (2004) Books, banks and bullets: Controlling our minds the global project of imperialistic and militaristic neo-liberalism and its effect on education policy. *Policy futures*, 2 (3 & 4). Retrieved from http:www.wwwords.co.uk/pfi e/

———.(2005) State Theory and the Neoliberal Reconstruction of Schooling and Teacher Education, in G. Fischman, P. McLaren, H. Sünker & C. Lankshear (Eds) *Critical Theories, Radical Pedagogies and Global Conflicts*. Boulder: Rowman & Littlefield.

———. (2007) Critical teacher education, New Labour, and the global project of neoliberal capital. *Policy futures*, 5 (2). Online at http://www.wwwords.co.uk/pfi e/content/pdfs/5/issue5_2.asp

———. (ed.) (2009a) *The Rich World and the Impoverishment of Education: Diminishing Democracy, Equity and Workers' Rights*. New York: Routledge.

———. (ed.) (2009b) *Contesting neoliberal education: Public resistance and collective advance*. London; New York: Routledge.

Hill, D. & Boxley, S. (2007) Critical teacher education for economic, environmental and social justice: An ecosocialist manifesto. *The Journal for Critical Education Policy Studies*, 5 (1).Online at *www.jceps.com*

Hill, D. and Kumar, R. (eds.) (2009) *Global Neoliberalism and Education and its Consequences*. New York: Routledge.

Hillcole Group. (1991) *Changing the future: Redprint for education*. London: Tufnell Press.

———. (1997) *Rethinking education and democracy: A socialist alternative for the twenty first century*. London: Tufnell Press.

Hursh, D. W. (2001) Neoliberalism and the control of teachers, students, and learning: The rise of standards, standardization and accountability. *Cultural Logic*, 4 (1). Retrieved from http://www.eserver.org/clogic/4–1/4–1.html

———. (2008) *High-stakes testing and the decline of teaching and learning: The real crisis in education*. Lanham, MD: Rowman and Littlefield.

International Finance Corporation (IFC). (2001) *Investing in private education: IFC's strategic directions*. Washington, DC: IFC. Online at www.ifc.org/../$FILE/Final%20Public%20Version%20Education%20Strategy%20Paper %202001.pdf–

International Viewpoint (2008) Online at http://www.internationalviewpoint.org/

Lipman, P. (2004) *High stakes education: Inequality, globalization, and urban school reform*. New York: Routledge.

Macrine, S.; Hill, D. & McLaren, P. (eds.) (2009) *Critical pedagogy: Theory and praxis*. London: Routledge.

Marx, K. & Engels, F. [1847] (1977) The Communist Manifesto, in *Karl Marx and Frederick Engels, Selected Works*. London: Lawrence & Wishart.

Mathison, S.; & Ross, E. W. (2002) The hegemony of accountability in schools and universities. *Workplace: A journal for academic labor*, 5 (1). Retrieved from http://www.louisville.edu/journal/workplace/issue5p1/mathison.html

McLaren, P. (2000) *Che Guevara, Paulo Freire, and the pedagogy of revolution.* Lanham, MD: Rowman and Littlefield.

McMurtry, J. (1991) Education and the market model. *Journal of the Philosophy of Education,* 25 (2), 209–217.

Pilger, J. (2002, November 4) The new protest movement: Something is stirring among the people. *New Statesman,* pp.11–12. Retrieved from http://www.zmag.org/content/showarticle.cfm?SectionID=15&ItemID=2579

Radical Notes (2008) Online at http://radicalnotes.com/content/view/12/26/

Rikowski, G. (2001) *The battle in Seattle.* London: Tufnell Press.

———. (2003) *The suppression and compression of critical space in education today.* Paper presented at University College Northampton.

Ross, E. W. & Gibson, R. (eds.) *Neoliberalism and education reform.* Cresskill, NJ: Hampton Press.

Sadgopal, A. (2006) Dilution, distortion and diversion: A post-Jomtien reflection on education policy. In Kumar, R. (Ed.), The crisis of elementary education in India. New Delhi: Sage Publications, pp. 92–136.

Tooley, J. (2000) *Reclaiming education.* London: Cassell.

———. (2001) *The global education industry* (2nd ed.). London: Institute for Economic Affairs.

World Trade Organization (WTO). (2003) *GATS: Fact and fiction. Misunderstandings and scare stories.* Geneva, WTO: http://www.wto.org/english/tratop_e/serv_e/gats_factfictionfalse_e.htm

———. (2005) *World Trade Organization services database online.* http://tsdb.wto.org/wto/WTOHomepublic.htm

Acknowledgments

With thanks to my daughter Naomi Hill for her proofing and corrections and help and smiles and wonderful sunniness in Brighton, England, and to her son, my grandson, Josh Akehurst, eighteen years old on the day this final set of proof corrections—the final manuscript—was sent off, 18th November, 2008. Thanks to Josh for the proofing work he has done on this book, and also for his work assisting with The Journal for Critical Education Policy Studies, www.jceps.com, where a number of these book chapters appeared in earlier incarnations. And thanks, too, to Eleanor Chan of IBT Global in Troy, New York for her proofing and efficiency and greatness to work with, and, with this book, for her tolerance!—the other three books in this series were on time!—this one was a little delayed. And thanks to Benjamin Holtzman at Routledge in New York for his support and encouragement and patience.

Thanks also to the radical academics, labour movement activists, and leftists and all those exposing and challenging the dominant neoliberal capitalist hegemony- and pointing the way to resistance to national and global economic, social and political injustices and oppression. Not all the writers by any means share my own democratic socialist/ Marxist beliefs and activism—writers in this book come from a variety of left and radical political and ideological traditions and perspectives. Some in this book are working to and wishing to reform capitalism. Others (such as me) wish to replace capitalism—characterised as it is by its essentially exploitative and oppressive relationships—while at the same time pushing for, working for, agitating for, progressive, egalitarian reforms. But, as a group of writers and activists, we, in this book, and this series of four books in the Routledge Education and Neoliberalism series, unite in our criticisms of neoliberal Capital, and in our belief at its replacement. A replacement, that at this current juncture of a crisis of capital accumulation—the near-global credit crunch and the discrediting of neoliberal policies in finance and economics at least, appears to be rather more likely than had previously been thought!

For a fairer, egalitarian and socialist world, and education systems, for the billions not the billionaires, for children and students and teachers throughout the countries of the Earth—and for my grandchildren Josh

Akehurst, Hannah Hunt, Jamie Beaton-Hill and Ella Beaton-Hill. With love, passion, hope, analysis and organisation.

Dave Hill
18 November 2008
University of Northampton,
England and The Journal for
Critical Education Policy Studies at
www.jceps.com

1 Introduction

Ellen Rosskam

CONTEXTUALIZING EDUCATION LIBERALIZATION THROUGH NEOLIBERAL REFORMS, STATE GOVERNANCE, AND STABILITY OF NATION-STATES

In low- and middle-income countries, relegating education from the state—as an essential public service—to the market, is often used as an often, but not always unspoken excuse for governments to reduce spending on public services. Governments can thus allocate their budgets differently than would have been considered essential and socially acceptable in the past, particularly prior to the mid and late 1970s.

Curriculum control through the state is, in most cases, equal and equivalent nationwide, in any country. Curriculum control through private, market driven educational institutions is often left up to the individual institution, often driven to some extent by the private funders of a particular private institution. Even in countries where the state requires *all* educational institutions—including private institutions—to follow state approved curricula, private institutions nonetheless often have much more scope and flexibility to alter or include non–state dictated curricula. In addition, where private institutions are state required to be nonprofit, all too often the state 'looks the other way' when investors make personal financial profit nonetheless.

Where private educational institutions have proliferated in low- and middle-income countries, as described in all of the chapters in this book, corresponding growth of government inspectors of educational institutions has not increased in the proportion needed to monitor schools properly. On the contrary, with the proliferation of private education institutions, in low- and middle-income countries in particular, most governments have actually decreased their budget allocations to state inspectorates, shifting public budget allocations elsewhere. Where financial commitment and the needed increase in human resources for inspectorates by the state are insufficient, the space and scope for maneuvering around state required curriculum can only grow in private institutions. The bottom line becomes clear—who really knows whether a given private institution is really following the state approved curriculum to its full extent? If followed to its full extent as in public/state schools, there would be little room left in the classroom for alteration, although patterns and methods of teaching certainly leave varying degrees of room for differentiation from school to school. Particularly in middle-income countries, there tends to be a continuum of evolution in pedagogical styles, as more teachers gain exposure to different learning and teaching techniques and concepts, and where more international exchanges take place. Thus what has often been a tradition of passive rote learning has the chance to shift to more interactive and student centered learning, as opposed to strictly teacher centered learning. Middle-income countries may have more opportunities to benefit from such openings due to a generally higher level of interaction with and exchange programs with different countries, as well as more possibilities, often financial, for teachers to attend conferences where new ideas can be presented and shared, or to obtain access to continued training or skills development.[1] This trend generally has more opportunity to take root in middle-income countries, in particular. Low-income countries[2] tend to have fewer opportunities for teacher exchange programs, and exposure to newer teaching techniques, dedicated to the development of critical, creative, and analytical thinking skills, as well as to active student interaction and engagement in the learning process.

Neoliberal reforms in education do not come alone. They are typically accompanied by similar reforms, particularly through privatization, of a range of essential public services, which have traditionally been viewed and socially deemed as a core role of government, and with governments playing their much needed role in *governing* essential public services. In additional to education, other core public services which have been reformed, privatized, marketized, commercialized to a degree or another in countries around the world include: health services, pensions, social services for the elderly and for children, labor market training services, public employment services, credit rating services, and criminal care services—prisons in particular.

While global trade union federations such as Public Services International (PSI) and Education International (EI) have produced a significant body of knowledge in the area of education privatization (PSI covers all areas of public services while EI concentrates exclusively on education), much more research is still needed, particularly to describe the changes and impacts of these reforms in low income and the least developed countries. Research is needed in developing and transitional economies to further describe the impacts of these neoliberal reforms on workers in core public services, on workers' ability to deliver quality services, and on the impacts of changes on the recipients of services. An important global state of the art review of what is known to date around the world (Rosskam [ed.] 2006) has revealed a dismal picture. The resulting trends globally indicate that a two tiered, class based system of services is appearing and which has already taken firm root in many developing and transitional economies, preceded by similar reforms in many industrialized countries. The trends indicate that those who can pay for services obtain what were, pre-1980s, essential government services—now private services. Those who cannot pay for private services either do not obtain any service at all (which is critical in all areas but which can be devastating and life altering in the areas of health and educational services), lack access to services, or get less quality services than those who can pay for private services. Concurrently, for workers in these areas of services, while the private sector in some cases may offer higher wages to attract the best workers, often conditions of work are worse than in the public sector (see, for example, Chapter 2 on Latin America, Chapter 8 on Pakistan, and Chapter 10 on Burkina Faso). Some examples of worse employment conditions in the private educational sector in low and middle-income countries include a lack of employment security, lack of severance pay requirement in the case of job loss, lack of pension contribution requirement by employers, lack of the employer requirement to provide notice in the case of laying off workers, longer working hours, weekend work, more teaching hours required per week or per month than in the public sector, lack of access to skills development and further training, and worse conditions of work in terms of occupational health and safety for workers (Schnall, Dobson, Rosskam [eds.] [forthcoming 2008]).

With a lack of government inspectors to monitor effectively the proliferation of private schools in addition to the existing number of public schools, many private educational institutions take advantage of this gap in government regulation, monitoring, and enforcement, and abandon educational workers to a life of increased insecurity. Typically, public sector schools provided and still provide employment security, a limit on working and teaching hours, pension accrual, and the requirement for the state to give notice, legally sound reason, and severance pay in the event that an educational worker was to be laid off (Hill, in Rosskam [ed.] 2006, pp. 3–54; Hartmann, Haslinger, and Scherrer, in Rosskam [ed.] 2006, pp. 55–119).

Since the 1980s, in low- and middle-income countries pressure driven by monetary loan based *requirements* to reduce government services and government size overall has left many countries with little choice but to reduce government spending on what were traditionally considered essential state provided services, and to shift such services to the market, with little or no control. The downsizing of core government services and corresponding state spending on such services has been accompanied by a worrying lack of governance in countries where the market has taken precedence over government provided services. Education is an area needing governance by an overarching state body. State governance is the only means of ensuring regulation and enforcement, more equitable provision of schools across country populations, and more equitable conditions and terms of work for education providers, preventing the creaming off of the best teachers and administrators to the private sector, leaving those who cannot pay for private educational services either without access or with access to poorer quality education than students attending private institutions.

It does not take much time before such inequalities reveal the inevitable social repercussions of reform catalyzed transitions. By marketizing educational services, population shifts occur in access to labor market opportunities and quality of jobs for the poor or lower-income groups who were not able to pay for private educational services prior to young people entering the labor market. This translates into increased class differentials and increased income inequality in countries that often cannot absorb the shocks that accompany the rapid growth in social disparities (see Chapter 7 on Turkey, for example). Even rich countries have difficulties in absorbing the shocks that accompany the growth in social disparities, although they are able to absorb such shocks better than low- and middle-income countries, which have little margin to address and redress even further increases in social inequality than already exist. Such shocks can manifest themselves as festering social wounds, which may take time, even decades, to emerge and require redressing to prevent social instability, particularly in low-income countries. Notwithstanding, the growth of social disparity and of income inequality must be seen as a risk factor for social instability. This is the case even for middle-income countries.

Upward mobility tends to be a myth of the promise of neoliberal economic reforms for most people, particularly those in developing countries and for the poorest segments of society in middle-income countries. Even in those developing countries where more children have gained access to primary and/or secondary education, this has not been equated with real upward mobility amongst the poor. In direct contrast, however, amongst families that can pay for private schooling and private university education in low- and middle-income countries, the social status value of private education, the financially backed and linked networks existing in and through such institutions, and the social value often equated with the quality of privately funded institutions compared with public educational services is very often a guarantee to upward mobility for young, newly educated people. Their access to quality jobs or skills based jobs in the labor market and the financially linked networks that enable parachuting graduates into good, well-paid jobs ensure a bright future for many young people in developing and transitional countries. This group tends to constitute what are viewed as the "winners" in society.

Those whose families cannot pay for such lifelong opportunities often witness their children remaining at the same socioeconomic status level as the parents or at the same level as that achieved before receiving any education at all. This group tends to constitute what are viewed as the "losers" in society. This is a major element in the cycle of poverty, and access to primary or secondary education is not the only answer to end the cycle. Equality and equity in the type and quality of education received across a population is needed to level the playing field, to help lift the poor out of poverty by providing them with equal access to opportunities on the labor market and equal access to real skills development. Achieving this requires political commitment and/or social mobilization to insist on change (see Chapter 11 on South Africa, for example).

In our post-9/11 world, there is increasing concern about creating and ensuring social stability, especially for countries considered as geopolitically "critical" to the more powerful countries. In those countries considered to be geopolitically "critical" (by the United States and member states of the European Union in particular), concerted attempts to ensure stability, to promote the rapid growth of "transitional democracy" in newly democratic or newly democratizing countries, to further democracy in already democratic states, and to ensure growth in free trade and market driven services globally are the main and often sole foci of foreign policy by the leading industrialized countries. Some of the outcomes of what is often a tunnel vision in foreign policy making include increased external pressures on sovereign states, interference in national policy making, increased pressure for market driven reforms of public services, pressure on governments to rapidly conform to international trade liberalization agreements in areas such as education, and a strong focus on militaristic action to help ensure national stability in countries considered as critical nations for the West.

These pressures are not necessarily based on principles of social justice, equity or equality. In fact, there would appear to be little, if any, concern at all for the impacts on populations from such external pressures. In addition, under such pressures and accompanying constraints, national governments often exhibit little concern for the most vulnerable groups in their countries, and frequently implement insufficient or inadequate measures to ensure equal access to quality education for all, to give one example. With the reduction in government size required as a condition of loans from international financial institutions during the 1980s and 1990s, many low- and middle-income country governments are simply unable to respond effectively to new and old challenges faced within their countries.

With many governments increasingly unable to govern effectively since the late 1980s, the private market for essential services, such as education, becomes essentially a free-for-all, with little control, regulation or enforcement by the state. Ironically, while Western foreign policy is concerned primordially with national stability in geopolitically "critical" countries, little or no attention from without or from within is given to the threat of instability as a direct result of the growth in income inequality and growth of social disparities in those same "critical" countries. History has shown repeatedly that where there is tunnel vision in policy making, there is a high risk of being blindsided, or made vulnerable from exactly where one was not looking.

The social impacts of education liberalization (and the liberalization of other essential public services) in low- and middle-income countries are a breeding ground for such risks of social instability. The repercussions may take decades to emerge, by which time probably only historians will attempt to look back and view social and foreign policies made decades earlier as correlated with the civil strife, national instability, and even wars that may have later ensued. Policy driven "social experimentation" continues (see Chapter 9 on India, for example). As such, it seems fair to wonder whether policymakers take the time to read and consider alternative policy recommendations, particularly those related to social protection and social and economic security, and to review the research findings that exist today which demonstrate how past policies that have since been viewed by many researchers and scientists as social experimentation (because they had not been previously studied or tried, but were nonetheless imposed on countries in transition or in development) resulted in widespread negative consequences, even devastating consequences, in many countries (Afford, 2003; Annycke, Bonnet, Khan, Figueiredo, Rosskam, Standing, 2004; Rosskam and Loos, 2003). Thus, who are the winners and who are the losers in society due to education liberalization needs to be viewed from a wider optic—one which attempts to assess what is good for the individual country overall, and not good only for selected groups or classes out of the general population. If national stability in "critical" countries is truly a key objective among Western countries, then investing heavily in health and education in those countries and promoting the introduction of strong social protection programs based on principles of universalism and citizenship rights are among the best measures to ensure long-term stability.

Whereas people in Western countries have achieved the right of freedom of speech and freedom of expression such that they are able to mock or criticize their political leaders on the front pages of newspapers, on television, and in all spheres of public life, it is worth noting that in the majority of countries in the world, such guaranteed rights to freedom of speech and expression still do not exist in real terms (see, for example, Chapter 12 on Mozambique and Chapter 10 on Burkina Faso). Democracy is a process, one that will be ongoing for a very long time in most countries. But even in countries with a long history of democracy, fundamental rights that were often won through bloodshed can be whittled away from citizens, and even offered up *by* citizens when they are sufficiently co-opted into thinking that weaker rights may help in protecting their country against potential enemies. The bottom line is that hard-won rights need to be guarded vigilantly at all times, even in existing democratic states (see Chapter 6 on Chile, for example).

THIS BOOK

This volume aims to explore the social consequences of the liberalization of education on low- and middle-income countries. Discussing from national country perspectives as well as one regional perspective for Latin America, the chapters in this volume bring together the diverse aspects of the impacts of neoliberalism on education, the mechanics of change from public education to private in low- and middle-income countries, and the various impacts on education workers. The chapters also present discussions of resultant negative social repercussions that have been witnessed and documented. Empirical findings are used as the basis for this global perspective of the range of impacts in low- and middle-income countries.

In **Chapter 2: Neoliberalism and Education in Latin America: Entrenched Problems, Emerging Alternatives, Adam Davidson-Harden and Daniel Schugurensky** examine the impact of neoliberalism on education in Latin America, and how it affected teachers and students. In Latin America, neoliberalism took off in Chile on September 11, 1973, with the coup d'état that overthrew the government of Salvador Allende. The military dictatorship of Pinochet immediately began to implement a set of economic policies recommended by the 'Chicago boys,' led by Milton Friedman. Friedman equated free markets with social and political freedom, but the only freedom—with political opposition incarcerated, killed, or exiled, and the Parliament closed—was the freedom of the government to pass policies without public deliberation. Sooner or later, with the spread of military regimes in the region, mounting external debts, conditionalities, and the hegemony of promarket ideologies in ruling circles, neoliberalism broadened to most countries in the region. Whereas neoliberal pundits promised that privatization and structural adjustment would bring a rising tide lifting all boats and that all classes would benefit through the spillover effect, during the last two decades Latin America was the most unequal continent on the planet. In the conclusions, the authors make note of recent changes in Latin American politics whereby many countries in the region are moving beyond the Washington consensus and are promoting viable democratic alternatives to neoliberalism in the economic, social, and educational arenas.

In **Chapter 3: World Bank and the Privatization of Public Education: A Mexican Perspective, Gian Carlo Delgado-Ramos and John Saxe-Fernández** provide a close inspection of current privatizing programs of public education, particularly higher education, for both the north and Global south, and the radical impacts and consequences as "market forces" reconfigure a) the number and type of potential students, b) the structure and content of study programs, c) teaching procedures, as well as d) the types of science and technology emphasized. The effects on the skill acquisition of labor, the growing "links" and dependencies created by the "marriage" of universities with multinational corporations, the increased brain drain—from the Global south to the north—as well as the chronic technological dependency of underdeveloped countries being fostered, are topics addressed in this chapter. An overall assessment of the World Bank's critical role in these processes through the "filtration" of its conditionality in the host country's public budget design is offered.

In **Chapter 4: Argentina: Growth, Height, and Crisis of Teachers' Opposition to Neoliberal Reforms 1991–2001, Julián Gindin** analyzes how the history of Argentina from 1991–2001 has been a history of neoliberal hegemony and decay. The "Convertibility Plan," sanctioned in April of 1991, pegged the peso to the dollar one-to-one. The Convertibility Plan began a new epoch of greater ideological consensus and political/economic stability by the Menem government. A little more than ten years later, in December of 2001, enormous social mobilization and unrest forced the early resignation of Fernando de la Rúa, who had been elected president because of his opposition to the policies of Carlos Menem, but had maintained the political policies of his predecessor.

In **Chapter 5: Venezuela: Higher Education, Neoliberalism, and Socialism, Thomas Muhr and Antoni Verger** analyze the Higher Education For All (HEFA) policies and practices in the Bolivarian Republic of Venezuela. In the construction of a 21st-century socialism, universal access to higher education has not only become a constitutional right but also assumes a pivotal role in both the repayment of the social debt and in the country's 'endogenous development.' The authors contextualize HEFA with exclusion from access to lower education levels under 1990s neoliberalism and draw attention to the nonformal education programs (missions), which support the HEFA policies. They explore the strategic role ascribed to higher education (HE) in the Bolivarian government's pursuance of social transformation and argue that HEFA poses a counterhegemonic challenge to the prevalent global HE agenda of commodification and privatization. Muhr and Verger conclude that Venezuela's holistic approach toward a more egalitarian society should receive substantially more attention by the international education and development community than is currently the case.

In **Chapter 6: Legacy Against Possibility: Twenty-Five Years of Neoliberal Policy in Chile, Jill Pinkney Pastrana** demonstrates that Chile is a country that can claim as its legacy an extremely well organized, relatively egalitarian, and effective public education system. It is also the first country to have systematically enacted and restructured its entire education system along neoliberal lines. In 1973, the political and economic changes that occurred following the Pinochet military coup created a number of interesting challenges concerning the organization and purpose of education in Chile. During the 1980s the ruling military junta directed the country and all of its institutions firmly toward the global marketplace. Neoliberal education reform and the 'market-logic' that ideologically grounds such reform, was imposed onto the educational system of Chile. These reforms created a new vision and organization for education in Chile. An educational system whose mandate had previously been firmly rooted in ideas of equity and opportunity was quickly shifted to one focused on efficiency and competition. These changes radically reformed the education system in Chile, both structurally and ideologically, and despite an ongoing series of reforms following redemocratization in 1989, neoliberal policies and their accompanying ideologies create numerous challenges for education in terms of quality, equity, and democratic participation.

In **Chapter 7: A Class Perspective on the New Actors and Their Demands from the Turkish Education System, Fuat Ercan and Ferda Uzunyayla** analyze changes taking place in the education system of Turkey. The analysis is based on the objective of uncovering the class dimensions of these changes. Before pointing to the new class demands on education, the authors consider the 'technical' and 'legitimizing' concepts currently related to education. Such an analysis is necessary as it uncovers both the structural transformations in capitalism and the demands of classes and actors within the process of transformation. The claims of organizations of education related groups on education are considered at two levels: national and international. At both levels changes taking place in education are considered as a 'technical' necessity despite the fact that the basic structural determinant of the changes is the self-production of labor power. Next, the authors consider new class demands on the reproduction of labor power through changes in education, and the resultant reforms (legal changes) and other state projects. The study tries to understand changes in the education system not through the state but through the agency of class, reflected in state action. The chapter points out that the main orientation of reforms and projects is to establish parallels between education and labor markets for the advantage of capital. The study claims that EU policies are one of the major components which pursue such parallels. In summary, this chapter analyzes the changes in the education system of Turkey departing from the demands of classes which constitute parties to the restructuring process, as well as the function of the state in the shaping and realization of these demands.

In **Chapter 8: The Neoliberalization of Education Services (Not Including Higher Education): Impacts on Workers' Socioeconomic Security, Access to Services, Democratic Accountability, and Equity—A Case Study of Pakistan, Ahmad Mukhtar** describes how Pakistan has put the education sector in the experimentation lab for a long time, like many other sectors in the country. However, due to the relatively nonelastic structure and longer waiting time for reform results, this sector has seen more policy changes than any other, primarily credited to a panic policy mechanism. One of the leading factors in recent policy experimentation is the deregulation and privatization of the education sector, which has led to a clear divide between public and private education providers. The public sector is left far behind due to lack of resources and attention while the private sector is emerging as the winner, but not necessarily a substitute.

Contrary to the improvement in quality, curriculum, and approach of the private sector education providers, this sector has failed to reciprocate this success in the impact on workers' socioeconomic security, access to services and democratic accountability. The teachers' salaries are just a fraction of the fee revenue of most of the private schools, while the job security, career development, and capacity building are rare elements to be found.

In **Chapter 9: State, Inequality, and Politics of Capital: The Neoliberal Scourge in Education, Ravi Kumar** delves into how the trajectory of capital across different stages of capitalist development becomes an important tool to understand the nature of changes in education policy making in India. Recently, the Indian government has tried to demonstrate its willingness to provide school education to every child. However, the policies that it has been pursuing as part of its neoliberal agenda indicate that education is becoming not only inaccessible but is also being distorted. Despite loans from international financial institutions and new programs for education, the problems of equality and quality in Indian education persist. This chapter reflects on the current status of school education in India as emerging out of the needs and policies of capital, which is represented by its neoliberal form today.

In **Chapter 10: Global and Neoliberal Forces at Work in Education in Burkina Faso: The Resistance of Education Workers, Touorouzou Hervé Somé** critically examines education in Burkina Faso, a third world country undergoing the backlashes of global and neoliberal forces. It is a thick description and analysis of a little known peripheral country on the periphery of the periphery.

Charting the educational situation of a former colonial country confronted with the disintegration of the concept of publicness, the chapter explores the impact of globalization and neoliberalism on education in Burkina Faso and workers' resistance. The chapter attempts to pry open the limits of trade unionism. It exposes the dangers of unchecked nongovernmental forces or incentives in education in an economy dependent on 'aid': the surrender of national sovereignty, the increasing inequality in education, the falling of standards, corruption that is eating into the fiber of education, teacher pauperization, the increasing number of workers without work who cannot afford the education of their dependents, and the erosion of national languages and indigenous cultures. It concludes with a cautious hope that local communities, unions, political parties, and civil society at large, through organization and action, can curb the effects of globalization and provide an alternative to the present educational system that is just a foreign cyst transplanted in a culture without any attempt to integrate the local realities.

In **Chapter 11: From "Abjectivity" to Subjectivity: Education Research and Resistance in South Africa, Salim Vally, Enver Motala, and Brian Ramadiro** examine the new independent social movements as they resist the impact of neoliberalism and increasing poverty and inequality in postapartheid South Africa. The analysis has as a context South Africa's proud history of resistance in and through education against racial capitalism, a praxis that still exists, but one whose centre of gravity today has shifted.

This chapter examines this resistance and specifically the role of research in enhancing the capacity of working class organizations to confront neoliberalism. It assesses the methodology of some mass based community initiatives that challenge the new state to fulfill its promises of social justice. The chapter specifically details the struggle to challenge the costs of education for working class communities, policy flaws, and the policy response of South Africa's state education departments.

In **Chapter 12: Mozambique: Neocolonialism and the Remasculinization of Democracy, João M. Paraskeva** aims to analyze the masculinization of Mozambique's society based on a western democratic platform—undeniably one of the most substantive issues in Mozambique's neocolonial epoch. In order to accomplish this task, the author digs into the impact of current neoliberal policies. In so doing, Paraskeva aims to understand how Mozambique's neocolonial moment is profoundly submersed in gender segregation, and how real democracy is a profound mirage for the huge majority of the population as well. The chapter concludes claiming for the need to transform the state as a new social movement as the only best way to build a true just and democratic society.

In **Chapter 13: From the State to the Market?: China's Education at a Crossroads, Ka Ho Mok and Yat Wai Lo** analyze the significant economic transformations and social changes that China has experienced in the last two decades. The economic reforms which started in the late 1970s have unquestionably enabled some social groups to become wealthy, but the same processes have also widened the gap between the rich and the poor, as well as intensifying regional disparities in China. Most significant of all, embracing the market economy has led to the growing prominence of ideas and strategies along the lines of neoliberalism in reforming not only the economic sector but also public sector management and social policy delivery. Having been influenced by the global trends of privatization, marketization, and commodification of education, China has appropriated neoliberal policies and far more procompetition policy instruments have been adopted to reform and restructure its education. As depending upon state financing and provision alone will never satisfy the growing demands for higher education, China has therefore increasingly looked to the market/private sector and other nonstate sectors to venture into education provision, hence diversifying education services and proliferating education providers. This chapter sets out in the wider policy context outlined above to examine how China's education has been transformed, especially when far more procompetition and market oriented reform measures are adopted. With particular reference to the intensified inequalities in education, this chapter also examines how the Chinese government has made attempts to address the problems which have resulted from the marketization of education in the last two decades.

NOTES

1. My own experience working in numerous middle-income countries has revealed this to be true, in countries such as Turkey, Brazil, numerous countries in Central and Eastern Europe, and in South Africa. In contrast, my

own work experiences in low-income countries and those countries included in the category of the least developed countries, has demonstrated that few opportunities for international exchanges or skills development and knowledge growth for education workers exist in such countries, such as Togo, Moldova, Ukraine, Tobago, Trinidad, Philippines, and Nepal; to name a few.

2. Some exceptions to this would include Romania and Bulgaria, for example, which are considered low-income countries but which have had a great deal of international exchange, opening and exposure to new ideas, practices and techniques in education, as well as in other fields, largely due to their EU accession process and now membership.

REFERENCES

Afford, C. (E. Rosskam and A. Leather, Eds.). (2003) *Corrosive reform: Failing health systems in Eastern Europe.* Geneva: International Labor Office.

Annycke, P.; Bonnet, F.; Khan, A.; Figueiredo, J.; Rosskam, E.; & Standing, G. (2004) *Economic security for a better world.* Geneva: International Labor Office.

Hartmann, E.; Haslinger, S.; & Scherrer, C. (2006) Liberalization of higher education and training: implications for workers' security. In E. Rosskam (Ed.). Winners or losers: Liberalizing public services. Geneva: International Labour Office, pp. 55–119.

Hill, D. (2006) Education services liberalization. In E. Rosskam (Ed.) Winners or losers: liberalizing public services. Geneva: International Labour Office, pp. 3–54.

Rosskam, E. (Ed.). (2006) *Winners or losers: Liberalizing public services.* Geneva: International Labour Office.

———. and Loos, G. (Eds.). (2003) *Balancing globalization with social responsibility: Perspectives on work security, health, and environment in the global economy.* Special issue of *New solutions: A journal of environmental and occupational health policy*, Vol. 13, No.1.

Schnall, P.; Dobson, M.; & Rosskam, E., (Eds.) (forthcoming 2008) *Unhealthy work: Causes, consequences, and cures.* New York: Baywood.

2 Neoliberalism and Education in Latin America

Entrenched Problems, Emerging Alternatives

Adam Davidson-Harden and Daniel Schugurensky

INTRODUCTION: SETTING THE CONTEXT: A REGIONAL HISTORY OF NEOLIBERAL EDUCATION RESTRUCTURING

The history of neoliberalism in Latin America can be traced at least to 1973, when a U.S.-backed coup deposed the democratically elected government of Salvador Allende in Chile. The new regime, a brutal military dictatorship led by Augusto Pinochet, immediately began to implement a set of economic policies recommended by the 'Chicago boys' under the tutelage of Milton Friedman, who equated free markets with social and political freedom, and had been advocating for school vouchers since the 1950s. Without need to pass policies through Parliament, Chile soon became the testing ground for neoliberalism. It is pertinent to remember this, because in Latin America neoliberalism did not fall from the sky. What fell from the sky were the bombs that destroyed the government building of La Moneda in Santiago on September 11, 1973. Neoliberalism emerged in a particular historical context, as a reaction against the 'Welfare State' and Keynesian approaches to economic development that originated in Roosevelt's New Deal and expanded after WWII. Neoliberalism consisted in a set of economic ideologies and policy priorities emphasizing a preference for the 'inherently efficient' market and private sector over the 'inherently inefficient' state and 'public sector' as principal means for regulating economic and social exchanges, including education (Teeple, 2000; Heneles and Edwards 2002).

After decades of experimenting with these free market models, Latin America continues to be one of the most unequal regions of the planet. Moreover, in most countries of the region, neoliberalism has increased both prior inequalities in income distribution and the external debt. In Latin American countries, more than 30 percent of total per capita income (35 percent in several countries) is concentrated in the top income decile. In contrast, the share of total per capita income corresponding to the poorest 40 percent of households falls between 9 percent and 15 percent (ECLAC,

2006; SEDLAC, 2006). For large sectors of the region's population, particularly in the 'heavily indebted poor countries,' inequality is associated with high levels of unemployment, underemployment, malnutrition, high rates of disease, and overall poverty. Presently, about 205 million Latin Americans, about 45 percent of the total population, are living in poverty. Among them, about 79 million are below extreme poverty, living in indigence (ECLAC, 2006). This is the context in which adult educators, for example, face a reality of 40 million illiterates. In Latin America, poverty cannot be understood in isolation from inequality. Likewise, poverty reduction programs can be effective if they address issues of inequality and promote redistributive policies. (ECLAC, 2006; ECLAC/UNDP/IPEA, 2002).

Concurrent with a process of economic polarization and social stratification, educational restructuring has facilitated a parallel process in access to educational and occupational opportunities by gender, race, and class. In terms of gender, women earn between 32 percent on the low end and 58 percent on the high end of what men earn in Latin American workplaces. This gender inequality has particular implications when one considers trends in teacher remuneration, as we do below. Social polarization also exacerbates the lack of access to basic services and parity in work opportunities/remuneration among both indigenous and Afro-Latin populations across the region (Grant et al, 2004, pp. 79–82), where poverty is also more heavily concentrated (a recent report focusing on matters of race and inequality in Brazil, Guyana, Guatemala, Bolivia, Chile, Mexico, and Peru found significant wage disparity between indigenous and Afro-Latin ethnic groups compared with white populations, with indigenous males earning 35–65 percent less than whites, while in Brazil Afro-Latin citizens of both genders were found to earn less than half of what lighter skinned/white individuals earn. In all cases across the countries studied, women bore disproportionately the burden of polarization through their position at the bottom of all scales showing distribution of assets and income (De Ferranti, 2003). In this atmosphere, educational attainment becomes a symbol and object of possibility in the quest to break a cycle of poverty:

> An emphasis on basic schooling in public spending enhances intergenerational mobility in Latin America. There, a person needs at least 10 years of schooling to have a 90% or higher probability of not falling into poverty or moving out of poverty. And having just 2 years less schooling means 20% less income for the rest of a person's active life. (UN HDR, 2002, p. 20)

However, policy discourses and practices around 'economic competitiveness' have been largely ineffectual to promote equity, rights, and poverty alleviation. The tide of 'free trade' represented by international regimes such as the WTO's General Agreement on Trade in Services (GATS) and the proposed (though now possibly defunct) Free Trade Area of the Americas

(FTAA) agreement, as well as the Dominican Republic-Central American Free Trade Agreement (CAFTA-DR) continues the push to increase further U.S. hegemony in the region. At the same time, educational privatization is disproportionately beneficial to those segments of society who can afford to pay for better educational opportunities, experiences and social connections. In this context, only a broad policy discourse confronting realities of inequality in the region can hope to address educational dilemmas. As Reimers (2000) notes:

> . . . the poor have less access to preschool, secondary, and tertiary education; they also attend schools of lower quality where they are socially segregated. Poor parents have fewer resources to support the education of their children, and they have less financial, cultural, and social capital to transmit. Only policies that explicitly address inequality, with a major redistributive purpose, therefore, could make education an equalizing force in social opportunity. (p. 55)

In Latin America, neoliberalism promised redistribution through trickle-down economics, but its policies generated a vacuum up effect. For most people in this region, neoliberalism represents an ideology and set of policies designed to favor domestic elites and global corporations, with the resulting effect of social and economic polarization and more inequalities in wealth distribution. Hence, it is not surprising that many Latin American societies are presently challenging neoliberal policies and promoting alternatives that could nurture that 'major redistributive' project necessary to transform the damage done by those policies into hope for the future.

In this context, education remains an embattled terrain, comprised of neoliberal pulls toward decentralization, privatization, and marketization on the one hand—along with these policies' attendant lack of capacity to address inequality—and repeated calls for adequately funded public education on the other. Voices representing the latter side of this debate continue to press for the realization of the 'redistributive potential' of universal access to education through unleashing significant public investment at all levels of education.

Taken in broad relief, the status of basic education in Latin America offers a picture of beguiling progress at the superficial level, with systemic and chronic dilemmas comprising an enduring picture connected integrally with the problem of inequality. While overall statistics show school enrollment and access has kept up a growing pace since the 1980s across the region (UNDP, 2006; UNDP, 2001; Carnoy, 2002; Winkler & Gershberg, 2000), at the same time aggregate funding cutbacks as well as wider issues of social inequity and poverty across the region have arguably compromised the 'quality' or the type of educational experiences teachers are able to provide for students (Carnoy, 2002, Borón and Torres, 1996), concerns that reflect types of 'measures' for education that are frequently omitted or ignored in conventional instruments emphasizing enrollment and retention (Stromquist, 2003).

Further, indicators such as gross or net enrollment must be complemented with those addressing dropouts or 'school survival' in order to get a fuller picture of the state of education in the region and in some of its poorest and most heavily indebted states. In particular, the region's ignominious distinction as the most unequal on the planet is borne out forcefully in statistics attesting to the inequality of educational attainment (or 'school survival') levels in Latin American countries, trends emphasizing divides along gender, urban/rural, and identity/race lines in terms of indigenous/ nonindigenous as well as Afro-descendant peoples (Umayahara, 2005; Hopenhayn, 2005). Indigenous peoples are shown to suffer pronounced inequality in primary completion rates and indeed across most educational indicator categories, with differences most pronounced between them and nonindigenous young people in Bolivia when it comes to educational attainment/school survival (ECLAC, 2005, p. 90–91).

Cutbacks and restructuring in education systems across the region have been achieved under what Carnoy describes as the 'finance-driven' imperative for education reform in Latin America (2002, p. 296), in accordance with neoliberal economic and social policy prescriptions and directives. Efforts at education reform in this context have been driven primarily and most significantly by an economic imperative to reduce aggregate social expenditures, whether as a measure of 'sound fiscal policy' or as conditions of structural adjustment programs and loans (SAPs and SALs) administered by the World Bank and International Monetary Fund (IMF) (Chossudovsky, 2003) designed primarily with debt servicing obligations in mind.

Frequently, neoliberal education policies in Latin America have taken the shape of 'decentralization' efforts, aimed at scaling down the role of central governments in direct responsibility for different aspects of education, toward increased provincial/regional, municipal and private involvement in education (Carnoy, 2002; Munín, 1998; Borón and Torres, 1996). Through conditionalities and other mechanisms, pressure remains high on Latin American countries to move toward neoliberal education restructuring as a purported solution to the problem of the pronounced social inequity in the region. Such efforts critically include movement toward 'privatized' forms of educational 'delivery,' a theme supported and promoted by key agencies such as the World Bank and OECD, as well as—importantly—the International Trade Centre of the UNCTAD and WTO. As noted above, Chile has been at the forefront of experiments with neoliberal economic and social policy since the 1973 coup, which included a test case for a system of voucher based schools, with subsidized private and independent private schools that left publicly funded 'municipal schools' underfunded and lower performing (Carnoy, 1998; Pinkney Pastrana, 2007; Ginsburg et al, 2005). This retooling undermined a long legacy of a strong education system dedicated to a project of universal access to quality public education ("Estado docente"). Educational decentralization, privatizing efforts and educational inequalities have been also noted in several other Latin American countries (Plank, 1995; Parrado, 1998; Rhoten, 2000; Gershberg, 1999; Tatto, 1999; Vanegas, 2003; Stromquist, 2003).

THE 'ELEPHANT IN THE ROOM': LATIN AMERICAN DEBT AND ITS SOCIAL CONSEQUENCES, WITH A FOCUS ON SELECTED 'HIPCS'

The foundation for the neoliberal policy ascendance that impacts education in the region is the continued leverage or power of policy based 'conditionality' attached to loans and debt relief schemes under the auspices of both multilateral and bilateral creditors. As such, it is relevant to consider the broad contours of this foundation toward understanding better the reason for the continued preeminence of the neoliberal 'toolkit' for education in Latin America. This chapter will not pretend to be able to comprehensively treat the subject of regimes of external debt across Latin America as a region. That much broader analytical task would expand the scope of the present argument beyond the capability for clarity and an attempt at a concise focus on education. Instead, using a few macroeconomic indicators and figures to paint a broad portrait of regimes of debt across the region, we will focus here on the cases of a few of the region's most heavily indebted countries—Bolivia, Honduras and Nicaragua—all officially recognized as 'Heavily Indebted Poor Countries' (HIPCs) by the Bretton Woods Institutions (BWIs),[1] each of which have been accountable for Poverty Reduction Strategy Papers (PRSPs), the most recent embodiment of neoliberal conditionality. Even within this somewhat narrower focus, the aim here is not to provide a comprehensive account of the complex picture of indebtedness and its parameters for education. Indeed, the complexity of the task of assessing the public debt and its consequences for citizens—a few of which will be explored here—represents a challenge that many civil society movements across Latin America and beyond have taken up with citizen driven 'debt audit' processes.[2] This being said, it is possible to evoke something of the debt driven political economy of education even through the limited means utilized here. The two most important factors concerning regimes of Latin American debt, driving the present argument are a) a consideration of substantial portions of foreign public debt, as 'illegitimate' or 'odious,' and b) a consideration of the 'strangling' effect of heavy indebtedness on social expenditure, including that on education.

The social consequences of heavy indebtedness and burdensome debt service priorities/obligations has been linked to systemic neglect for proper funding and involvement on the part of the state in education. The orientation of the state away from social investment and public services and toward

BWI driven export economics and financial/trade liberalization constitutes the fundamentals of the neoliberal shift required by the Washington consensus. What social movement activists and citizens have been arguing for years, in the meantime, has finally been recognized by some multilateral lenders themselves. Lora and Olivera (2006), for example, confirm in their working paper for the IDB that higher levels of indebtedness as well as the burden of debt servicing obligations have contributed to a trend of declining social expenditures in Latin America as a region, leading to an incidence of marked lower contributions as measured in percentage of GDP in Latin America as a region as compared with other parts of the world. They note that a particular shortfall occurs in education expenditures comparatively, with the gap between education expenditures as a percentage of GDP in the region as compared with "developing countries of East Asia, Europe and Central Asia, and Africa" totaling 1.2 percent (Lora & Olivera, 2006, pp. 14–15). The authors also argue that default on external debt in this context could be beneficial in removing the 'debt burden' from the shoulders of states to be able to allocate funds to social programs of various kinds. Along these lines, the authors note that resources directed toward payment of debt interest payments (debt service) average 2.8 percent of GDP across Latin America annually, and that this amount would be enough to increase total social expenditures by 25 percent. (Lora & Olivera, 2006, p. 4). Across Latin America as a whole, debt servicing obligations as a percentage of GDP rose from 4.0 to 7.8 percent just from 1990–2004 (UNDP, 2006), while education expenditures as a percentage of GDP in Bolivia, Honduras, and Nicaragua outstrip debt service payments in 2004 by only a slim margin (UNDP, 2006).

IFIS, INTERNATIONAL TRADE REGIMES, AND ENCOURAGEMENT OF THE ROLE OF THE PRIVATE SECTOR

Among the International Financial Institutions (IFIs), the World Bank has taken full advantage of the leverage of debt to both require and recommend policy changes. Particularly through the International Finance Corporation (IFC) and its 'Edinvest' service, the Bank is conspicuously involved in ongoing attempts to encourage (via strategic loans) the growth of private, including for-profit, educational initiatives throughout Latin America. Ambiguous language (similar to that of the WTO secretariat's above) can also be found in the WB's literature around its so-called 'private sector advisory service' and 'private sector development strategy.' In a document discussing overall strategies for private sector development, the authors make references to education which, while less explicit than the WTO secretariat's note, contain elements of a marketizing agenda in contradiction with statements of the potential market value of public education. As is typical of this literature, these elements are couched in contradiction with statements about the necessity of 'basic education.' While this type of position nominally seeks equity, it also encourages the growth of an 'educational private sector,' the mandate of part of which may indeed be to provide paid access to 'basic' as well as other (including tertiary and adult) educational 'services.' This approach is also emphasized in another IFC document entitled 'Investing in Private Education: IFC's Strategic Directions' (IFC, 2001).

The IFC rationalizes educational cutbacks through 'efficiency' measures and privatization through the stated goal of improving equity. The rationale for this argument is based on the assertion that through privatization of education at various levels, 'subsidies' for wealthier families are removed as these groups transfer their education 'investment' into the private sector, leaving state funding for the rest of the public school system. However, as evidence from Latin American countries such as Chile shows, these types of modes of increasing the role of private (including for-profit) education provision at the basic and secondary (as well as tertiary) levels create gaps in access to schooling of an adequate quality based on social class, despite compensatory measures from IFIs intended to defray these stratification effects of privatized voucher systems (Carnoy & MacEwan, 2001; Carnoy, 1998; Carnoy, 2002). A corresponding dilemma of this dynamic is the phenomenon of private school 'cream-skimming' of wealthier families' children who are more equipped to succeed at school, with a corresponding burden on public system schools to absorb students from groups with higher educational needs and challenges and long histories of social exclusion and oppression. In this way, existing negative equity effects in education based on rampant social polarization are exacerbated by market style restructuring efforts, a dynamic also observable in other international contexts (Gewirtz et al, 1995; Whitty et al, 1998).[3]

Toward the objective of encouraging an 'equity of choice,' the IFC has directly supported (through financing) various private education initiatives across Latin America. These have included, for example, a loan to help Mexican private universities develop a student loan program for private university students, a loan to support voucher schemes in Colombia (IFC, 2001, p. 23), and also a loan to assist the capitalization of an online fee paying educational service in Brazil called 'Escol@24Horas' (IFC, 2001). A current list available on the IFC's Web site highlights twenty-eight projects supporting initiatives as diverse as operating expenses for private, for-profit universities, to financing student loans, as well as private for-profit companies relating to basic education.[4] In an earlier article, we argued that this type of development can be seen in tandem with the phenomenon of the growth of interest in the capacity of international trade regimes such as the WTO's GATS to reinforce trends of privatization in education. Such regimes seek through supranational legal mechanisms to entrench a dynamic of commodification of various aspects of 'education services,' assisting interested private sector actors in this pursuit globally as well as in Latin America specifically (cf. Schugurensky & Davidson-Harden 2003).

EDUCATION FUNDING, RESTRUCTURING, AND TEACHERS IN LATIN AMERICA

This excerpt from the WB's 2004 WDR represents a salient note from which to begin a brief overview of the plight of teachers in the region. Aside from this excerpt's negative characterization of teachers and their role in labor struggles, the report—as mentioned above—emphasizes a preference for various types of 'decentralized' systems of governance which could de-emphasize the role that teacher compensation plays as a cost driver in education funding. In contrast to the type of perspective offered above, the perspective adopted here both bemoans the poor status of teachers (and underfunded systems) in the region according to international benchmarks, as well as celebrates teachers' efforts to safeguard—and struggle for—adequate investment in public education,

---

BOX 7.8 *Education reform and teachers' unions in Latin America*

Reforms to promote greater parental involvement, more school autonomy, more emphasis on results, and changes in the training, selection, assignment, and compensation of teachers are politically explosive—particularly with teachers' unions. A study of five attempts at education reforms that included many of these elements in Latin America in the 1990s found that teachers' unions opposed nearly all of them—emphatically and stridently.

"Teacher's unions in Mexico, Minas Gerais, Brazil, Bolivia, Nicaragua, and Ecuador followed similar strategies in opposing education reform. All used strikes to assert their power . . . against unwanted changes. The power to disrupt public life, to close down schools and ministries, to stop traffic in capital cities, to appeal to public opinion—were familiar actions to them." In April 1999 the announcement by the Bolivian Ministry of Education of its intention to transfer teacher colleges to public universities set teachers and students at those colleges "rioting in the streets, breaking windows, attacking police, throwing rocks, and setting cars on fire" (images the government used to mobilize public opinion against the unions).

Teachers' unions wanted governments to address the issues of teachers' wages and working conditions and were concerned that decentralization and school autonomy would intrude on more familiar relationships and negotiations between a centralized school administration and a centralized union.

Even when governments pushed reforms through, conflicts with the unions made implementation problematic, since successful reform requires teacher participation.

Source: Grindle (forthcoming).

Figure 2.1 Excerpt from the 2004 World Development Report. (World Bank Group, 2004, p. 129.)

reflecting both collectively agreed upon national and international goals. The aforementioned tendency under IFI imperatives to restructure education systems in Latin America under the ideologies of decentralization as well as privatization has indeed led to a predictable dynamic of confrontation with embattled teachers in public education systems across the region. A comparative report by leading educational scholars that looks at Mexico and Argentina along with other countries internationally (including in North America) sums up the trend of decentralization and its effect on teachers in terms of an erosion of the power of teacher unions through both direct means (legislation rescinding unions' right to bargain) and indirect means, including the proliferation of noncertified or unionized teaching personnel effected through decentralization measures (Torres, C. et al, 2004, pp. 3–4)

These types of problematics in the education systems of Latin American countries are borne out through the documentation of workers' challenges through the ILO and tracking of progress (and lack thereof) toward the goals set out in the ILO/UNESCO Recommendation Concerning the Status of Teachers (1966), monitored by the Joint ILO/UNESCO Committee of Experts on the Application of the Recommendations Concerning Teaching Personnel (CEART). The following excerpt from a recent report from a meeting sponsored by the ILO on educational personnel illuminates well many of the dynamics set out by C.A. Torres and his co-authors concerning decentralization and privatization. In addition, it alludes to the more foundational concern with the very freedom to associate and wage collective action and struggle. In Ecuador, El Salvador, and Guatemala, a CEART related research team found violations of the rights of teachers to either associate toward discussion of relevant provincial or national level issues, or conduct strikes or other types of collective job action. Teachers responded to decentralization trends emphasizing 'democratic participation' in educational governance by criticizing and resisting such trends when they threatened to further impinge on the rights of teachers through, for example, devolution to parents and small associations of the right to hire and fire personnel, or recruit unqualified personnel (International Labour Office, 2000, pp. 26–27).

These trends witness to the dynamics of the intensification of work as well as a general low job security and status for educators across the region comparatively as a result of neoliberal education restructuring trends. In some countries, declining teachers' working conditions and threats to their livelihoods have reached tragic proportions in the context of generalized social conflicts. A case in point is Colombia, where paramilitary squads have targeted and murdered many teacher union members in past years (Schierenbeck, 2004). Education International (EI),[5] in its own response to CEART in 2006, confirmed the continuing poor status of teachers in Latin America particularly as consonant with similar trends in Central Eastern Europe, as well as African and Southeast Asian countries. Consistently, teachers' salaries compare unfavorably with other professionals' remuneration, citing that "the relative social value of the teaching profession, as expressed by the public remuneration level compared with other professions, is in long-term decline." (Education International, 2006, p. 5) In Latin America, EI found through its regional office that decentralization programs that devolved responsibility for staffing in schools to local, often private authorities (including families) contributed to the worsening status of teachers in terms of deteriorating wages, job insecurity, and a growing preference for nonaccredited teachers. Further, the problem of already poor teachers' salaries not keeping pace with rates of inflation has comprised a serious problem across many Latin American countries, contributing in EI's terms to the "impoverishment of teachers" (Educational International, 2006). This impoverishment, in turn, is significantly gendered in the region: In particular, EI's report cites Chile, Colombia, El Salvador, Honduras, Panama, and Paraguay as particularly egregious cases of gender disparity in terms of teachers' salaries (2006, p. 6). In addition to existing threats to teachers' work security, current statistics also illuminate the context of fiscal restraint under policy regimes that have set the stage for the challenges faced by teachers in the current context. Puiggrós sums up the dilemma of teachers in Latin America as caught in a vicious circle of underfunding:

> Salaries remain the biggest chunk of education budgets, even though teachers have been underpaid. Primary school teachers in Latin America earn between $100 and $400 a month in countries where the minimum wage is between $80 and $120. In nearly all countries, teachers earn only about as much as unskilled workers. Neoliberal economists do not address this problem because fair wages for teachers would require permanent increases in school budgets. Instead, the Bank recommends paring down teachers' already measly salaries (Puiggrós, 2002).

Following the 'lost decade' of the 1980s and its legacy of neoliberal cuts that in some case continued into the 1990s, the last decade has not seen an adequate improvement enough in expenditures on education to account for the emasculation of education systems under structural adjustment regimes and neoliberal policy agendas. This trend is evidenced by current statistics relevant to the topic and touching on the neoliberal trends of debt, low social spending, and reproduction of inequality touched upon above.

With stagnant variation in education funding predominating, the above table (Figure 2.2 'ECLAC Statistics on Education Expenditures') shows even a decrease over the past—eight to ten years in education funding as a percentage of GDP in Colombia and Ecuador, while many other countries have not seen any appreciable changes whatsoever. The table

LATIN AMERICA (18 COUNTRIES): PER CAPITA PUBLIC SOCIAL EXPENDITURE ON EDUCATION (1997 dollars, percentages of GDP and absolute variations)							
Country	Period 1996–1997		Absolute variation in relation to 1990–1991		Period 2000–2001		Absolute variation in relation to 1996–1997	
	In per capita dollars	% of GDP	In per capita dollars	In point of GDP	In per capita dollars	% of GDP	In per capita dollars	In points of GDP
Argentina	336	4.2	110	0.6	385	5.0	49	0.8
Bolivia	59	5.9	...	...	66	6.5	7	0.6
Brazil	157	3.2	-5	-0.5	185	3.8	28	0.6
Chile	169	3.1	82	0.7	238	4.1	69	1.0
Colombia	126	4.8	64	2.1	97	3.9	-30	-0.9
Costa Rica	148	4.4	35	0.6	189	5.0	41	0.6
Ecuador a/	56	3.4	11	0.5	45	3.0	-11	-0.4
El Salvador	43	2.3	...	...	51	2.6	8	0.3
Guatemala	28	1.7	4	0.2	46	2.6	18	0.9
Honduras	28	3.5	-5	-0.8	45	5.8	17	2.3
Mexico	153	3.7	49	1.2	190	4.1	37	0.4
Nicaragua	21	5.0	2	0.7	28	6.1	8	1.1
Panama b/	181	5.8	56	1.1	199	6.0	19	0.3
Paraguay	73	3.9	51	2.7	70	4.0	-4	0.2
Peru	57	2.5	27	0.8	58	2.5	1	0.0
Dominican Rep.	41	2.3	25	1.1	67	3.0	26	0.7
Uruguay	198	3.0	68	0.6	213	3.4	16	0.4
Venezuela	119	3.1	-10	-0.4	178	5.0	59	1.9
Latin America c/	118	3.6	35	0.7	139	4.2	21	0.6

Source: ECLAC, social expenditure database.
a/ The figure in the 2000–2001 column refers to 2000, and the absolute variation in relation to 1990–1991 refers to 1991.
b/ The figure in the 2000–2001 column refers to 2000.
c/ Simple average for the countries shown, except Bolivia and El Salvador.

Figure 2.2 ECLAC statistics on education expenditures. (ECLAC, 2003, p. 184.)

below (Figure 2.3 'Education Expenditures and Debt Servicing'), from a 2004 ECLAC report on education finance, additionally compares rates of spending on education as a percentage of GDP with countries' commitments to debt servicing as a percentage of GDP. Here the legacies of structural adjustment loans and programs are starkly evident, with the comparison between public spending at the primary and secondary levels on a par in many cases to levels with expenditures on debt servicing.

In the context of increasing teacher union unrest over the severe stagnation and lack of progress in overall funding as well as in remuneration for teachers' work, 2003 saw a spate of teachers' strikes across the region (Montero, 2003; Stubrin and Gindin, 2004). A news report covering recent labor unrest cited statistics showing that teachers in Argentina and

LATIN AMERICA AND THE CARIBBEAN (22 COUNTRIES): PUBLIC EXPENDITURES FOR EDUCATION AND PUBLIC DEBT SERVICING, 2000

Country	GDP per capita (1995 US$)	Combined enrolment rates in pre-school, primary and secondary schools [a]	Total public spending for education as % of GDP	Public spending for pre-school, primary and secondary education as % of GDP	Annual interest payments on public debt [b]	
					% of GDP	(US$ mill.) [c]
Argentina	7283	79	4.6	3.65	3.4	9124.3
Bolivia	941	63	5.5	3.85	1.9	147.3
Brazil	4324	72	3.8	2.98	3.9	28839.7
Chile	5790	68	4.2	3.66	0.4	368.0
Colombia	2285	60	5.1	3.58	3.9	3765.0
Costa Rica	3775	66	4.4	3.51	3.7	551.4
Cuba	3861	92	8.5	7.08		
Ecuador	1682	68	1.6	1.47	5.9	1255.2
El Salvador	1756	49	2.3	2.09	1.3	141.6
Guatemala	1562	49	1.7	1.70	1.3	232.9
Haiti	436	38	1.1	1.09	0.5	18.8
Honduras	714	45	4.0	4.00	2.0	91.4
Jamaica	2009	84	6.3	4.39		
Mexico	4811	75	4.4	2.72	3.0	14306.3
Nicaragua	800	48	5.0	5.00	3.3	134.7
Panama	3205	69	5.9	4.37	4.2	400.7
Paraguay	1552	65	5.0	3.49	1.1	95.1
Peru	2333	73	3.3	2.24	2.1	1285.8
Dom. Republic	2052	55	2.5	2.48	0.7	117.0
Trinidad and Tobago	5584	72	4.0	3.68		
Uruguay	5826	68	2.8	2.23	2.1	403.6
Venezuela	3082	61	3.0	1.44	2.6	1965.4
Latin America and the Caribbean [d]	3938	69	4.1	3.06	3.2	63244.3

Source: Economic Commission for Latin America and the Caribbean (ECLAC), based upon "World Education Compendium, 2003. Comparison of World Education Statistics", Montreal, 2003, UNESCO Institute of Statistics (UIS).

[a] Average net school enrolment rates at their respective levels.
[b] Average annual expenditures for interest on public debt, 1999-2001
[c] Figures are expressed in millions of 1995 dollars.
[d] Corresponds to country weighted averages.

Figure 2.3 Education expenditures and debt servicing. (ECLAC, 2004, p. 16.)

LATIN AMERICA AND THE CARIBBEAN (12 COUNTRIES): MINIMUM WAGE AND PER CAPITA GDP, 2002

Country	Monthly minimum wage (at current 2002 prices)	Currency	Monthly minimum wage (in 2002 dollars) a/	Urban poverty line in dollars b/	Urban real minimum wage index, 2002 (1995=100)	GDP per capita, 2002 (in constant 1995 dollars) d/
Bolivia	430	Boliviano	60.0	49.8	147.1	941.8
Brazil	200	Real	68.5	53.5	129.9	4 343.8
Chile	111 200	Chilean peso	161.4	62.5	142.3	5 919.1
Colombia	309 000	Colombian peso	123.4	70.0	105.4 d/	2 271.0
Cuba	100 e/	Cuban peso	–	–	–	–
Ecuador	128	US dollar	128.0	73.3	96.7	1 516.0
El Salvador	109 f/	US dollar	109.1	72.4	91.9 d/	1 763.7
Guatemala	900 g/	Quetzal	115.1	85.9	121.2 d/	1 763.7
Honduras	2 099 g/	Lempira	127.7	89.6	121.3 d/	704.9
Mexico	1 192 g/	Mexican peso	123.4	153.9	89.6	4 708.6
Peru	410	Nuevo sol	116.6	64.2	217.7	2 376.3
Uruguay	1 110	Uruguayan peso	52.2	75.0	86.0	5 023.6

Source: ECLAC, based on official information supplied by the countries in response to the ECLAC survey conducted in September–October 2002, and other official figures (minimum wage index and per capita GDP).
a/ Calculated using the IMF "rf" series, with the exception of Guatemala, for which the "wf" series was used.
b/ Poverty line values around 1999 were converted to 2002 prices based on the annual averages of the General Consumer Price Index available on the IMF online database (http://imfstatistics.org) because the CPI for food, a more suitable index for this type of conversion, was not available.
c/ Provisional figures subject to revision.
d/ Information for 2001.
e/ Minimum wage established in 1987 for certain service occupations. Other differential minimum wages have been established based on the complexity of the work, with ranges by category.
f/ Based in the simple average of daily minimum wages for industry, trade and services, multiplied by 30.
g/ Based on daily wages multiplied by 30.

Figure 2.4 ECLAC minimum wage statistics. (ECLAC, 2003, p. 200.)

Brazil earn $120 on average per month, in Bolivia $170, in Peru and Uruguay $200, in Ecuador $250, and in Colombia, Mexico and Venezuela, $300 (Montero, 2003). As the following table (Figure 2.4 'ECLAC Minimum Wage Statistics') from ECLAC's Social Panorama (2003) shows, these figures barely meet or exceed concurrent, and conservative, figures reflecting minimum wages in the region:

In addition, remuneration for teachers at the primary and secondary levels in Latin American countries compare unfavorably in the main internationally, as evidenced by the following tables (Figures 2.5 'ILO Statistics on Teachers' Salaries in Primary Education' and 2.6 'ILO Statistics on Teachers' Salaries in Secondary Education') which show teacher remuneration in selected Latin American countries in comparison with other countries, including some from the richer North:
2002, p. 38.)

Yet another perspective on teacher remuneration in Latin America can be achieved by looking through the lens of purchasing power parities (PPP), putting ability to purchase a basic 'basket' of goods in context in terms of U.S. dollars:

Here the stark contrast with the richer United States system lays bare the comparative disadvantages and challenges teachers face in underfunded Latin American education systems.

With teachers' working conditions being students' 'learning conditions,' it is clear that Latin America faces a struggle in achieving adequate support for public education in the face of still regnant neoliberal ideologies in education policy. Struggles over adequate funding for education across Latin America have been spearheaded by teachers, and in many cases have formed important linkages with other workers and movements in the context of a broader struggle to protect what social

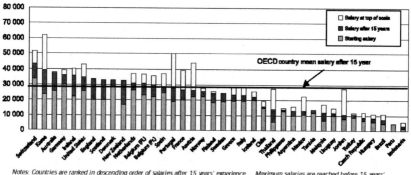

Notes: Countries are ranked in descending order of salaries after 15 years' experience. Maximum salaries are reached before 15 years' experience in Australia, Denmark, England, New Zealand and Scotland, so that the mid-career part of the bar in the above chart shows in fact maximum salaries.
Source: OECD, 2001.

Figure 2.5 ILO Statistics on teachers' salaries in primary education. (Siniscalco, 2002, p. 37.)

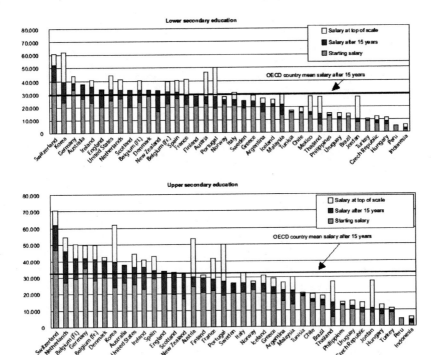

Note: *Countries are ranked in descending order of salaries after 15 years' experience.*
Source: OECD. 2001.

Figure 2.6 ILO statistics on teachers' salaries in secondary education. (Siniscalco, 2002, p. 38.)

table 3.2	STARTING SALARIES OF TEACHERS IN US$ PPP, BY LEVEL OF EDUCATION, 1998		
Country	Primary	Lower Secondary	Upper Secondary
Argentina	8,906	14,426	14,426
Brazil	4,818	11,970	12,598
Chile	9,067	9,067	9,067
Mexico	10,465	13,357	n.a.
Peru	4,282	4,282	4,282
Uruguay	5,241	5,241	5,703
USA	25,707	25,155	25,405

Source: UNESCO/OECD WEI. See annex for data and notes.

Figure 2.7 Regional education indicators project teacher salaries by PPP. (Regional Education Indicators Project, 2002, p. 74.)

gains remain from a more expansionist welfare state, as well as to extend public services and interests.

FINAL REMARKS: RESISTANCE AND ALTERNATIVES IN LATIN AMERICAN EDUCATION AND THE NEW EMERGING 'POLITICAL MAP' OF THE REGION

While international organizations such as UNESCO have endorsed the agenda of 'Education For All' (with a current target of 2015), it is clear that such broad-minded goals are constrained by persistent social inequalities in the region, as well as chronic funding issues compounded by equally persistent neoliberal policies and external imperatives. Indeed, UNESCO estimates that in order to meet the goals set out in Dakar in 2000, a massive investment is required, the equivalent of $149 billion U.S. across the region of Latin America and the Caribbean (ECLAC, 2004, p. 8). In an ongoing context of struggle over positive objectives for education systems across the region, several organizations, representing both teachers as well as other concerned citizens within and across countries, have come to the fore both as agents of resistance and as sources of alternatives to the current order. In Latin America, teachers have been at the forefronts of many of the emergent social movements confronting neoliberal policies.

Already noted above were the waves of teachers' strikes which have typified conflicts in Latin American education in recent years. One example of a more unorthodox move of resistance can be found in recent experiences in Argentina. The example that Argentine teacher unions have offered through their innovative and creative movement in the late 1990s stands out as an example of alternative resistance to neoliberalism in the contemporary context. Beginning in 1997, Argentine teachers waged hunger strikes and set up a White Tent (the 'Carpa Blanca') outside of the National Congress. This protest action blossomed, gained widespread public support and became a site of cultural creativity and life. Moreover, the action did not attempt to interfere with classes, possibly drawing further sympathy from the populace for this reason. Larger federations of teacher unions, such as Education International's Latin America office, have also been in the forefront of efforts and initiatives to raise challenges to the predominating neoliberal order of restructuring and underfunding in the region, as it affects teachers and the system as a whole (Education International Latin America Regional Office, 2003).

The Hemispheric Secretariat on Education (HSE) emerged out of a meeting under the auspices of the People's Summit (the 'Hemispheric Forum on Education,' an alternative meeting that took place in the shadows of the 2001 FTAA meetings in Québec City, Canada.) This juxtaposition illustrates the conflict in values which such a body reflects in comparison to the narrow neoliberal agenda reflected by the support of an international trade regime such as the FTAA, with its focus on a move at all costs toward 'liberalization' of trade in services, including various types of education services. The principles which Forum participants derived from their meeting in 2001 reflect the common consideration of those who, across the region, share a resistance to neoliberal imperatives for education and seek to strengthen the role that states can play in educational development (Hemispheric Secretariat on Education, 2001).

The World Education Forum, held three times in Porto Alegre, Brazil,[6] as well as in other cities like Caracas and Nairobi, represents another important, hopeful, and ongoing venue for the articulation of an agenda organically connected to that espoused by the HSE and the World Social Forum. The Forum's statement affirms an alternative agenda to neoliberalism on a broad and comprehensive scale (World Education Forum, 2004). These principles reflect not only a concern with the defense of adequately funded public education systems, but also an alternative vision supporting equity oriented principles and programs. Together with reaffirmations of the goal of EFA in the Latin American context with broad support across the region[7] (Torres, R-M., 2001), these principles and actors continue to mount an impressive struggle for the defense of public education in the Americas.

Perhaps these principles and the actors behind them will be able to rejuvenate the somewhat stagnant struggle toward alleviating the educational equity goals that EFA attempts to address. However, instead of aligning with IFIs and private investment goals for education in continued efforts at neoliberal types of education restructuring, these new actors and movements seek a qualitatively different sort of agenda, that of democratic control over educational governance. Remediation of the ills which plague most Latin American educational systems is not reducible to one measure, however, and even well-funded education is not a panacea for the development problems impacting the region (Heneles & Edwards, 2002). As such, newly emerging lines on the political map of Latin America arguably hold promise in terms of competing ideologies and alternatives to hegemonic neoliberalism.

From the strong and vibrant social movements in Bolivia (including teacher union members), active in the context of contesting the privatization of water and the intensification of neoliberalism from 1999–2003, to alliance between teachers and the Landless Workers' Movement in Brazil (Diniz-Pereira, 2005), to solidarity with the nonviolent campaign of the Zapatistas in Mexico as well as recent protests in Oaxaca, trends of resistance have flourished across Latin America in response to the continuing demands of neoliberal hegemony. Gentili, Suarez, Stubrin and Gindin (2005) note the growing militancy of teachers' unions in Latin America in the context of the late period of structural adjustment in the 1990s and the new 'era' of poverty reduction (2005), which has seen a precipitous rise in collective action on the basis of a variety of factors, but notably in solidarity with other social movements and concerning other issues than education per se.

It is clear that education alone cannot reverse the social and economic damage caused by neoliberalism. For this, a larger policy shift is required, and in recent years, growing numbers of Latin American citizens reacted favorably to electoral choices for progressive political parties and coalitions—some moderate, some more radical—in several countries, including Uruguay, Argentina, Brazil, Chile, Paraguay, Nicaragua, Ecuador, Bolivia, and Venezuela. Publics in countries affected strongly by neoliberalism continue to tilt toward political options—both electoral and nonelectoral—that can help realize the goal of alternative paths to development. Along these lines, arguably the strongest example of alternative policies to neoliberalism in the region can be found in Venezuela. In addition to its own bold advances in promoting equity in education (access to higher education is now enshrined as a constitutional right) (Muhr & Verger, 2006), Venezuela's advancement of alternative trade regimes for the region in the Bolivarian Alternative for the Americas (ALBA) promises to be an ambitious experiment that promotes a more horizontal economic and social integration in the hemisphere. Already ALBA members Venezuela, Nicaragua, and Bolivia have withdrawn from the Bank controlled International Centre for the Settlement of Investment Disputes (famously implicated in the Cochabamba water conflict), with Venezuela having paid off its loans to the IMF. Similar actions took Argentina and Brazil in order to gain more autonomy in developing economic policies. More recently, the Bank of the South was launched in order to provide an alternative to external lending. Perhaps the most salient feature of these new emerging lines on Latin America's political map is the strong counterreaction to neoliberalism's prescriptions, including those for education, and a renewed emphasis on the role of the state to promote the common good and to curb the inequalities generated by the market. Where these alternatives lead the region is of course, a matter of history unfolding.

NOTES

1. We use this term as well as international financial institutions (IFIs) to refer to the World Bank and International Monetary Fund as historical artifacts of consensus between powerful states at meetings in Bretton Woods in 1944. From this point on the terms 'the Bank' and 'the Fund' will be used as a shorthand to refer to the World Bank and IMF respectively.
2. Citizen movements in Ecuador have been the first to implement this type of process, and momentum is building for related processes across Latin America. See http://www.choike.org/nuevo_eng/ifis/informes/443.html
3. For a discussion of the equity argument for tuition and fees in tertiary education, see Schugurensky (2000) and Puiggrós (2002).
4. www.ifc.org
5. EI is an international organization comprised of 280 teacher unions and associations across the globe (http://www.ei-ie.org/).
6. http://www.portoalegre.rs.gov.br/fme/default.asp?mst=5
7. To access a copy of the actual statement including a list of supporters current to 2001, visit http://www.cies.ws/PaperDocuments/WordDocs/LATIN%20

AMERICAN%20STATEMENT%20ON%20EDUCATION%20FOR%20
ALL.htm

REFERENCES

Ball, J., Fischman, G., and Gvirtz, S. (eds.), Crisis and hope: The educational hopscotch of Latin America. New York and London: Routledge Falmer, pp. 45–65, 2003.

Borón, A. & Torres, C. (1996) The impact of neoliberal restructuring on education and poverty in Latin America. *The Alberta Journal of Educational Research* 62, (2), pp. 102–114.

Carnoy, M. (2002) Latin America: The new dependency and educational reform. In *Educational restructuring in the context of globalization and national policy*, ed. H. Daun. New York: RoutledgeFalmer.

———. (1998) National voucher plans in Chile and Sweden: Did privatization reforms make for better education? *Comparative Education Review* 42, (3), pp. 309–337.

Carnoy, M. & MacEwan, P. (2001) *Does privatization improve education? The case of Chile's national voucher plan*. Stanford: Stanford University School of Education.

Chossudovsky, M. (2003) *The globalization of poverty and the new world order*. Ottawa: Global Research.

De Ferranti, D. (2003) *Inequality in Latin America & the Caribbean: Breaking with history?* Washington: World Bank Group.

Diniz-Pereira, J. (2005). Teacher Education for Social Transformation and its Links to Progressive Social Movements: The case of the Landless Workers Movement in Brazil. Journal for Critical Education Policy Studies, 3 (2). Retrieved February, 2007 from http://www.jceps.com/?pageID=article&articleID=51

ECLAC. (2005) *The millennium development goals: A Latin American and Caribbean perspective*. Santiago, Chile: The Author.

———. (2004) *Financing and management of education in Latin America and the Caribbean: summary*. Santiago, Chile: The Author.

———. (2003) *Social panorama of Latin America*. Santiago, Chile: ECLAC.

ECLAC/UNDP/IPEA (Instituto de Pesquisa Econômica Aplicada) (2002). Meeting the millenium poverty reduction targets in Latin America and the Caribbean. Santiago: The Authors.

Education International. (2006) *Education International Report to the Expert Committee on the Application of the 1966 ILO/UNESCO Recommendation on the Status of Teachers and the 1997 UNESCO Recommendation on the Status of Higher Education Teaching Personnel*. Brussels: The Author.

Education International Latin America Regional Office. (2003) *Retos Docentes y Sindicales en el Nuevo Contexto*. San José, Costa Rica: Education International Latin America Regional Office.

Gentili, P., Suarez, D., Stubrin, F., & Gindin, J. (2005) Educational reform and teachers' struggles in Latin America. Hemispheric Secretariat on Education Newsletter, 3.

Gershberg, A. (1999) Education "decentralization" processes in Mexico and Nicaragua: legislative versus ministry-led reform strategies." *Comparative Education* 35, (1), pp. 63–80.

Gewirtz, S.; Ball, S. J.; & Bowe, R. (1995) *Markets, choice, and equity in education*. Buckingham, UK: Open University Press.

Ginsburg, M.; Espinoza, O.; Popa, S.; & Terano, M. (2005) Globalisation and higher education in Chile and Romania: The roles of the International Monetary Fund,

World Bank, and World Trade Organization. In J. Zajda (Ed.), International handbook on globalisation, education and policy research. Springer: Dordrecht, pp. 221–234.

Grant, U.; Hulme, D.; Moore, K.; & Shepherd, A. (2004) Understanding chronic poverty in Latin America and the Caribbean. In the chronic poverty report 2004–2005. Manchester: The Chronic Poverty Research Centre, pp. 79–82.

Hemispheric Secretariat on Education. (2001) Final declaration of the Hemispheric Forum on Education, Second People's Summit of the Americas, Québec City, April 17 and 18, 2001. Retrieved August 15, 2004 from http://www.secretaria.ca/eng/declaration.htm

Heneles, L. & Edwards, B. (2002) Neoliberalism and educational reform in Latin America. *Current Issues in Comparative Education*, 2 (2).

Hopenhayn, M. (2005). Recognition and distribution: Equity and justice policies for discriminated groups in Latin America. Retrieved February, 2007 from http://siteresources.worldbank.org/INTRANETSOCIALDEVELOPMENT/Resources/Hopenhayn.rev.pdf

International Finance Corporation, Health and Education Group. (2001) *Investing in private education: IFC's strategic directions*. Washington, DC: International Finance Corporation.

International Labour Office. (2000) *Note on the proceedings. Joint meeting on lifelong learning in the twenty-first century: the changing roles of educational personnel, Geneva, 10–14 April 2000*. International Labour Organization Sectoral Activities Programme, document number JMEP/2000/10.

Larsen, K.; Morris, R.; & Martin, J. (2002) *Trade in educational services: trends and emerging issues*. Working Paper. Paris: OECD.

Lora, E. & Olivera, M. (2006) *Public debt and social expenditure: friends or foes?* Interamerican Development Bank Research Dept. Working paper 563.

Munín, H. (1998) "Freer" forms of organization and financing and the effects of inequality in Latin American educational systems: Two countries in comparison. *Compare* 28, (3), pp. 229–243.

Montero, D. (2003) "Education—Latin America: Thousands of teachers strike amid regional crisis." Globalinfo news service. Retrieved August 15, 2004 from http://www.globalinfo.org/eng/reader.asp?ArticleId=23483

Muhr, T., & Verger, A. (2006). Venezuela: Higher education for all. Journal for Critical Education Policy Studies, 4 (1). Retrieved from http://www.jceps.com/index.php?pageID=article&articleID=63

Parrado, E. (1998) Expansion of schooling, economic growth, and regional inequalities in Argentina. *Comparative Education Review* 42, (3), pp. 338–364.

Pinkney Pastrana, J. (2007) Subtle tortures of the neo-liberal Age: Teachers, students, and the political economy of schooling in Chile. *Journal for Critical Education Policy Studies*, 5 (2).

Plank, D. (1995) Public purpose and private interest in Brazilian education. In C. Torres (Ed.). Education and social change in Latin America. Albert Park, Australia: James Nicholas.

Puiggrós, A. (2002) World Bank education policy: Market liberalism meets ideological conservatism. In V. Navarro (Ed.), The political economy of social inequalities: consequences for health and quality of life. Amityville, NY: Baywood, pp. 181–190.

Regional Education Indicators Project. (2002) *Regional report: Educational panorama of the Americas*. Santiago, Chile: UNESCO Regional Office for Education in Latin America and the Caribbean.

Reimers, F. (2000) *Unequal schools, unequal chances: The challenges to equal opportunity in the Americas*. Cambridge, MA: Harvard University Press.

Rhoten, D. (2000) Education decentralization in Argentina: A "global-local conditions of possibility" approach to state, market, and society change. *Journal of Education Policy* 15, (6), pp. 593–619.

Sáinz, Pedro (2006). Equity in Latin America Since the 1990s. DESA Working Paper No. 22. New York: United Nations Department of Economic and Social Affairs.

Schierenbeck, J. (2004, August 14) Getting away with murder: Colombia's death squads target unionists; teachers hard hit. *United Federation Of Teachers—Labor Days*. Retrieved August 15, 2004 from http://www.uft.org/?fid=245&tf=1238&nart=1091

Schugurensky, D. & Davidson-Harden, A. (2003) From Cordoba to Washington: WTO/GATS and Latin American education. *Globalisation and Societies in Education*, 1 (3).

Schugurensky, D. (2000) Syncretic discourses, hegemony building and educational reform. *Education and Society* 18 (2), pp. 75–94.

Siniscalco, M. (2002) *A statistical profile of the teaching profession.* Geneva & Paris: International Labour Office and United Nations Educational, Scientific and Cultural Organization.

SEDLAC (Socio-Economic Database for Latin America and the Caribbean) (2006). Website: https://www.depeco.econo.unlp.edu.ar/cedlas/sedlac/default.html

Stromquist, N. (2003) "While gender sleeps. neoliberalism's impact on educational policies in Latin America." In S. Ball, G. Fishman, and S. Gvirtz (eds.), Crisis and hope: the educational hopscotch of Latin America. UK: Routledge

Stubrin, F. & Gindin, J. (2004). Conflictividad docente en América Latina. Boletín De La Secretaría Continental Sobre Educación Número 2, Marzo. Sao Paulo: OLPED.

Tatto, M. (1999) "Education reform and state power in México: the paradoxes of decentralization." *Comparative education review* 43, (3), pp. 251–282.

Teeple, G. (2000) *Globalization and the decline of social reform.* Aurora: Garamond.

Torres, C.A.; Cho, S.; Kachur, J.; Loyo, A.; Mollis, M.; Nagao, A., & Thompson, J. (2004) "Political capital, teachers' unions, and the state. Conflict and collaboration in educational reform in the United States, Canada, Japan, Korea, Mexico, and Argentina." Retrieved August 15, 2004 from http://www.isop.ucla.edu/lac/cat/montim.pdf

Torres, R-M. (2001) "3000 voices from Latin America: The Latin American statement for education for all.'" Retrieved August 15, 2004 from http://www.fronesis.org/otros/3000voices.htm

Umayahara, M. (2005). Regional Overview of Progress toward EFA since Dakar: Latin America. Paris: UNESCO Executive Office, Education Sector.

United Nations Development Programme (UNDP). (2006) *Human development report*. Washington: The Author.

———. (2002) Human Development Report 2002: Deepening Democracy in a Fragmented World. Washington: The Author.

United Nations Economic Commission for Latin America and the Caribbean (ECLAC). (2006) *Social panorama of Latin America*. Santiago: ECLAC.

Vanegas, P. (2003) "The northern influence and Colombian education reform of the 1990s." In S. Ball, G. Fishman, and S. Gvirtz (eds.), Crisis and hope: the educational hopscotch of Latin America. UK: Routledge.

Whitty, G.; Power, S.; & Halpin, D. (1998) *Devolution and choice in education: the school, the state and the market.* Melbourne: ACER.

Winkler, D. & Gershberg, A. (2000) Education decentralization in Latin America: the effects on the quality of schooling. *LCSHD Paper Series No. 59.* Washington: World Bank Group. (2004) *Making services work for poor people: world development report 2004.* Washington: The Author.

World Education Forum. (2004) "Declaration of the Third World education forum."

3 World Bank and the Privatization of Public Education
A Mexican Perspective

Gian Carlo Delgado-Ramos
and John Saxe-Fernández

INTRODUCTION

The notion of the dissolution of the state's role in key public issues is a myth. Neither the role of the state—in central or peripheral countries—has diminished nor are we under "decisions" made by abstract, overreaching, and automatic "market or globalization forces."

The World Bank's programs are an example of "road maps" or basic designs which, far from diminishing the role of the state, foster it. Once the loans are formalized by the national governing class, the country must accept, willingly or not, rigid protocols which involve specific clauses of conditionality, "recommendations and suggestions," and even in some cases, "simple observations" and "offerings."

ON THE WORLD BANK (WB)

At the intiative of Washington, the Bretton Woods conference was celebrated in mid-1944 in New Hampshire. Its aim was to provide the United States (US) with a "new economic order" that "could keep the nation's economy pumping away so that the war shocked world could be rebuilt and the US system saved from a possibly fatal shock of another 1930s-like depression" (La Feber, 1989, p. 410). To solve these problems, two new organizations were established: the International Bank for Reconstruction and Development (IBRD or World Bank) and the International Monetary Fund (IMF). Since the US at that time controlled two-thirds of the world's gold, the Roosevelt administration insisted that the postwar economic system rest on gold and the US dollar. Both institutions were designed, as Gabriel and Joyce Kolko point out, not merely to implement disinterested principles, "but to reflect the United States' control of the world's monetary gold and its ability to provide a large part of its future capital. The IBRD was tailored to give a governmental framework for future private investment, much of which would be American." (Kolko and Kolko, 1972, p. 16)

The US dominated the WB and the IMF, and were used by Roosevelt "to force the British Empire to open up to the American goods and investment" (La Feber, 1989, p. 411) and soon after, as powerful tools to do the same with the rest of the world. To Dean Acheson, the aim was to create not just an American dominated international marketplace, but one that did not need excessive state interference or high tariffs (Acheson, 1969, n.p.). The GATT arrangement was central to these aims.[1]

In this paper the WB and IMF are treated as state and class instruments of US national private interests and not just "international financial institutions" or "multilateral instruments" To us, they are vital tools of "Pax Americana."

The US holds 16.39 percent of the voting power within the IBDR and 23.68 percent in the International Finance Corporation (IFC).

Considering that 80 percent of the votes is needed to approve any proposal within the WB, the US has the power to "neutralize" any action that threatens its interests, which is tantamount to veto power. At the IMF it controls 14.17 percent of the voting power. Eighty-five percent of the votes are needed to ratify any decision.

As former U.S. Treasury Secretary Henry Morgenthau pointed out, under the encouragement of the WB, " . . . international trade and international investment can be carried out by businessmen on business principles." (Kolko and Kolko, 1972, p. 16) Morgenthau refers, of course, to American and other entrepreneurs from the "North."

This is amply demonstrated by IFC's modus operandi. Functioning on an organizing mechanism of "clusters" or work groups, it encourages international private "partners" to engage actively in the business of privatizing and denationalizing the main—and strategic—assets of host nations. Among IFC partners in the "Water & Sanitation Cluster," there are companies such as Vivendi, Ondeo (Suez), and Thames Water. Companies and state institutions in the "Natural Resources Cluster" include, among others, Conservation International, the U.S. Agency for International Development (USAID), World Trade Organization (WTO), and Inter-American Development Bank (IBD). All other "work groups" are also linked, by this mechanism, with "selected" multinational companies, most of them US based.

As we have documented elsewhere (Delgado and Saxe, 2005), the private sector agenda, together with its denationalizing thrust, has deepened in the last few years. As stated by the WB in México: " . . . a new relationship with the World Bank Group has been established" (World Bank, 2007, p. 1), exemplified by a substantial increase of ongoing projects and advisory missions.

After paying 56 percent of México's debt with the WB in 2006, the country still owes U.S. $5.73 billion and as of 2007 new loans are being negotiated for at least U.S. $1.6 billion.

World Bank and the Commercialization of Higher Education

The commercialization of higher education is basically carried out as part of the "Washington Consensus," which includes the privatization of public universities. According to Santos, this has been a two-stage process. The first stage, from the 1980s to 1990 aimed at the expansion and consolidation of a national market for higher education. The second stage, from 1990 on, centered on stimulating the creation of a "transnational" market in higher education, under the US-European dominated World Trade Organization (WTO) and, the WB. Higher education is defined and treated exclusively as a mercantile operation (Santos, 2004, p.17–18).

By 1998, when the "second stage" was well underway, the WB published a report, "The Financing and Administration of Higher Education" which laid out an agenda for educational "reform."[2] With the intention of adjusting the educational system to "present and future needs," the Bank followed the suggestion of Frans van Vught (van Vught, 1994) in the sense that " . . . the reform agenda of the 90s, and almost certainly extending well into the next century, is oriented to the market rather than to public ownership or to governmental planning and regulation" (Johnstone, 1998, n.p.). Central to WB's higher education programs, the report calls for its privatization, deregulation, and "orientation by the market." (Ibid)

Notwithstanding the historical experience of European universities as hubs of humanistic and scientific knowledge, and as a key public institution, for the WB education, science and technology are commodities, and consequently they must be conceived and managed through "market" mechanisms. Thus education is framed in a context of limited supply and is available for a certain price.

Looking at the demand side of the phenomenon, the financing of higher education acquires a peculiar connotation. This has to do, in the Bank's own words, with the fact that " . . . when the government shifts cost to the students, it must introduce a parallel system of financial assistance." (Ibid, p. 7) The WB proposes (Ibid, p. 5, 7):

a. Introduction of substantial increases in registration costs
b. Charging full fees for room and board
c. Introduction of mechanisms to investigate economic resources of students applying for grants and loans
d. Loans for students based on market interests rates
e. Improvement of the students' loan payments by subcontracting private companies
f. Implementation of a graduation fee imposed on all students
g. Promotion of philanthropy to establish foundations for direct operation of universities or to grant scholarships
h. Improving the quality of education by entrepreneurial training

i. Offering for sale research projects findings, training courses, and all university services through concession agreements or subsidies

j. Increasing the number of private institutions with a progressive decrease in public education

On these, the WB states:

" . . . much of what may look like the agenda of the neoliberal economist may also be more opportunistic than ideological. With taxes increasingly avoidable and otherwise difficult to collect and with competing public needs so compelling on all countries, an increasing reliance on tuition, fees and the unleashed entrepreneurship of the faculty may be *the only* alternative to a totally debilitating austerity." (Ibid, p. 5)

In México, these have been "well" understood by the local and powerful elite. Since the 90s, through its deputies and senators the private sector has introduced in the legislative agenda new bills that call for opening the education and public health sectors to private investment based on "service-rendering projects" agreements; an operational scheme similar to that of multiple service contracts sponsored by the WB in México's public oil and electric enterprises, leading to the "sector's *de facto* privatization (Saxe-Fernández, 2002).

The WB and its "country managers"—from the "president" and its cabinet, all the way down the federal bureaucracy—argue for drastic reductions in "non-productive" expenditures (public education is considered as such), so that money can be spent in health, security, or infrastructure. This is the same argument used for privatizing such services.

Fostered by both the WB and a "conventional wisdom" built on a massive and costly "public relations campaign," the privatization of public assets is propagandized as the only alternative to current economic stresses and distresses. It really responds to the private sector's interest in pillaging the public treasury, strengthening what has been described as a key feature of this process: "the privatization of profits and the socialization of costs."

The educational system as a whole is now being thrown into this scheme. Presented to the public as a major effort at "educational reform," its privatization is being fostered through highly conditioned WB loans to the public ministry of education, universities, and research and development units such as the National Council on Science and Technology (CONACYT) and to the major public universities of the country. By encouraging the "entrepreneurial spirit" in the educational institutions at all levels, the Bank is basically eroding the fragile position of academy and scientists in defining study plans and scientific and technological development programs. Since according to the Bank's reasoning, the "market" (i.e., the private sector) should "decide" on these matters, there is a growing gap between the problems affecting the population at large and the national research and development agenda. The WB, through linguistic gymnastics, conceals the main beneficiaries of privatization. James Petras[3] has pointed out that "the market" is an analytic category. It does not "demand" nor does it "decide" or "urge." What we are facing is an anthropomorphic distortion. It is the chief executive officers, the decision makers of organisms such as the WB, the IADB, and the IMF who really "demand," "decide," and "urge." Not "the market."

This helps to understand the real meaning of WB's jargon:

> . . . a greater reliance on market signals brings a shift in decision making power not just *from government*, but also *from higher educational institutions*—and especially from the faculty, to *the consumer or client*, whether student, business or the general public (Johnstone, 1998, p. 5).

The WB's main campaign motto is centered in the virtual destruction of the university as such when it calls for the suspension of "the isomorphic reproduction" of the "classic university" based on free research and teaching, and what it claims as the existence of an "excessive power of the faculty."

According to Santos, worldwide spending in education is estimated at 2 *trillion* dollars, more than global automotive sales. Merrill Lynch analysts quoted by Santos indicate that capital growth in education has been exponential with one of the market's highest earning rates: 1,000 pounds invested in 1996 generated 3,405 pounds four years later; an increased value of 240 percent in contrast to a 65 percent valorization rate in the same period in the London Stock Exchange (Santos, 2004, p. 27). Current commercialized education, incomplete as it is, already generates around 365 billion dollars in profits worldwide.[4] Indeed a profitable business that could greatly expand if higher education is formally defined and treated as a "commodity" under the WTO's General Agreement on Trade and Services (GATS).[5]

Four modes of service supply have been explained by Rikowski to carry out such commercialization under GATS's requirements to avoid "discrimination against foreign multinationals entering services markets": 1) through "cross-border" supply (as the online educational services or online universities already in a boom stage), 2) through the supply concerned with the "consumption abroad" where the consumer travels to the service supplier (tightly linked to the brain drain process), 3) through what is called the "commercial presence" where the services suppliers establish themselves in the foreign market as a legal entity in the form of a subsidiary or branch (i.e., the University of Florida of Panama), and 4) by the "presence of natural persons" from another country which means that those subsidiaries might operate with employees from the matrix country (Rikowski, 2001, n.p; Santos, 2004, p. 32–37). In such a context, any dispute must be solved through the WTO's Dispute Settlement Process under the operation of tribunals in which only member states are allowed to participate with no outside appeals procedures (Rikowski, 2002, n.p.).

Up to now, the United States, New Zealand, and Australia have been most enthusiastic with the "benefits" of the GATS since, as Santos points out, these countries are at the top of the exporting education services business. The European Union, on the contrary, has "liberalized" the education sector with some restrictions in order, first, to get prepared to compete in the world market. It is a policy geared at strengthening the internal market in education as well as the homogenization and standardization of the general education framework policy, prior to completing the "liberalization" of the sector. For the business interests involved, bilateral and multilateral agreements on education liberalization and privatization are the best bet, at least in the short term (Santos, 2004, p. 36–37).

WB insists that to achieve quality and efficiency in higher education, "a great productivity" is required. Adding that, ". . . the main higher educational productivity problems lie not so much with excessive costs, but with insufficient learning." (Johnstone, 1998, p. 6) "Therefore the following step, according to the WB, is to redefine the evaluating parameters of the universities' budget in terms of a commercially verifiable performance." (Ibidem) This means measurements based on standardized indicators focused on criteria "that are of interest" to the market: in other words, a criteria based on national and foreign entrepreneurs' requirements and interests.

As a case in point, the WB states that, ". . . among Mexican universities there is an increasing realization that regular operating subsidies from the government will not grow. Hence, the private sector will be the source for the extra income required, involving faculty and students in this effort. Some departments are beginning to generate income on their own, through the sale of services, specialized courses, etc. Even in disciplines where this was once unthinkable, this is happening by imitation." (Ibid, p. 17)

In a similar vein, the WB's *Country Assistance Strategy 2002–2006* (for México) encourages a "new educational culture" in which ". . . supervisor and parent participation will have to focus less on process and more on actual results, as measured by published student scores in standardized national tests" (World Bank, 2002, p. 12). Everything indicates that, for the WB, the content of teaching and the process of educating new generations are no longer relevant.

In early 2004 and following the WB recipes, the Mexican government announced its intention to condition any new funds to public universities on the application of standardized proficiency examinations. By this type of funding, said the government, it would benefit the "competitiveness" of the private sector. By 2007 this scheme was being partially implemented through random evaluation exercises, the application of diagnostic tests at the beginning of the university career—an implicit prerequisite to apply for a Conacyt or a WB/Pronabes scholarship (México's National Scholarship Program)—and the formalization of an optional placement and ranking test at the end of the bachelor's stage.

Actually the "authorities" are not talking about any real increase in public expenditure for higher education. Such budget has not only been frozen, but with Calderon it has been reduced in real terms, while it has been substituted by highly 'conditioned' loans, donations, or other arrangements of this kind. In addition, the remaining public budget would be assigned to different functions because, as the WB has indicated, the ". . . Mexican government is very keen to increase demand-side financing—that is, financing students rather than institutions, to improve access to higher education." (Johnstone, 1998: 11) This is precisely the purpose of the WB/Pronabes program formalized by Fox in 2001 with the WB. In 2006, 58 percent of the program's resources came from the WB.

Private sector presence is felt not only in study plans or evaluations of scholarship assigning but also in major public universities' internal decision making, particularly with regard to budgetary decisions. Major public universities' autonomy is being shattered by being forced to accept funding from the private sector, national and international foundations or the IFI's funding for infrastructure, equipment, scholarships, etc. In UNAM's case, the major university in Latin America, ranked as 68 worldwide, this is particularly true as it is illustrated by the IADB's "Science and Technology Program" (IADB, 2002), among other WB loans such as the one for the "Corruption and Transparency Analysis and Documentation Lab" (www.corruption.unam.mx). Another case in point is UNAM's Foundation, in charge of managing important university assets and key cultural and social events. Top Mexican businessmen, the crème of the crème, are members of the Foundation's board of trustees: such as Carlos Hank-Rohn, Alfredo Harp, and Guillermo Ortiz, all of them presided by Carlos Slim, the leading Mexican businessman at the very top of the Forbes list of billionaires.

Ironically, while the economic crisis worsens, unemployment among the young grows the most and salaries shrink to a critical point, the tendency to privatize higher education is dramatically reducing the number of total enrollments as public options are becoming "limited." This is a recipe for widespread class conflict. By placing private institutions as the alternative, higher education is transformed into a commodity that can only be afforded by high income families and only partially by the middle class. This scheme is central in any objective assessment of a "standardized evaluation system" being fostered by the WB and local functionaries, which clearly responds to the necessity of employers to rank the workforce according to the amount that the client (the student) is "willing" to pay.

In an extraordinary statement on the "externalities" of its agenda, the WB acknowledges that in Latin America, ". . . the statistics indicate that the proportion of students attending private institutions has more than doubled over the last fifteen years. But, at the same time the proportion of people being educated nationwide is dropping at a worrisome rhythm." (Ibid, p. 14) This is a case either of institutionalized schizophrenia or cynicism that becomes more striking if one takes into account that in 2004, Cuba, the only country in Latin America not under WB modernizing programs, ranked at the very top of the region's educational achievement list (measured by the population's years of schooling) with an average of 11 years of education nationwide in contrast to Colombia with around 7 years, Chile with 8.5, México with 7.3, Argentina with 9, or Brazil with 6.1 years.[6]

In México, while in the decade of 1980 the primary and secondary cycles were mainly covered by public institutions, according to Organization for Economic Cooperation and Development (OECD) data, by 1999 the percentage of students attending private institutions accounted for 7.4 percent in primary (first six years of schooling), 13.4 percent in "lower secondary" (7th to 9th year) and, 21.4 percent at the upper secondary (10th to 12th year of schooling).

This privatization trend of public education, along with the recent emphasis on technical schooling of middle and higher education (basically training a skilled workforce), is better understood in the context of the worldwide trends and changes being observed in the workforce and in the "South-North/North-South" transfers of workers.

EDUCATING THE WORLD'S WORKFORCE

Chart 3.1 indicates a general approximation of the composition of the workforce and the transfer tendency between the North or capitalist central states (left block) and the South or the capitalist periphery states (right block). The classification of the workforce segments does not respond to just "years of schooling," which can be tricky when, among other things, it takes into account those individuals that have just one year of schooling in each level. Even so, here we take the years of schooling into account. In part this is because the national and international data are made in such a way, and the segments employed are also based—and named—by the type and content of education as a function of the workforce to be prepared. This is a way of partially avoiding the multiple "black boxes" behind the official indicators that make it a difficult comprehensive analysis. For example, the difference of years that each country takes into account for primary, secondary and tertiary education levels had recently allowed China, by reducing the years of its primary education program, to achieve the United Nations' Millennium goal of "universalizing the primary education" (Conference sponsored by the UN and the WB in Jomtien, Thailand, 1990).[7]

Keeping all this in mind, from Chart 3.1 it can be said that the illiterate group (I) or those with no schooling at all, is almost nil in the North, but is a considerable proportion of the South's population—in some regions almost half. For example, the Mexican illiteracy national average is around 11 percent,[8] but in the southern regions of the country, like Chiapas and Guerrero, the illiteracy rate increases to nearly half of the population, particularly within the indigenous one.[9] In other Latin American countries the percentage is higher. In

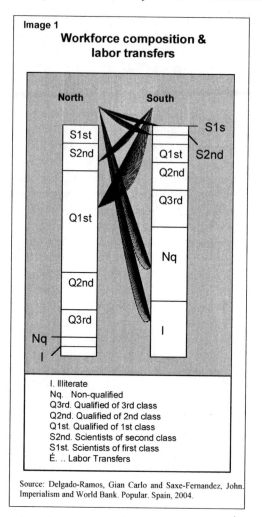

Image 1

Workforce composition & labor transfers

I. Illiterate
Nq. Non-qualified
Q3rd. Qualified of 3rd class
Q2nd. Qualified of 2nd class
Q1st. Qualified of 1st class
S2nd. Scientists of second class
S1st. Scientists of first class
É. .. Labor Transfers

Source: Delgado-Ramos, Gian Carlo and Saxe-Fernandez, John. Imperialism and World Bank. Popular. Spain, 2004.

Chart 3.1 Workforce composition and labor transfers

Brazil (21.2 percent). In Colombia (19.8 percent) (Barro and Jong-Wha, 2000, n.p.). The illiterate population in Latin America and the Caribbean is around 39 million (AFP, 2005, n.p.).

The same proportion within the North and the South is present with the "not qualified" (NQ) segment, where we would locate elementary education (this category includes the population that has some or has completed the first six years of schooling).[10] In México this segment accounted for between 37.8 percent and 47.3 percent of the population in 2000.[11] In other Latin American countries, the percentage is around half of the population or even more: in Argentina 49.6 percent, in Brazil 56 percent, in Chile 42 percent, in Colombia 19.8 percent (Barro and Jong-Wha, 2000, n.p.).

Qualified people of the third class (Q3) have an education corresponding to technical junior high school (some lower secondary education or between the 7th and 9th year of schooling). In the North, this is also a minority group, while in the South, they are in a third position, although of course, smaller than that of the NQ, and obviously of the I segment. In México, Q3 accounts for 24.4 percent of the total population, and 19.1 percent of those with the three years of schooling are included (www.inegi.gob.mx).

Qualified workers of the second class (Q2), who have senior high school or some "upper secondary education" (10th to 12th year of schooling), whether in the technical, scientific, or humanistic fields are of significant importance because of their number in both regions (the North and the South). They fill most of the ranks of "technicians" in both South and North. Particularly those enrolled in private institutions are employed as some type of First class segment's (Q1) workforce in the South, which is different from the Q1 of the North. In the last one, that labor segment (of "first class" technicians) mainly include those that hold either a technical bachelor's degree or, going to the top of this group and in a smaller proportion, a technical master's degree. The percentage is difficult to determine because the group is not defined mainly by the number of schooling years but by the "type" of education. The percentage of Mexican population that has at least one year of "upper secondary education" is 16.8 percent (Ibid). If segments Q3 and Q2 are added in order to get what it is generally known as "secondary education level," the average for México falls between 29 percent and 41.2 percent, depending on the data.[12] In other Latin American countries, for example, Q3 and Q2 accounts for 13.5 percent of the total population in Brazil, 36 percent in Chile, or 21.4 percent in Colombia (Barro and Jong-Wha, 2000, n.p.).

Scientists of the second class (S2nd) are those having a nontechnical bachelor's, a master's degree, or a PhD degree, and who carry out, at the most, basic activities of science and technology research. This is the smallest group after that of the scientists of the first class (S1st) or of those scientists involved in the development of advanced science and high tech. It should be noted that the S2nd and S1st in the North are considerably larger groups than in the periphery, probably because they receive larger *stimuli* and resources than those in the South. Again, the percentages are difficult to determine because the different categories are defined by the type and quality of education and not mainly by the number of years of schooling. Even though, in México, if we include in the S2nd category some Bachelor's degree (undergraduate) education (at least one year) and we add the S1st to same group usually known as the "tertiary level of education," the percentage from the total population is only 11 percent.[13] In other Latin American countries, such percentage is 8.4 percent in Brazil, 15.8 percent in Chile, and 9.9 percent in Colombia. All these numbers shrink when we look at the percentage of the population holding a bachelor's degree. In México this accounts for only around 7 percent of the population. This figure includes those with a master's degree, a PhD, or postdoctoral degrees. These represent no more than the 2.5 percent of the country's population.

While the metropolitan tendency is to increase the Q1 groups, reducing all blocks under this segment, and to open the possibilities of augmenting slightly those located above, although not necessarily so (due, among other factors, to the extended privatization of the sector); the 'Peripheral' countries, on the other hand, tend to widen the Q3 block (and, to a much lesser extent, the Q2 segment), specially to satisfy the demand of trained technicians capable of meeting the necessary requirements to operate, maintain, and fix the machine tools that the North transfers to the South, whether by sale of technology or through *maquila* factories in the periphery's territory.

This is one of the fabulous "comparative advantages" that some well placed "personalities" in the social sciences tell the periphery to use to their advantage. The groups downward could be little reduced but to the extent in which the demand of Q3 and Q2 encourages them. The S1st and very few S2nd of the periphery will continue being financially preempted by the capitalist central states (brain drain), especially if the extended scenery in which resources for their education—in the periphery—continue to diminish or are privatized, and this situation persists.

For instance, México's Conacyt has reduced by almost two thirds the number of scholarships for graduate studies abroad, and has cancelled the formal mechanisms established to repatriate scientists that benefited from the scholarships. This started occurring at a time when the president of that institution proudly announced that the brain drain phenomenon must not be seen as such, but as "a natural export" of "Mexican ambassadors" (Rodríguez, 2004, n.p; Castaños-Lomnitz, 2004). This line of "reasoning" seems to be compatible with the basic posture and aims of a government then presided over by a former CEO of Coca-Cola. But it is important to realize that the brain drain phenomena has important costs to the Global south because these countries pay for those "ambassadors'" education and because it directly affects, in the most negative way, the capacity of the South to develop its own scientific, technological, and research and development agenda. But, most importantly, because the loss of brains also implies grave loss of highly qualified social leaders.[14]

The "brain drain" figures speak for themselves. In the last forty years Latin America has "exported" to the North 1.1 million scientists and researchers, an average of 27,500 experts per year. Direct economic cost for the education expenditures of this massive transfer of highly trained human resources has been estimated to be at least 30 billion dollars (Schlachter, 2005, n.p.). However, this might grossly underestimate the real direct costs, as we are dealing with all governmental investment in education, which includes the financing of teaching and research infrastructure, general overhead expenditures for each professional career being lost to the North, etc.

And that means, from kindergarten to the attainment of at least masters or doctoral degrees. That cost is estimated at U.S. $200 thousand dollars per career. If this is correct, the direct cost of the "brain drain" over 4 decades, would be around 200 billion dollars. Needless to say, the "qualitative loss" of this brain drain is immensurable.

The aforementioned "guidelines" did not originate within the walls of national educational ministries or research and development institutions but rather in the WB. Most of Conacyt's funds assigned for scholarships abroad, come from Nacional Financiera, a public institution functioning as a "clearing house" of many of heavily 'conditioned' loan packages "granted" by the WB to México. Consequently, for graduate aspirants, while the options to access to what is left of the national science and technology establishment continue to diminish, their opportunities to study abroad also tend to lessen. This shall result in an increase of Q1 due to the loss of subjects in S2nd and S1st that have to compete with their peers not only in the North, but also in their own country, as a consequence of the relative ease with which the metropolitan workforce in those categories can move between the metropolis and the periphery.

In contrast, the opportunities that the periphery's workforce has of legally moving toward the North are highly restricted and selective (including that of S2nd and S1st). This is in striking contrast to the neoliberal rhetoric of the urgent and "necessary" liberalization and deregulation of the economy as a whole.[15]

It is well known that when men and women of the periphery migrate to the North (if they do not die in the attempt) their services (generally of the I and Nq categories) are bought in the "market" under the stigmatized label of "illegal work," and thus they carry out the worst jobs for the lowest salary. What we have is a recipe for fostering underdevelopment, through liberalizing trade and capital, and implementing high restrictions to the workforce's cross national mobility.

This labor capital "arrangement" is an upside down welfare state on a global scale and has been all along the expected result of the application of "neoliberal policies," free trade agreements, and "competitiveness regional alliances" promoted in the Global south by the metropolis and the WB.[16] Thus, it is not surprising that WB's loans for the Latin American education sector have been dramatically increasing during recent decades. The total of the WB's highly conditioned loans for education from 1990 to 2004 is estimated at more than $4.6 billion.[17]

WORLD BANK'S EDUCATION LOANS IN MÉXICO

In the Mexican case, the co-participation of the national power elite has been a key factor to successfully achieve the WB's agenda in education, which is closely related to the Mexican workforce qualifications, as demanded within the context of the North American Free Trade Agreement (NAFTA). In 1990, former Secretary of Public Education Manuel Barttlet signed an agreement with México's private sector to establish new institutes of higher education under the direct management of Mexican businessmen. By 1999 there were 40 of these "modern" institutes initially financed through WB loans and rapidly under a *de facto* private sector management (National School of Professional and Technical Education—CONALEP) (World Bank, October 2004). In 2006 there were 268 such CONALEP schools organized in 30 state colleges and one operational unit in the Federal District (covering all the federal territory). This is more than all existing public universities (Ibid). At the same time a national Fund for the Modernization of Higher Education (FOMES) was established with the goal of promoting the private interests and perspectives in the "public institutes" by promoting short specialization courses (usually lasting two years).[18] In addition, a National Center for the Evaluation of the Higher Education (Ceneval) started operation. Its function is to evaluate, for a price, all candidates that apply for entrance in any public institute. This is done through a unique test designed by specialists and scientists selected by the business community (Aboites, 2000).

After "preparing" the national market for private higher education in 1994, the same year NAFTA was signed, and at a time when the so called "trinational mercantile parameters on education" (US, Canada, México) were established, as Aboites' pointed out, "former Public Education secretary of México, and later President of México Ernesto Zedillo, adopted as his own the WB's Agenda" here described. One of the first measures he adopted was the Program for the Improvement of Faculty—PROMEP (a kind of a market "certification" program not only on the quality, but mainly on the content of what is to be taught). It reinforced the FOMES program and the Ceneval's unique test (see Aboites, 1997).

By 1998, the WB lunched a 180 million dollar "Higher Education Financing Project" cosponsored with public funds from Conacyt and private donations (World Bank, June 1998, p. 4). The project, said the WB " . . . would have a positive impact on the coverage, quality and equity of higher education." By " . . . developing a private sector student loan scheme, it will contribute to increased equitable opportunities for participation in higher education," and, at the same time, "it will improve the quality of the education" because, as the Sonora Student Loan Institute (ICEES) and university administrators have pointed out, " . . . the students who bear some part of the costs of their education, whether they pay this up-front or borrow against their future earnings by taking out student loans, tend to be more motivated and academically successful" (Ibid, p. 1–2, 5).

The basic aim of this student funding program was to stimulate either the enrollment of students in private institutions (through direct WB's funding of the Society for the Promotion of Higher Education—SOFES; a financial intermediary of private universities; and members of the Mexican Federation of Private Universities—FIMPES, which represents the most important private institutions in México), or to obtain some sort of social legitimacy by using the high fees already being charged by the University of Sonora (a public institution). The idea was to settle all discussion on fees, thus avoiding any public discussion, and by further modulating the social reaction with a strong scholarship program financed by the WB (through the Sonora Student Loan Institute). It is important to take notice that Sonora was chosen because its public university already charged high tuition fees, before the WB's project came into action, therefore the WB's program stimulated the privatization of a public university minimizing "political risk."[19] The goal was not to educate poor people. If that had been the case, the Bank could have selected a Mexican state with a high percentage of the national undergraduate population, such as Oaxaca or Chiapas, and not Sonora with just 4 percent of the total.

All these have deeply impacted UNAM, as indicated by the adoption of a wide "modernization" of teaching programs' content of its schools and faculties; a reduction in public financing and a considerable increase in private grants and loans for high quality research now being carried out by UNAM's scientists and researchers. Charging higher registrations costs and board fees has been an explosive issue in México. By proposing such an increase, the then administration had to face a student and faculty strike that lasted a whole academic year (1999–2000). The former rector and his advisers were forced to resign, and the imminent divestiture process then being implemented by that administration under WB and IADB guidance as well as the privatization of the university were stopped.

Student and societal rejection of UNAM's divestiture, privatization, and outsourcing has been labeled by WB technocrats as a "ferocious resistance." In response, the Bank and its *country managers are devising and implementing new mechanisms to defuse such "ferocious opposition."* According to a WB statement, the Fox administration agreed to " . . . change the culture of Mexico's educational system, a change that will take time but that can start during the current administration." (World Bank, 2002, p. 12) In fact, this was one of the main "missions" carried out by the Fox administration in this sphere.

Fox continued the WB's "Knowledge and Innovation Project" (4349/ME), approved by the Zedillo administration (1994–2000) by renovating it for 2005–2009, as "Innovation for Competitiveness Project" (7296/ME). Both projects totaled 550 million dollars in WB's loans and are aimed at a) establishing formal links among universities and private (national and/or foreign) enterprises, b) the expansion of a peer evaluation system, c) the decentralization of decision making processes, d) the identification and promotion of new research and development fields under public/private collaborative schemes, and e) the monitoring and evaluation of Conacyt's institutional capacities.

As a consequence of implementing this "project," the WB through the Fox administration proceeded to sponsor the reform of the National Science and Technology Law and Conacyt's Organic Statues. The aim was to promote a program for sector funding managed by Conacyt, the corresponding state department—agriculture, energy, education, etc.—and the private sector. As a result of implementing these programs, the science and technology agenda became a highly mercantile affair while any hope for building a coherent national science and technology program, vital for the future of the country, has evaporated, at least for the time being.

The short-term WB's blueprint has been clearly defined in its report "Mexico's Challenge of Knowledge-based Competitiveness" (World Bank, 2006):

> México's strategic objective should be a dramatic increase in productivity through knowledge-based integration into global value chains and participation in knowledge networks. To achieve this Mexico will require reform of its system of national innovation and enterprise upgrading. A dynamic and flexible innovation system must be led by private demand and it must respond to private sector needs (. . .) in the short term the policy agenda should focus on formulating a cohesive strategy, improving incentives, and increasing the role of the private sector in public programs (Ibid, p. 15).

Regarding Conacyt, the WB adds:

> the government could enhance its catalytic function by i)supporting research and training linked to joint ventures between international and domestic technology companies, ii) prompting international technology companies to create research teams in México through a staff-exchange scheme, iii) moving science and technology researchers from government institutions to companies through specific public-private incentive programs, iv) leveraging innovation spillovers from FDI through targeted investment promotion, and v) expanding programs supporting innovation start-ups with matching grants through private venture capital firms and incubation assistance (Ibid, p. 16).

More WB projects are on line: In 2005 it planned a 200 million dollar Conacyt-II Project yet to be approved.

CONCLUSION: RESISTANCE

In 1908 Thorstein Veblen warned about the commercialization of higher education—including science and technology development. He noticed that the scholarly goals of inquiry and the pursuit of truth were being substituted by a businesslike attitude, " . . . a merchantable commodity, to be produced on a piece rate plan, rated, bought and sold in standard units, measured, counted and reduced to staple equivalence by impersonal mechanical tests." (Veblen, 1965, n.p; Vidich, 1994, p. 639–668)

The consequences of all these trends and policies being implemented are deep-seated because the public university is being estranged from national public interests, losing its critical capacity and that of generating the type of knowledge and technology required by the societies and economies of the Global south. All of this is happening at a time when multinational corporations, and to a lesser degree local entrepreneurs, are placed as "the key agents" in the transformation of higher education; as the new architects of universities; the guiding light that defines what scientific technological research should be done; how, when, and what must or must not be taught in school rooms, thus seriously undermining the autonomy required to carry on theoretical and scientific advancement based on objective or "idle intellectual curiosity."

To reverse current trends and give impulse to a truly educational project based on the national public interest, we consider, as a prerequisite, to reclaim the instruments of decision, which have become increasingly alienated in favor of institutions such as the WB through the conditionality linked to all their credit lines. This is the foundation upon which to build a re-articulation of an economic model that centers on fostering the well-being and interests of the population as a whole.

NOTES

1. By 1971, Nixon unilaterally imposed a surcharge on imports, thus violating the spirit and the letter of the Gatt, a cornerstone of the economic structure of Pax Americana.
2. Even that the report was 'only' supported by the World Bank as part of *its* contributions to the UNESCO World Conference on Higher Education (Paris, France. October, 1998), it widely reflects the views of the Bank's Board, as it can be proved by the blueprint of the diverse WB's programs on education around the globe; some of them are pointed out here. On this, see: Saxe-Fernández, 2003, p. 55–66.
3. "Remarks" at Seminario Internacional, Programa El Mundo Actual, Centro de Investigaciones Interdisciplinarias en Ciencias y Humanidades, National Autonomous University of México (UNAM), fall 2000.
4. The tendency of commercialization is already taking place. As Glenn Rikowski had written, " . . . on information gleaned from the EU GATS Infopoint, it appears education has already been lost to the GATS. For primary education, 20 countries committed themselves to GATS disciplines in 1994, and for secondary education 22 countries took the plunge. The EU is GATS-committed for both primary and secondary education." (Rikowski, 2002). For profits data, see: Avilés, 2004.
5. The WTO agreements are: Trade Related Investment Measures (TRIMS), Trade Related Intellectual Property Measures (TRIPS), General Agreement on Trade in Services (GATS), Sanitary and Phytosanitary Standards Agreement (SPS), Financial Services Agreement (FSA); and specific agreements on agriculture, information technology and telecommunications.
6. The data of Cuba is taken from the Ministry of Economy and corresponds to the year 2004, México's from INEGI (www.inegi.gob.mx) for the year 2004, Chile from the Government of Chile for the year 2002, Brasil from the

National 2001 Indicators, Colombia from the National Ministry of Education for the 2004, and those for Argentina are approximated based on Barro and Jong-Wha's data for 2000.

7. For a critical analysis of the primary education transformations around the world in the last decades, read: Andrade, 2000.

8. Barro and Jong-Wha's data for 2000 indicates that the illiterate population in México (that does not reads and write properly) was the 12.4 percent of the total population. INEGI's (Nacional Institute for Geographic and Stadistic Information of México) data indicates that for the same year, it was only 10.3 percent. Here we have used an average number. (See: Barro and Jong-Wha, 2000; and www.inegi.gob.mx).

9. Accordingly with INEGI's data for the year 2000, the illiterate indigenous population in the country accounted for 33.8 percent. In Chiapas the percentage was 43 percent, and in Guerrero it was 52.1 percent (www.inegi.gob.mx).

10. In Latin America and the rest of the South, large shares of the population have only a few years of education. Limiting the analysis to only the population who have completed at least one education level would discard a significant fraction of the population with some level of schooling. Therefore in the official statistics, considered into each level are those individuals who at least have one year of schooling in each level.

11. On one hand, INEGI's data indicates a 37.8 percent of the population. Nearly the half of this percentage (18.4 percent of the total population) represents the population with an incomplete primary education that ranges between the first to the fifth year of schooling. Only the rest (19.4 percent) of that group of the population has a complete primary education (six years). On the other hand, Barro and Jong-Wha's data indicates that the population with some primary education accounts for a 47.3 percent of the total population.

12. INEGI's data for the year 2000 indicates that the percentage is 41.2 percent while Barro and Jong-Wha's data gives a 29 percent. Assuming that the Mexican governmental data is accurate, we can say that there is an increased "technical trend" in México's workforce, a number that would increase if we take into account the Q1 workforce with a bachelors technical degree.

13. INEGI's and Barro and Jong-Wha's data are the same in this case with 11.3 percent and 11 percent, respectively.

14. In addition to that aspect, the exponential specialization of education had been generating a lost of memory, particularly a loss of historical memory, increasingly reducing the production of critical and utopian thinking.

15. For example, the US policy on the issue clearly shows the need in that country for foreign brains, but at the same time, its tight regulations. Foreigners working in areas considered "sensitive" by the government, such as chemistry, engineering, and pharmacology, among others, are subject to a strong but attractive residence regulation. It is a type of control determined by specific length of the clearance, recently extended for up to four years for students and two years for working scientists, with the goal of making it easier for them to remain in the United States for the duration of their work or study programs. As stated by Asa Hutchinson, under secretary for border and transportation security in the Department of Homeland Security, " . . . this change sends a clear message that the U.S. highly encourages those with great scientific minds to explore studying and working in our country." (Lee, 2005, n.p.).

16. We follow the suggestion of Costa Rican former president Rodrigo Carazo who, when using that term, is referring to the Latin Americans holding higher offices in power, who follow as if blind mice the Bank's prescriptions.

17. The amounts are in current U.S. dollars (of 2004). See the World Bank Statistics on Education: http://econ.worldbank.org

18. Also the Inter American Bank (IDB) has been stimulating the WB's Agenda in the country. In this case, for example, by a grant for the Autonomous University of Guadalajara, to evaluate, adapt and expand two-year university programs that are closely linked with employment (See: World Bank, June 1998, p. 8).

19. Literal: " . . . limiting activities to the strengthening of the ICEES loan scheme and the establishment of the SOFES program was preferred for the following reasons: (a) cost-sharing is still rather controversial in Mexican public higher education institutions and focusing on these two activities would allow a growth in the country's experience while minimizing political risk; (b) the experiences of a public and private institution would provide fruitful lessons for future investments; (c) there is a strong sense of commitment and ownership for these programs; and (d) the conditions in other statuses are not yet sufficient for the establishment of a local version of ICEES." (World Bank, June 1998, p. 7)

REFERENCES

Aboites, H. (1997) *Viento del Norte: TLC y privatización de la educación superior en México*. México: Plaza y Valdés.

————. (2000) La privatización de la Universidad y la huelga en la UNAM. *Memoria*. No. 133. March. México.

Acheson, D. (1969) *Present at the creation*. New York: Norton.

AFP. (2005) En AL y el Caribe hay 39 millones de analfabetos, reportan CEPAL y UNESCO. *La Jornada*. February 3. México.

Andrade Oliveira, D. (2000) *Educaçao Básica: gesao do trabalho e da pobreza*. Editora Voze. Brazil.

Avilés, K. (2004) Sería un grave error dejar la educación al libre comercio: De la Fuente. *La Jornada*. June 29.

Barro, R. & Jong-Wha, L. (2000) *International data on educational attainment: updates and implications*. Cambridge, MA: Harvard University Press.

Castaños-Lomnitz, H. (2004) *La migración de talentos en México*. México: UNAM-Porrúa.

Delgado-Ramos, G. & Saxe-Fernández, J. (2004) *Imperialismo y Banco Mundial*. España, Cuba: Popular and Marinello.

Delgado-Ramos, G. & Saxe-Fernández, J. (2005) *Imperialismo en México*. México. Arena.

IADB. (2002) *Informe de Terminación del Proyecto*. Science and Technology Program. Loans 804/OC-ME and 001/SPQ-ME. México.

Johnstone, D. Bruce. (1998) *The financing and management of higher education:A status report on worldwide reforms*. World Bank. Buffalo, New York: State University of New York.

Kolko, G. & Kolko, J. (1972) *The limits of power*. New York: Harper and Row.

La Feber, W. (1989) *The American age*. New York: Norton.

Lee, K.A. (2005) U.S. relaxes visa rules for some scientists. *Herald Tribune*. February 15.

Rikowski, G. (2001) *The battle in Seattle: Its significance for education*. London: Tufnell Press.

Rodríguez, U. (2004) Cerebros mexicanos en fuga. *El Independiente*. January 24th. México.

Santos, Boaventura de Sousa. (2004) *A universidade no século XXI*. Brasil. Cortez.

Saxe-Fernández, J. (2002) *La Compra-Venta de México*. Mexico. Plaza y Janés.

————. (2003) La Banque mondiale et l'enseignement supérieur en Amérique latine et ailleurs. *Alternatives Sud*, X (3).

Schlachter, A. (2005) Ciencia, globalización y sostenibilidad. *Granma*. February, 10th.

United Nations. (1990) *World Declaration on Education for AU*. Jomtien, Thailand. Available at http://www.unesco.org/education/efa/ed_for_all/background/ jomtien_declaration.shtml.

van Vught, F. (1994) Autonomy and accountability in government/university relationships. In Jamil Salmi and Adriaan Verspoor, Eds. *Revitalizing higher education*. London: Pergamon Press.

Veblen, T. (1965) *The higher learning in America*. Fairfield, NJ: Augustus M. Kelley.

Vidich, A.J. (1994) The higher learning in America in Veblen's time and our own. *International Journal of Politics, Culture and Society*, 7 (4).

World Bank. (1998) *Higher education financing project*. Report No. 17174. Washington. June.

————. (2002) *Country assistance strategy*. Report No. 23849-ME Washington. April 19.

————. (2004) *Country assistance strategy 2004–2008*. Report No. 28141-ME. Washington, C.D. April 15.

————. (2004) *Technical education and training modernization project*. Report No. 30232. Washington, October.

————. (2006) México's challenge of knowledge-based competitiveness: challenges and opportunities. *Colombia and Mexico Country Management Unit*, Volume 1. Washington DC. June.

————. (2007) *Country partnership strategy progress report for the United Mexican States for the period FY05–08*. Washington, D.C. January 8.

4 Argentina
Growth, Height, and Crisis of Teachers' Opposition to Neoliberal Reforms 1991–2001[1]

Julián Gindin

INTRODUCTION

My objective is to analyze the policies of the Argentina Republic Confederation of Education Workers (CTERA) in respect to the neoliberal offensive from 1991–2001. Neoliberal reforms in the 1990s promoted discussions about the worker's pension systems, the working conditions of teachers, the criteria to define remunerations, and educational system management. Even if the balance of the process was clearly negative for teachers, they managed to keep most of their contracting conditions and led the erosion of the neoliberal education reform projects. CTERA became stronger as a political union and educational actor, and in 1997 installed in front of the National Congress the "Carpa Blanca de la Dignidad Docente" (White Tent of Teacher Dignity). It was probably the principal union protest of the decade, and allowed CTERA, during two years, to lead the opposition to neoliberal policies, defending education as a social right and partially transcending the professional interests of teachers. Showing the relation of the CTERA with the federal government and opposition parties and describing the political process as a whole, the chapter concludes by focusing on the difficulties and the political conditions of the universalization of the worker's struggle.

NEOLIBERAL REFORMS AND THE TEACHING PROFESSION

The neoliberal agenda appeared in Argentina together with the last military dictatorship (1976–1983). The final dictatorship had an important social, political, and economic role. Drastic repression marked an era of increasingly open markets and shrinking internal industrialization and market expansion.

After the military dictatorship, in 1983 Raúl Alfonsin became the first candidate for the presidency of the Radical Civic Union (UCR) that defeated the Justicialist Party (PJ).[2] The PJ maintained its tough opposition to the government from the provincial governments and the workers' movement: There were thirteen general strikes during the six years of Alfonsin's presidency. The impulse of the neoliberal policies lost strength during the Raul Alfonsin government (1983–1989), partially because of political paralysis and economic recession, and recuperated force in the 1990s during the Carlos Menem presidencies (1989–1995 and 1995–1999).

After the high inflation of the eighties, economic stabilization was one of the most important demands of the reformist agenda. The parity between the peso and the U.S. dollar was fixed by law and the inflation index was stabilized during the Convertibility Plan.[3] The relative stabilization of real salaries, which were devalued until then, contributed to the workers' demobilization, but this wasn't the only factor. The repression of the military dictatorship—marked by the murdering of thousands of union base leaders—the large ideological offensive, the market labor changes, the fact that the PJ was in government, the policies to integrate the unions into the reforms, and the economic crisis contributed to the hegemony of the neoliberal program of capitalist restructuring.

With the exception of a short recession in 1995, the Argentine economy grew during the nineties until 1998. This growth was attributed to the policies of free markets, privatization, and fiscal adjustment, making Argentina one of Latin America's "examples" for international credit organizations. In the beginning of the Menem government, economic growth and falling inflation rates made possible increased employment. After the implementation of neoliberal reforms, however, dramatic effects upon the labor market began to crystallize. In the last years of the Menem presidency, external debt accumulation, increased interest rates, and less foreign investment resulted in economic recession in 1998.

The effects on the labor market and income inequality were deep. Informal labor, which is labor not protected by labor legislation, increased during the 1990s. Unemployment grew from 6.3 percent in 1991 to 14.7 percent by the end of 2000. In the same period, the richest 10 percent of the population increased its control of total income from 35.5 percent to 40.3 percent. The Gini index, which measures income inequality, increased from 0.44 to 0.48 within the decade (Damill, Frenkel, & Mauricio, 2002).

A political opposition front won the 1999 elections, but continued with neoliberal reforms which led to a rapid loss of its legitimacy. In December of 2001, a spontaneous insurrection forced the resignation of President Fernando de la Rua. The political crisis was expressed by massive mobilizations shouting "que se vayan todos, que no quede ni uno solo" (everybody get out, no one remain). Sectors of the bourgeois took advantage of the unstable political situation to press for the devaluation of the currency, suggesting that the devaluation would end the economic recession. The devaluation did indeed end the economic recession in 2003, but the popular sectors suffered as a result of super inflation and salary contraction.

The reformist wave during the nineties in the educational arena, as in society as a whole, was expressed in a large offensive against social and labor rights. The Teachers Statutes, particularly in those aspects concerned with stability, license regimes, and salary structures were considered rigid by the reformers of the nineties, who tried to introduce different policies of payment for productivity and specific tasks.[4] They argued that the teacher's salary structure, because of its universal character, discouraged teacher initiative. This fact, they argued, added to the nonexistence of an evaluation system that would reward bad professors.

The teacher's social welfare system endured a profound offensive, the goal of which was to open the administration of the pension and health care funds to private administrators, or at least to introduce market logic into their administration.[5] Another objective was to deal with the fund shortages produced by an aging population and declining pension contributions—stimulated by the increase of nonregistered employment.

Teacher wage devaluation, part of the state policy in the decade, preceded the period in which we are interested. In fact, the economic recession of the eighties had a dramatic impact on teachers' salaries. In the nineties, when the economy grew, their wage situation did not improve. According to Rivas (2004) teachers' salaries decreased from 100 percent of the Gross Domestic Product per capita in 1980 to 63 percent in 1991 and 56 percent in 1999. In the nineties, despite the economic growth, their wage situation did not improve. From 1993 to 1998, there was an increase in the GDP though salaries remained low. The relation between teacher's salaries and economy became closer in the recessive last years of the decade until the 2001 dramatic crisis—when, with a common base of 1993:100, salaries exceeded the GDP evolution (General Study Coordination of the Educational System Costs, 2008).

Neoliberal reforms in education questioned teacher's pedagogical capabilities. The curriculum modifications in teacher training were part of this, requiring further training for teachers. This process was referred to as "professionalisation," but it is important to consider that, in this context, "professionalisation" is understood as a training technique, without taking into account the autonomy of teachers at work (Oliveira, 2003). In fact, the "professionalized" reform is a part of educational policy that increases control over teachers.

The growth of social inequality and the need for investment in education also contributed to modifications in teachers' working conditions. Teachers were forced to play the role of social workers, infrastructure conditions declined, violence increased inside schools, and teacher dissatisfaction grew because of low social valorization to their work. More teachers began to work in more than one institution—to compensate for salary devaluation—intensifying their workload. The whole transformation strained teachers' physical and mental health. More teachers reported mental health problems such as depression and emotional tiredness (OREALC/UNESCO, 2005; Tenti, 2005).

The material and symbolic deterioration of the teaching profession had profound consequences on teacher subjectivity, promoting a transformation in professional identity, with vocational elements having less importance. It also led to a transformation of the sociological composition of the teaching body, with the entry of teachers from the lower class sectors. In a deteriorated labor market, teaching is a profession desired for the job stability it represents (Birgin, 1999).

Teachers responded to the difficult social, economic, and professional situations in various individual and collective ways. My objective is to analyze the growth, the height, and the crisis of national teacher collective opposition to neoliberal reforms.[6]

THE CTERA'S POLICIES IN THE 1990s

The CTERA, created in 1973, evolved into a national federation of state level unions for public school teachers. In 1987 the Light Blue slate, linked to the PJ, won CTERA's elections.[7] A year later was the most important teacher strike since Argentine democratization took place. Lasting more than fourteen days without classes, teachers demanded a salary update and collective bargaining negotiations with the government.

Elected in 1989 in the middle of hyperinflation, Carlos Menem's (PJ) presidency began early because of the dimension of Alfonsin's government problems, which couldn't control either the economic or social crisis. Menem's presidency began an aggressive policy of public company privatizations, labor, and state reforms. These policies caused important conflicts, but they were not centralized. The first years of the Menem government were still politically and economically unstable until the Convertibility Plan.

In this difficult situation, various items appointed in the democratic pedagogical agenda of the 80s—related to teaching universalization and the education system's democratization—were completely dislocated by a new discourse focusing on poverty reduction using compensation policies and market logic promotion. Neoliberal discourse appropriated some concepts presented in leftist pedagogical discourse such as "autonomy," "decentralization," and "teacher professionalization." It also hid the responsibility of the state and blamed the teachers and the schools for unsatisfactory education results (Imen, 2005).

With respect to teacher's work, two examples of the difficulties to keep any advance into the hegemonic neoliberal context are clear. In April 1991, the Collective Bargaining Teacher Workers Law was sanctioned, a late result of the 1988 strike. It was never applied. The same year, the "Teacher's Special Pensions Law" was sanctioned. It established a special regime for the retiring age of national professors. Women aged 60 and men aged 65 with 25 years of teaching service could become eligible for pension benefits of up to 82 percent of their salaries.[8] Years later, the 78/94 decree revoked the law of teacher pensions and other special regimes. The legal attempt to protect the special regimes, in the teachers' case, was not successful until 2005.

Two laws reformed the elementary educational system. The first one was the Transference Law of 1991, which concluded the task began in 1978 by the last military dictatorship, when national primary schools were transferred to the provinces. The law transferred to the provinces the schools remaining under federal jurisdiction—basically secondary schools. The process finished in 1994. The second law was the Federal Education Law, sanctioned in 1993.

The Federal Education Law redefined the educational concepts in neoliberal terms by promoting privatization policies, orienting education to the labor market and "employability," and redefined the role of the state. The law reformed the education system structure by establishing two cycles of nine (General Basic Education) and three years (Polymodal), instead of the old cycles of seven and five years. Associated with the creation of the new cycles, a large curricular transformation was made. The law also created new mechanisms of control and regulation with a national evaluation system and national "Common Basic Content" defined by education "experts." After the transference of schools and the reform of the education system, the federal government kept their control mechanisms, such as the quality evaluation system and the definition of acceptable teachers' formation courses, and compensatory policies, with the "Educational Social Plan." The provinces had their educational systems enlarged, but lost capacity to manage them.

More aggressive reform projects were in the agenda in 1992, but they were moderated because of opposition from the education community. The CTERA wasn't hegemonic among teachers in the large mobilizations of 1992 because of the presence of other national unions and an important autonomous mobilization process. The CTERA criticized the reform projects, but seemed to concentrate on financing issues and in guaranteeing free public education. Both goals were finally achieved because of the mobilization of the educational community. Years later, CTERA's attitude evolved into a general discussion against Menemist education policy.

Unions were divided between agreement and confrontation with Menem. Within the latter group, there were two principal actors. One created in 1992 the Argentinean Workers Congress (CTA), an alternative central to the Work General Confederation (CGT). CTERA was part of this more creative and socially active group, but it also faced more difficulties in dialogue with the remaining unions. The other group, the Movement of Argentinean Workers (MTA), was created in 1994 and tried to lead the CGT, the major central union. The MTA, because of its importance in the transportation unions could carry successful general strikes with the CTA even without the participation of the CGT.

Apart from the CTA and the MTA, other unions kept relative autonomy from Menem's government and were by no means disposed to resign power positions. The liberalization of the unions' monopoly in health services contracting and the reform of the collective bargaining law were two of the neoliberal offensives that faced more union resistance.

The social costs of Menem's economic program increased national social movement opposition beginning in 1994 with the "Federal Mobilization" and several general strikes (see the diagram in page 68). After the government retreated from hard line reform in some respects, and after the resignation of the Economy Minister Domingo Cavallo—author of the Convertibility Plan—many unions became closer to Menem. The CTA and the MTA kept an opposition attitude, but between 1997 and 1999, the political discussion took an electoral course: In 1997 the PJ lost the legislative elections, and in 1999 lost the presidential elections. Both elections were won by the Alliance for Work, Education, and Justice—known as the "Alliance." The Alliance consisted of the UCR and the Solidarian Country Front (FREPASO), a new party integrated by CTERA's leadership which came in second place in the 1995 elections, breaking the polarized Argentinean electoral system. Despite this, the new president, Fernando de la Rua, belonged to the UCR.

EDUCATIONAL REFORM AND TEACHER'S UNIONS IN THE PROVINCES

With the new education legal structure sanctioned, the transference concluded, and the Federal Education Pact signed in 1994, the circumstances of the educational reform implementation and the relationship between the governments and the teachers' unions became principally provincial. Implementing the Federal Education Pact, the federal government allocated resources to the provinces, in exchange for the province's compromise with the application of educational reform. In this way, the decentralization rhetoric hid the fact that the national government kept the leadership of the reform in the provinces more dependent on federal funds (in a lot of cases, more than half of the provincial budget was composed by federal funds).

Also within the provinces, the educational system management became more authoritarian and teachers lost influence. In some provinces, supervisors (the highest position in the teaching profession) lost power and governments froze Qualification and Discipline Boards (see footnote 4). In Neuquén and Río Negro, two provinces in which during the 80s there were some democratic advances in the system, the situation regressed. The Education Councils, which should have been independent and democratic organisms in charge of education management, were eliminated or relegated to an advisory role. In only four small provinces, the councils kept their original function (Rivas, 2004).

One of the most important changes established in the Federal Education Law was the creation of the two academic cycles already referenced. Only in Buenos Aires City and in the provinces of Río Negro and Neuquén was this change not implemented. In Buenos Aires City and in Río Negro, political differences between the authorities and the federal government prevented changes. In Neuquén, radical teacher opposition halted alterations (Rivas, 2004).

The most ambitious neoliberal project was the "2001 Schools Project" of the San Luis province, sanctioned in 1999 and inspired by the charter schools' experience. In this initiative, Educational Associations were created and made responsible for the schools' management, the educational projects, teacher contracting and financial administration.[9] It was a politically important experience, but limited to a few schools. In general there were few advances in the more radical neoliberal educational management policies, educational transference to the municipalities, or in the liberalization of teacher contracting. In general, the Teachers Statutes survived the decade.[10] The only Teacher Statute sanctioned in the decade, that of Salta province, expressed the reform spirit: It permitted a link between completed teacher training courses and teacher salaries (Saforcada; Jaimovich; Pasmanik; Migliavacca, 2004). In the salary scheme, the principal modification was the perfect attendance gratification (known as "*presentismo*"), implemented to deal with teacher strikes and with working absences denounced by the government. In February 1999, 15 of the 24 jurisdictions, including the biggest ones (Buenos Aires City, Córdoba, Santa Fe, Buenos Aires, and Mendoza), paid *presentismo*. The costs of *presentismo* valued more than half of the basic salary of Santa Fe and Córdoba, and even exceeded it in Santa Cruz (Iñiguez, 2000). It constituted an important change, but the provincial, and particularly the national government, wanted further advances in this direction.

During this period, the public resources for education, as a GDP percentage, grew from 3.1 percent in 1990 to 3.6 percent in 1997 and 4.6 percent in 2000 (National Direction of Educational Quality Information and Evaluation). At least until the economic recession started in 1998, this increase meant also an increase in absolute terms. However, its growth wasn't used to increase teacher's salaries, but rather was used to carry out compensatory policies, to expand the educational system with new schools and teachers' jobs, and to finance educational reform as a whole (Rivas, 2003; 2004).

Meanwhile, the provincial fiscal deficits also affected teacher's salaries. In effect, working conditions, especially wages, were more affected by the fiscal situation than by the ideological and political positions of the government. In several jurisdictions salaries were frozen, delayed or even unpaid for months during the decade, but the situation became worse with the economic recession. In the "Federal Compromise" of December 1999, the provinces compromised to sanction fiscal adjustment laws. These laws established restrictions for the resources spent on employees (freezing gratifications, for example). On top of this, the provinces began to issue Bonuses, a kind of provincial currency, frequently devalued, with which they paid workers (Cetrángolo et al, 2002). Even without fiscal crises, Bonus or unpaid salaries, teacher's wages were regressively affected. In Buenos Aires city, a "rich" district, between 1985 and 1998 the basic teacher salary fell by 59% and the total teacher salary fell by 34% (Iñiguez, 2000).

At the same time, the reduction of employers' contributions and the aging population increased the deficit of the social security system. In 1993 the Pension Reform Law reformed the social security system and created the Integrated Pension System which incorporated the possibility of private management funds in a personal capitalization regime (with the partial transference of the contributions to that new regime, the deficit of the social security system grew even more). Two years later the Pension Solidarity Law was sanctioned. This made the salaries of active workers and pensioners independent, leaving to the Yearly Budget Law the decision about the value of the pensions of workers that did not migrate to the capitalization regime. The provinces also promoted reforms in their social security systems in order to increase worker contributions and the age of retirement. Some of these provincial funds were transferred to the federal government and the Integrated Pension System jurisdiction.[11]

Even without reaching the depth of the level of the mobilizations characteristic of the 1980s, teacher protests continued to happen. Provincial governments reacted with the *presentismo*, to avoid strikes; certification laws, to appease professors; and adjustments to substitute licensing requirements to save money without directly confronting teachers (Rivas, 2004).[12] These were only short term solutions which led to real long term stability.

When the application of some key educational reforms began, such as changes in the cycles' structure and the curricula, the educational community was restless. This context allowed for very interesting experiences of social articulation in some provinces between teachers, students, and other political and social organizations. Córdoba and Neuquén were two of the best known examples. The former because of the agreement between the government and the union after the end of the hegemony of the UCR in the province which meant benefits for the teachers. The latter, because of the blocking of reforms due to teachers' opposition. It is interesting to note that, even though the unions were in the political extremes of CTERA national politics, in both cases, the unions became stronger in social opposition to the educational reforms in 1996 and 1997. In these cases, as in the Buenos Aires province, teacher unions headed a front integrated by the educational community and the social and political opposition to the government. From those educational fronts, the teachers' union disputed the directions of the reforms, and managed to include discussions about associated worker problems. These struggles indicated the legitimacy of the opposition to the educational reforms and of teacher unions as its architects. Both the legitimacy of the opposition and the central role of the teacher unions would be expressed on a national scale in 1997.

At the same time, in the first half of the 1990s, the CTERA leadership moved further away from the Justicialist Party and participated in the creation of the FREPASO.[13] It also worked for the consolidation of the federal union structure, promoting a stronger organization of individual provincial unions. Finally, it worked on the necessity of constructing a pedagogical proposal coming from teacher unionism as opposed to government proposals.[14] In 1997, four years after the Federal Education Law was sanctioned, the CTERA made the First National Educational Congress. Universities, social organizations, and researchers participated. Its final declaration reads:

> We declare the need for a new National Education Law, built from the abolition of today's law and from consensus, popular participation, that will include the conclusions agreed upon in this Congress. (...) We reject the educational reform implemented by the national government because it is a faithful reflection of the construction of an anti-popular state. It deepens social differences, promotes an individualist and authoritarian way of life and reduces school to a mere place to acquire competence for insertion into the actual market model, minimizing the political, pedagogic, and socio-affective aspects that Argentinian Schools still promote.[15]

The opposition to the government's educational policies and the participation of the CTERA leaders in the FREPASO, at a federal level, converged with the provincial struggles in 1997.

The *Carpa Blanca de la Dignidad Docente*

1997 began with teacher conflicts in some provinces, particularly in Neuquén, where a strike was declared on March 10th and lasted for weeks. The strikers' demands were linked to implementation of the Federal Education Law and to provincial salary reductions. The Neuquén protest was repressed by the police, became more radical, and was nationally known. (Petruccelli, 2005)

On March 31st, the CTERA called a national strike and protest, to demonstrate national solidarity with the provincial teachers' protests. Three days later, with the Neuquén's strike still in progress, professors of the CTERA began a hunger strike in the *"Carpa Blanca de la Dignidad Docente"* (White Tent of Teacher Dignity). The tent was installed in front of the National Congress in Buenos Aires and demanded the application of a financing fund for the educational system. The fund would include salary recuperation for teachers. The CTERA also proposed progressive taxes (on the privatized companies, for example) to finance it.

From this moment on, the core of the teacher struggle was based at the *Carpa Blanca*.[16]

The support of the protest was enormous, putting the CTERA at the crest of a social and political wave of opposition to Menem's government. In this political context, the Alliance won the 1997 legislative elections.

The response of the Minister of Education was a project aligned with the neoliberal proposal, which included a working conditions reform. The Teachers Statutes were criticized by the government, and the reformers talked about "teacher professionalization." The CTERA didn't accept the project, and the National Congress, renewed since the election, rejected the proposal.

The government went forward with the proposal to create a National Fund for Teacher Incentive, financed with an unpopular tax on vehicles. The object of the tax, implemented in 1999, was to eliminate the social base of popular support for teacher demands. In October 1999, the first half-year quota of the Teacher Incentive was paid.

The Teacher Incentive was a step back for decentralization policy and a victory for teacher mobilizations, which rarely achieved improvements in salaries. Nevertheless, CTERA didn't halt the *Carpa Blanca* because of its opposition to the tax and because it was uncertain whether the following quotas would be paid.

After ten years of Menem government, the Alliance won the 1999 presidential elections. The CTERA removed the *Carpa Blanca* after 1,003 days of protest, in December, when the Teacher Incentive was included in the annual budget law and the tax for vehicles was abolished. According to CTERA, 1,500 teachers participated in the hunger strike and more than two million people supported the protest by participating in mobilizations, festivals, and conferences (CTERA, 1999/2000). Eleven national teacher's strikes (three in 1997, five in 1988, three in 1999) were carried out during the protest.

THE ALLIANCE GOVERNMENT

The short Alliance government maintained the same economic policies as the previous government and had to deal with the growth of social protests, promoted by the unions and organizations of the unemployed. With a weaker president, the same policies, and a tired people, the political situation became explosive.

Carlos Alvarez, FREPASO's leader, resigned the vice presidency in 2000, and this Alliance crisis demonstrated the difficulties of a center-left political project coveted by the FREPASO. The CTERA quickly distanced itself from the Alliance and rejected the new Education Minister, who participated in Menem's government. In spite of this, teachers couldn't achieve large social support after the vehicles tax, with ex-leaders in the government, and in a context in which educational issues weren't at the top of the political agenda.

As a consequence of the economic recession, the fiscal crises became worse. Teacher Incentive was overdue, in most of the provinces wages and annual complementary salaries went unpaid, payments were made in vouchers (in Corrientes representing up to 30 percent of wages) and food stamps (up to 20 percent of wages, in Jujuy), salary reductions were common (up to 13 percent, in Misiones), and seniority gratifications were frozen.

Important economic conflicts and strikes shook the CTERA. In Buenos Aires province, the largest one, teachers carried out the most important protest of the decade. Unlike the strikes of 1997 and 1998, which permitted the hegemony of the CTERA leadership in the union, these strikes strengthened the leftist opposition.

Union movements as a whole achieved greater importance. Seven general strikes were carried out in two years, lead by the MTA leadership. On top of that, a new actor appeared in the Buenos Aires suburbs, which until that moment had only been a force in the interior of the country: the mobilization of the unemployed. Surfacing in center-left and leftist organizations were the unemployed blocked routes and avenues demanding unemployment benefits. The government could neither control the unions nor the protests by the unemployed. In March 2001, a new economic minister announced an economic adjustment plan, which included the end of the Teacher Incentive. The mobilizations against it forced the resignation of the minister. A few months later, the government lost the legislative elections.

This situation was the prelude to the popular insurrection of December 2001 which led to the fall of the De la Rua presidency. Without a political alternative since then, different leaders of the Justicialist Party occupied the presidency in the next weeks. The political situation only became a bit more stable when Eduardo Duhalde, a PJ leader who had lost the 1999 elections against De la Rua, was elected by the parliament as president in 2002 January.

The first measure Duhalde's government took to deal with the economic recession was a deep devaluation of the currency. But even if initially salaries were crushed, it allowed, in the short run, new economic growth. Massive daily mobilizations and constant critiques of all political institutions put on hold some reforms and forced a change in political discourse. It was the end of neoliberal ideological hegemony.

CONCLUSIONS

Because of salary devaluation, teachers in the 1980s were especially active in labor disputes. Neoliberal reforms in the 1990s made more complex the teacher labor agenda, promoting discussions about working conditions of teachers, the criteria to define remunerations, etc. During the disputes established in the beginning of the 1990s, teachers managed to keep most of their contracting conditions, avoiding the Statutes reform. Pension regimes and working conditions were the areas that suffered the most. Specifically, salaries had been affected in different ways. Regressively, because of the reductions forced by the fiscal crises and of the weight of non-salary benefits (such as the *presentismo*). Another modification in remunerations, this time in a positive direction, was the Teacher Incentive.

Certain political developments cannot be understood without considering the teachers' protest period from 1991–2001. They led the erosion of the neoliberal education reform projects and put teachers' working conditions at the forefront of the political agenda. Despite strong continuities in some important aspects, there have been significant changes since 2002. Several provinces have made the *presentismo* less rigid or incorporated it into the salary. The 137/05 Decree abolished the 78/94 Decree and validated the teachers pension law. The new Decree included teachers who belonged to the federal system and also the teachers of the districts who transferred their social security funds to the Integrated Federal System. Also in 2005, the government sanctioned the Educational Financing law. It proposed that educational financing reach 6 percent of the GDP in 2010. The law also created a program to diminish salary differences between provinces, and mentions an agreement between unions and national as well as provincial educational ministries. This article was regulated in 2007 and allowed the desired collective bargaining for union teachers, and was implemented for first time in 2008. Before that, a new educational law supported by CTERA was passed.

CTERA was one of the unions which maintained worker activism during the nineties and even became stronger as a political union and educational actor. This was achieved partially because of teachers' responses to the educational reforms, sometimes as catalysts of the social opposition to educational policies and even to the neoliberalist program as a whole. Defending education as social right, teachers were part of a very important ideological struggle in a difficult context for social activism.

It is interesting to contrast national union protests of the three-year period of 1994–1997 with the 1997–1999 protests. In the first period, there were four CTERA strikes and six general strikes. In the second one, CTERA conducted thirteen strikes and took part in two general strikes. (In both periods, there was no general strike without CTERA's intervention). This expresses, on the one hand, a partial retraction of the CGT and the MTA. The retraction of the CGT and the MTA was a result of the government halting some reforms and because of the growth of the Alliance as the main government opposition. Most of the unions were not linked with the Alliance, and were partially dislocated by the political context. On the other hand, it shows CTERA's success in the nationalization of teachers' protests and the positive relationship between this process and the Alliance growth.

Unionism aims at immediate interests of specific professions linked to its common situation in the labor market (Hyman, 1992). In this sense, it can be said that unionism is "corporative" and that is why it has difficulties disputing for the hegemony in the society as a whole. This dispute for hegemony is, in some sense, the role of political movements and parties. But there also exists, within unionism practice, elements that point toward overcoming corporativism, because in the experience of particular interest defense, workers build meaning and recuperate traditions that allow the universalization of struggle. Unions preserve, strengthen, empower and give directions to these meanings and traditions.

In spite of its particularities, teacher unionism doesn't contradict this general characterization. The *Carpa Blanca* is a good example of this. The key to understanding the protest's success is the political erosion of the neoliberal project personified by Menem. In this context, the defense of public education and the opposition to the government functioned as a common cause of teachers and society, and in fact it allowed CTERA to lead demands that transcended the profession, in particular the opposition to neoliberal policies. This doesn't discredit CTERA's considerable experience of struggle, its strength within the profession, its political cleverness, but it contextualizes the protest. Social support of the teachers' demands had a meaning that transcended the demands inside and outside the profession: The demands were against the government. The *Carpa Blanca* would have been practically impossible in 1994. It began a few months before the Alliance victory in the legislative election and it finished with the end of Menem's presidency.

There were times that *Carpa Blanca* seemed to be a social or political movement because of its partial transcendence of the professional interests of teachers. Nevertheless, CTERA is a professional organization. This explains why one of the most important struggles for the defense of public education finished with an incentive economic fund specifically for teachers. This outcome was a major success for CTERA, but was a setback in regards to the teachers' partial corporative transcendence of 1997–1998.

CTERA remained active after the *Carpa Blanca*, and led six national teacher strikes in 2000 and 2001. Despite this, CTERA couldn't recuperate the legitimate role it maintained in civil society nor keep its own large base of support achieved in the previous period during its opposition to neoliberal measures. This was partly caused by Menem's clever policy regarding the vehicle tax, but also because the CTERA and the *Carpa Blanca* supported a political front which did not mean to, and in fact didn't carry out, a rupture with neoliberal policies.

Table 4.1 National CTERA's Strikes 1991–2001

CTERA' Strikes	General Strikes	Presidencies
6/5/1991		First Menem's Presidency
8/7–8/1991		
11/27/1991		
7/3/1992		
8/6/1992		
8/26/1992		
8/10/1993		
9/3/1993		
3/29/1994	8/2/1994	
9/29/1994		
3/13/1995	4/21/1995	
	9/6/1995	
3/21/1996	8/8/1996	Second Menem's Presidency
	9/26–27/1996	
	12/26/1996	
3/24/1997	8/14/1997	
3/31/1997		
4/14/1997		
6/20/1997		
11/27/1997		
4/2/1998		
7/10/1998		
9/10/1998		
10/14/1998		
11/11/1998		
4/6/1999	7/6/1999	
5/11/1999		
11/24/1999		
8/30/2000	5/5/2000	De la Rua's Presidency
	9/6/2000	
	23/11/2000	
20 e 21 /3/2001	21/3/2001	
28/6/ 2001	8/6/2001	
22/8/ 2001	19/07/2001	
4/10/2001	13/12/2001	
22/11/2001		

Source: Data based on the annual CTERA's Union Memories (1990–2000) in the Union Teachers' Action/Latin-American Observatory of Educative Policies Database (www.olped.net), and in Carreras (2001).

Note: In several CTERA's Strikes other teachers' unions—not integrated in the CTERA—also participated. Regarding general strikes, CTERA only didn't participate in the general strike of 9/11/1992.

Table 4.2 Teachers, Affiliation, and Remunerations

Jurisdiction	Public Teachers (2004)	CTERA's Affiliations (2001)	Remunerations in pesos (1999)		
			Basic	Total	With 10 years of seniority
Buenos Aires	222.892	62.863	234	364 (**)	481
Santa Fe	46.478	30.397	145	437 (**)	509
Buenos Aires City	42.618	10.003	213	351 (**)	536
Córdoba	42.205	27.543	226	575 (*)(**)	688
Mendoza	33.836	15.393	83	453 (**)	531
Entre Ríos	25.171	8.644	205	347 (*)	449
Chaco	22.498	879	222	313 (*)	424
Tucumán	21.911	1.103	186	352 (*)	445
Salta	18.781	8.565	155	346 (*)(**)	439
Misiones	16.592	6.885	201	329 (*)(**)	429
Corrientes	16.452	2.055	204	365 (*)	467
Jujuy	16.183	7.883	194	339	452
Santiago del Estero	15.783	210	329	478 (*)(**)	642
Neuquén	15.114	8.237	285	544 (*)	687
Rio Negro	14.645	9.434	232	376 (*)	492
San Juan	12.499	9.433	151	490 (*)	566
Formosa	11.076	7.361	230	310 (*)(**)	425
Catamarca	10.192	1.341	219	556	665
Chubut	9.922	3.689	273	362 (*)(**)	499
La Rioja	8.620	3.028	330	562 (**)	727
La Pampa	7.696	3.093	284	394 (**)	522
San Luis	7.187	1.072	280	375 (**)	516
Santa Cruz	6.624	3.537	161	866 (**)	947
Tierra del Fuego	3.396	956	205	832 (**)	955
Total	641.696	233.585			

Teachers: Teachers whose work in more than one jurisdiction were numbered more than once. Source: National Direction of Educational Quality Information and Evaluation (2005).
CTERA's affiliations: There are important unions apart from CTERA in some jurisdictions (Tucumán, Chaco, Santiago del Estero, Buenos Aires, Corrientes, Buenos Aires City). The Córdoba union also includes private teachers. Source: CTERA's electoral roll (2001).

Remunerations: Remunerations of primary school teachers. They don't include the Teachers' Incentive, received n 1999's second semester. Source: Iñiguez (2000).

* Provinces which in 1996 applied remuneration reductions (Birgin, 1999).

** Provinces which in 1999 paid perfect attendance gratification (Iñiguez, 2000)

In May 2001, according to the Argentina National Institute of Statistics and Census, people who earned between 350–500 pesos were between 40 percent and 60 percent of the total wage earning population in the Buenos Aires' metropolitan area (www.indec.gov.ar).

NOTES

1. I would like to thank both Jason Wozniak M.Ed. and Dr. Gabriel Calsamiglia for their helpful critiques and some reflections included in this work.
2. The PJ is a traditionally labor based party created by Juan Domingo Perón, one of the most emblematic leaders of the Latin-American populist regimes. Even if the UCR isn't a conservative party, it became the greatest PJ opposition in elections until 1995.
3. According to the Economic Commission for Latin America and the Caribbean (ECLAC), a United Nations organization, the consumer price index, with a base of 1995–100, grew from 24.7 in 1990 and was stabilized with the Convertibility Plan to around 100 and even declined to 98.4 in 2001. In 2003 the index reached 140.5 (data from the Buenos Aires and the metropolitan area). (ECLAC, 2004).
4. Teacher's work conditions were, and in general still are, unilaterally defined by the state, most of the time by Teachers Statutes. The sanctioning of these Statutes was a demand of the teacher's associations in the 1940s and 50s. Since 1958, when the Statute for national teachers was created, they established a mechanism for career promotion and contract conditions which put a limit on the employer's arbitrariness. They guaranteed stability for teachers with permanent positions, while substitute teachers and other non-permanent teachers remained with weaker contract conditions. The Statutes created the Qualification and Discipline Board with teacher representatives. It allowed relative impartiality in the selection and promotion of teachers. Apart from this, the Statutes established license regimes and wage definition criteria. With some variations across the provinces, they included position, seniority, localization, and family benefits (Saforcada; Jaimovich; Pasmanik; Migliavacca, 2004).
5. Teacher social welfare was marked by parallelism. In the case of provincial teachers, the social security and health care systems of provincial employees were managed by the provincial governments. National teachers were included in a unified pension system with the workers of the private sector and the body of national government employees. In spite of this, in 1990 national teachers achieved the incorporation into the special regime for public employees, which fixed their pension values at 82 percent of the remunerations earned by the active teachers, and the age of retirement of 65 for men and 60 for women.
6. The history of teacher unionism has some peculiarities in the Argentinean unionism context, which had been analyzed in Gindin (2008).
7. Initially in fact, CTERA divided itself into two national organizations. The principal organization was run by the Light Blue slate. The other organization also opposed the Alfonsín government, but was integrated by communist, Trotskyites, and leadership linked to the UCR.
8. In 1991 special regimes of the national state employers—including teachers—were abolished.
9. Those Educational Associations that can't charge tuition fees and have resources allocated per student guaranteed by the province. They can spend up to 85 percent of their funding on teacher's salaries, which in no case can be no less than or higher than 50 percent of what teachers contracted by the province earn (Rodríguez, 1999).
10. According to Rivas (2004) the Teachers Statue was only eliminated in Tierra del Fuego in 1999.
11. Eleven jurisdictions transferred their social security funds (Buenos Aires City, Jujuy, Salta, Tucumán, Santiago del Estero, Catamarca, La Rioja, San Juan, San Luis, Mendoza, and Río Negro).

12. Some of those laws were rejected by the unions because they did not include public competition for jobs. Nevertheless, those laws meant a progressive change in the contracting situation of teachers.
13. Also in 1995, Mary Sánchez, General Secretary of CTERA until that moment, was elected national deputy by the FREPASO.
14. Even if it is linked to program positions of this union's sector, it grew as an answer to neoliberal educational policies.
15. My translation. The whole declaration can be consulted on the union website: www.ctera.org.ar
16. An internal struggle was part of the conflict. In Neuquén, leftist union groups were particularly strong and were the inspiration for national leftist opposition to the CTERA leaders.

REFERENCES

Birgin, A. (1999) *El trabajo de enseñar. Entre la vocación y el mercado: las nuevas reglas de juego* (The Work of Teaching. Between Vocation and the Market: the new rules of the game). Buenos Aires: Editorial Troquel.

Carreras, N. (2001) *Las huelgas generales, Argentina 1983–2001: un ejercicio de periodización* (General Strikes, Argentina 1983–2001: A Periodization Exercise). 5th. National Congress of Work Studies. Buenos Aires: ASET.

Damill, M., Frenkel, R., & Mauricio, R. (2002) Argentina: A Decade of Currency Board. An Analysis of Growth, Employment & Income Distribution. Santiago: International Labor Organization.

ECLAC (2004) 2003 Statistical Yearbook for Latina America and the Caribbean. Santiago: ECLAC.

General Study Coordination of the Educational System Costs (2008) *Informe Indicativo de Salarios Docentes. Periodo Octubre/Diciembre 2007* (Indicative Report on Teachers' Salaries. October/December 2007). Buenos Aires: Ministry of Education, Science and Technology.

Gindin, J. (2008) Sindicalismo docente en México, Brasil y Argentina. Una hipótesis explicativa de su estructuración diferenciada. (Teacher Unionism in Mexico, Brazil and Argentina. An Explicative Hypothesis of their Different Structuration). *Mexican Review of Educational Research* 13th. N°37. México: COMIE.

Hyman, R. (1992) Trade unions and the disaggregation of the working class. The future of labour movements. Ed. by Marino Regini. *Sage studies in international sociology*, Vol. 43. London: Sage Publications Ltd.

Imen, P. (2005) *La escuela pública sitiada. Crítica de la transformación educativa* (The Public School Besieged. Critique of the Educational Transformation). Buenos Aires: Cooperation Cultural Center.

Iñiguez, A. (2000) *El salario docente: un síntoma del estado de la educación en Argentina*. Cuadernos del Instituto de Investigaciones Pedagógicas "Marina Vilte"/CTERA, Serie: II Congreso Educativo Nacional. (The Teacher's Salary: A Symptom of the Education Condition in Argentina. Working Papers from the Pedagogical Research Institute "Marina Vilte"/CTERA, Series: II National Educational Congress). Buenos Aires: CTERA.

National Direction of Educational Quality Information and Evaluation. (2002) *Anuario Estadístico Educativo 2000* (2000 Educational Statistical Yearbook). Buenos Aires: Ministry of Education, Science and Technology.

———. (2005) *Censo Nacional Docente 2004. Resultados preliminares* (2004 National Teachers' Census. Preliminary Results). Buenos Aires: Ministry of Education, Science and Technology.

Oliveira, D. (2003) *Reformas educacionais na América latina e os trabalhadores docentes* (Educational Reforms in Latin America and Education Workers). Belo Horizonte: Auténtica.

OREALC/UNESCO. (2005) *Condiciones de trabajo y salud docente. Estudios de caso en Argentina, Chile, Ecuador, México, Perú y Uruguay* (Teacher's Working & Health Conditions. Case Studies in Argentina, Chile, Ecuador, México, Peru and Uruguay). Santiago: OREALC/UNESCO.

Petruccelli, A. (2005) *Docentes y piqueteros. De la huelga de ATEN a la pueblada de Cutral Có.* (Teachers and Picketers. From ATEN's Strike to Cutral Có's Riot). Buenos Aires, El cielo por asalto / El Fracaso.

Rivas, A. (2003) *Mirada comparada de los efectos de la reforma educativa en las provincias. Un análisis de los resultados y de la dinámica política de la nueva estructura de niveles en las provincias a 10 años de la Ley Federal de Educación* (A Comparative View of the Educational Reform Effects in the Provinces. An Analysis of the Results and the Political Dynamic of the New Level Structure in the Provinces after 10 Years of the Federal Law on Education). Buenos Aires: CIPPEC.

———. (2004) *Gobernar la educación. Estudio comparado sobre el poder y la educación en las provincias argentinas* (Governing Education. Comparative Study on Power and Education in the Argentine Provinces). Buenos Aires: Granica.

Rodríguez, L. (1999) *Tendencias privatizadoras en educación* (Privatization Trends in Education). Buenos Aires: CTERA.

Saforcada, M. F., Jaimovich, A., Pasmanik, Y., & Migliavacca, A. (2004) *Reformas neoliberales, condiciones laborales y estatutos docentes* (Neoliberal Reforms, Working Conditions and Teachers Statutes). Buenos Aires: Educational Department/ Cooperation Cultural Center.

Tenti, E. (2005) *La condición docente. Análisis comparado de la Argentina, Brasil, Perú y Uruguay* (Teacher's Condition. A Comparative Analysis of Argentina, Brazil, Peru & Uruguay). Buenos Aires: Siglo XXI Editores.

DOCUMENTS

CTERA, 1999/2000, Memorias Gremiales (Union Memories).

CTERA, 2001, Padrón electoral (Electoral Roll)

Declaración final del I Congreso Educativo Nacional de CTERA (1997) (Final Declaration of the I CTERA's National Educational Congress).

Decreto (Decree) 78/94.

Decreto (Decree) 137/05.

Ley de Negociaciones Colectivas de Trabajadores Docentes (Collective Bargaining Law on Education Workers) (23.929/1991).

Ley de Jubilación Especial Docente (Teachers' Special Pension Law) (24.016/1991).

Ley de Transferencia a las provincias y a la Municipalidad de Buenos Aires de Servicios Educativos (Transference of Educational Services to the Provinces and to the Buenos Aires' Municipality Law) (24.049/1991).

Ley Federal de Educación (Federal Law on Education) (24195/1993).

Ley de Reforma Previsional (Pension Reform Law) (24.241/1993).

Ley de Solidaridad Previsional (Pension Solidarity Law) (24.463/1995).

Ley de Financimiento Educativo (Education Financing Law) (26.075/2005).

5 Venezuela
Higher Education, Neoliberalism, and Socialism

Thomas Muhr and Antoni Verger

INTRODUCTION

Under Hugo Chávez's government, the Bolivarian Revolution has dramatically changed the social, economic, and political landscape of Venezuela. The ratification of the Constitution of the Bolivarian Republic of Venezuela (CBRV, 2000) by popular referendum in 1999 provides the normative base for the "re-founding of the Republic" (now 'Fifth Republic') as a social and inclusive participatory democracy. Education is ascribed a pivotal role in achieving this objective. The government's integral, expressly anti-neoliberal and anti-neocolonial development model is rooted in 'endogenous development' as conceptualised by Osvaldo Sunkel and collaborators (1993), in which repayment of the historically accumulated social debt constitutes a key dimension. However, the Bolivarian revolution has radicalised the original proposal in the process of constructing a Socialism of the 21st century. The government's commitment to repaying the social debt manifests itself in a constant increase of social spending, from 8.2 percent of gross domestic product (GDP) in 1998 to 13.6 percent in 2006, which does not include the US $13.3 billion directly transferred by the state oil company Petroleos de Venezuela (PDVSA) in 2006 in order to finance a multitude of social programs, called missions. Over the same period, the education budget was raised from 3.4 percent of GDP to 5.1 percent (Weisbrot & Sandoval, 2007, p. 9).

We first explore exclusion from access to basic and medium diversified and technical education[1] under 1990s education 'decentralisation,' implemented by Venezuela between 1989 and 1998 under the 'Washington Consensus.' This contextualisation is necessary because exclusion from HE originated at the basic and medium diversified levels under the previous regime. That repayment of the social debt is by far not mere rhetoric is illustrated by the fact that in early 2007 around 15.3 million Venezuelans—approximately 55 percent of the total population—were in some form of compulsory formal or voluntary nonformal public education.[2]

As Venezuela is approaching universal basic education,[3] the right to free HE up to the undergraduate level, as established in article 103 of the CBRV (2000), probably constitutes the most revolutionary dimension of Bolivarian education. To guarantee this right, HEFA is supported by a range of nonformal missions at all educational levels. Our analysis of the strategic role of Bolivarian HE in national development illustrates why HEFA poses a counter-hegemonic challenge to the prevalent global HE agenda of commoditization and privatization. HEFA differs from European (post-second world war) liberal-democratic massification in that the primary motivation is not individual social mobility, but empowerment and endogenous development. Coordinated by the Ministry of Higher Education, created in 2002, the HEFA policy operates through the *Universidad Bolivariana de Venezuela* (UBV) and *Misión Sucre*, both launched in 2003 as the first nationwide public HE system in the country's history.[4] In accordance with the government's holistic approach to national and regional development, UBV is a considerable contributor to social justice not only by including those historically excluded from HE, but from social, political, economic, and cultural participation altogether.

Our knowledge derives from 13 months of fieldwork between 2005–07, drawing on government policy proposals and reports, un-semistructured interviews, and participant observation. However, this study neither constitutes an exhaustive empirical contrasting of discourses and their practical implementation, nor should it be understood as an evaluation of current policies and programs.

NEOLIBERALISM IN 1990S VENEZUELA

Contrary to the prevailing notion of Fourth Republic Venezuela (1958–1998) as having been Latin America's 'model democracy' (e.g. Ellner, 2003), Michael Derham's (2002) cogent analysis of Venezuela's recent history arrives at the conclusion that Fourth Republic exclusionary 'democracy' "was never democratic and was never meant to be." (p. 193) The Punto Fijo Pact (1958) between the two dominant parties *Acción Democrática* (AD) and *Copei* installed a regime of elite consensus politics similar to William Robinson's (1996) concept of polyarchy, where for forty years power alternated between the two parties accompanied by, especially in the 1960s/70s, state terrorist means to repress oppositional forces. However, the system's profound crisis of legitimacy of the 1980s originated primarily in the unsustainability of the oil rentier economy driven modernization doctrine (Puerta, 1992), which manifested itself in growing large scale structural impoverishment in the aftermath of the brief oil boom of the 1970s.[5] According to income based estimates, poverty increased from 33 percent in 1975 to 54 percent in 1988, and critical poverty from 13 percent and 22 percent (Riutort, 1999).

To re-legitimate the state and party politics, a political decentralization process—essentially a territorial deconcentration of central power to lower levels of the state apparatus—was implemented from 1988 onward. Its unquestionable merit was the introduction of direct, universal, and secret elections of state representatives at the subnational levels (governors, mayors), who up to then had been appointed by the central power holders. However, as elsewhere, decentralization under Chávez's predecessors Carlos Andrés Pérez (1989–1993), Ramón J. Velázquez (1993/1994), and Rafael Caldera (1994–1998) came as part and parcel of the general World Bank and International Monetary Fund (IMF) macroeconomic adjustment policies, referred to as the 'Washington Consensus.'[6] Both Pérez and Caldera had been elected on an explicitly anti-neoliberal platform, thus lacking the popular mandate for such policies, which caused violent reaction by the popular sectors and its bloody suppression by the state security forces (the '*Caracazo*'). However, the neoliberal reforms did, from 1988 on, allow increased opposition representation in the national parliament and other, mainly municipal, public offices. Nevertheless, Venezuelan education sociologist Orlando Albornoz (1999) argues that the ideological praxis of consensus prevailed due to a "re-issued Punto Fijo Pact," where the hitherto 'progressive' forces allied with the reactionary conservative sectors (p. 156).

Under structural adjustment, which in Venezuela followed the orthodox Washington Consensus prescriptions (López Maya & Lander, 2000, p. 230), the social contradictions of Fourth Republic governance intensified: Macroeconomically, the historical oil dependency could not be diminished, external debt and inflation increased, accompanied by ongoing devaluation of the national currency (Battaglini, 2000); politically, federal states' fiscal dependency continued, and citizen participation and trust in the political system remained absent (Mascareño, 2000); socially, the trend of exclusion aggravated. By 1997, income based poverty had reached 67 percent, and critical poverty 36 percent. The middle class shrank from 57 percent in 1975 to 44 percent in 1988 and to 31 percent in 1997 (Riutort, 1999). By 1998, income distribution had deteriorated to the 1970 level, when the poorest fifth of Venezuelans received 3 percent of income compared to 53–54 percent of the richest quintile (World Bank, 1979; 2003).

The illegitimate imposition of structural adjustment on the people in conjunction with the economic, political, and social bankruptcy of the corrupt and clientelist '*ancien regime*' provoked two failed military civilian uprisings in the years following the *Caracazo*, one of which staged by Colonel Hugo Chávez in 1992 in an attempt, as he recalls, to restore democracy (Chávez Frías, 2005). As Albornoz argues (1999), the most urgent social issues (social/ethnic exclusion, extreme social indiscipline) were "in the hands of exactly those that exclude and employ fascist and pernicious practices in a democracy." (p. 167)

NEOLIBERAL SCHOOL DECENTRALIZATION

Firmly embedded in the Washington Consensus redefinition of the role of the state, educational decentralization of basic and medium diversified education paralleled political decentralization in deconcentrating Ministry of Education bureaucracy and shifting fiscal responsibility to lower, primarily federal state levels, combined with school autonomy of neoclerical private schools (Estaba, 1999). As elsewhere, rooted in the neoliberal education rationales of improving "quality," efficiency, managerial transparency and school community "participation" and "empowerment" (ibid.), these World Bank-, IDB, and IMF-promoted finance-driven reforms pursued a shift of the cost of education to the 'users' through privatization, simultaneously instrumentalizing 'participation' as pecuniary and nonpecuniary household/community contributions (Carnoy, 1999), which in Venezuela took the form of unofficial and unconstitutional fee charging (Casanova, 2005). This occurred within the context of the unresolved issue of how education should be financed under 'decentralisation,' as the decreased national education budget, at a historical low of 3.0 percent of GDP in 1990, was not accompanied by legislation and strategies of cofinancing, such as raising tax revenues at the subnational levels (Gamus, 1999, p. 35). The rejection of financial responsibility especially on part of the federal state governors resulted in no definite transfers of authority to that level, and decentralization never got beyond the experimental stage (Casanova, 1999). In addition, teacher union resistance prevented the introduction of the charter school model (Bruni Celli, 2004).

The inherent ideological element of competition was most explicitly exposed by Pérez's education minister Roosen in stating that a "war of comparison" had to be introduced in national schooling (cited in Bruni Celli, 2004: 447). Parentocracy, i.e., free market and parental choice policies (see Brown, 1990), alongside a populism that rejected the authoritativeness of professional and technocratic expertise (schools, teachers, universities) (Lauglo, 1995; Albornoz, 1999), were discursively driven and legitimated by a "crisis of qualitative deterioration" which was attributed to the previous rapid massification and the centralized administration (García et al., 1992). Under the Roosen doctrine, public education was systematically denigrated and the constitutional thesis of the Estado docente, i.e., state leadership in the direct provision of education, dismantled (Albornoz, 1999). The proliferation of private schools was facilitated by a state subsidized market, where the Catholic Church as the major provider regained its historical leadership role in national education and reestablished substantial ideological control over the social microcosmos (school, home, family) (ibid.).

Privatization further meant companies assuming control over employee training, paralleled by their financing of Technological University Institutes, while *Programa Galileo* facilitated HE for the privileged sectors in the Northern countries, especially the US. Simultaneously, the prolonged underfunding of the public system produced deteriorating infrastructure, class cancellations, noncompliance with programmatic guidelines, shortage of didactic resources, and under-trained and noncommitted teachers (Pucci & Mundó, 1999). In order to cover up the great contradictions, the neoliberal state employed inherently populist social mechanisms to accompany the IMF's adjustment program, such as the glass of milk in school and food vouchers (León Sanabria, 1992) or direct subsidies to households for each child enrolled in the public school system, which replaced the free school lunch and was not necessarily spent on the food for children (Bruni Celli, 2004).

In accordance with the World Bank ideology of a minimalist four- to six-year primary education (World Bank, 1995), the policy of a nine-year basic education cycle as established in the 1980 Education Law was undermined as only one tenth of public schools (central government, federal state, municipal) offered the full cycle, joined by another 10 percent that provided grades 7–9 exclusively (Pucci & Mundó, 1999, p. 65). This means that the majority of the school population in the public sector could at best attend grades 1–6 (ibid., p. 66). Accordingly, between 1988/89 and 1997/98, private sector enrolment increased significantly at the upper basic education level (grades 7–9), from 19.0 percent to 27.9 percent and, more expressly, at the medium diversified and professional levels, where private institution enrollment went up from zero to 35.2 percent over the same period. Simultaneously, enrollment in central and federal state provided medium diversified and professional education decreased from 99.4 percent to 64.5 percent (see Mascareño, 2000, p. 120). Consequently, educational discrimination at the secondary and subsequently HE levels aggravated, produced by both direct exclusion from access to grades 7–9 and, indirectly, underfunded low quality public education (García et al., 1992).[7] Whilst there was no dramatic class related bias in primary school enrolment (7–12-year-olds), between 1990 and 1999, secondary school access deteriorated for the poorest 40 percent of 13–19-year-olds from 68.4 percent to 62.8 percent (CEPAL, 2006).[8]

This trend was matched at the HE level (Table 1): Firstly, between 1981 and 1997, the share of HE participation of the poorest 20 percent decreased dramatically, while access of Quintile 2 decreased almost 4 percentage points; that of Quintile 3 virtually stagnated over that period. Quintiles 4 and 5 could increase university attendance. Secondly, comparing Quintile 1 with Quintile 5, inequality between these two sectors of Venezuelan society increased from 4.8 percentage points in 1981 to 27.4 percentage points in 1997, and reached a historical climax of 33.9 percentage points in 2002. Thirdly, although between 1997 and 2002 *all* social classes enjoyed an increase in access to HE, it was the wealthiest 20 percent who, with an increase of 10.9 percentage points, were the absolute 'winners.' This counterargues the elite's insistence upon being the overall victims of the Bolivarian Revolution.

Table 5.1 HE Attendance of 20–24-year-olds According to Social Strata (in %)

	1981	1997	2002
Quintile 1	28.5	16.4	20.8
(poorest)	23.7	20.0	27.8
Quintile 2	23.9	24.5	29.7
Quintile 3	25.9	31.1	39.3
Quintile 4	33.3	43.8	54.7
Quintile 5			
(richest)			

Source: developed from Cepal, 2006.

EDUCATION AND THE BOLIVARIAN REVOLUTION

The Bolivarian Republic's holistic approach to education implies countering the previous notion of education as an 'independent variable' that would function independently of the unequal and inequitable social structures within which it is embedded (Casanova, 2005). For this reason, since 2002, the government has launched a range of temporary social emergency programs called missions (*misiones*) that tackle exclusion from cross-institutional angles.[9] In education, the formal system is complemented by *Misión Robinson I, II, III* (basic literacy; grades 1–6; consolidation of functional literacy in combination with the creation of production units, respectively), *Misión Ribas* (medium education), *Misión Vuelvan Caras* (work related education and training), and, as stated, UBV/*Misión Sucre*, that provides free HEFA for primarily the most impoverished and historically excluded sectors. As the worldwide achievement of the Millennium Development Goals (MDGs) is becoming increasingly illusionary (Social Watch, 2005), Venezuela was declared illiteracy free in 2005, and universal basic education (nine years) is aimed to be achieved in school year 2007/08.

As regards the formal system, the government has acknowledged that the distribution of schooling according to individual resources starts at the preschool level, which previously was primarily provided by the private sector (Albornoz, 1999). The 288 percent increase of the education budget between 2001 and 2005 (MF, 2006), in 2006 amounting to 15.5 percent of total government spending (MF, 2007, p. 366), ensures a universal supply policy that starts at the preschool level (the *Simoncitos*). Investment in infrastructure, where most Bolivarian schools now have been equipped with computer centers, laboratories, and the like, in conjunction with outlawing illegal fee charging is showing results: Net nursery school enrollment has gone up from 40.3 percent in 1998/99 to 54.6 percent in 2005/06;

over the same period, basic education (i.e. nine years) enrollment increased from 82.8 percent to 91.9 percent, and that of medium diversified and professional education from 21.6 percent to 33.3 percent (RBV, 2007). Considering that in 2006 over three million Venezuelans studied in one of the missions, the average Venezuelan of 15 years and older received 8.89 years of education in 2005, compared with 8.22 years in 1999.[10]

The Role of Education

The Bolivarian education paradigm is firmly embedded in the CBRV, which implicitly and explicitly incorporates the major UN human and educational rights norms and instruments for citizen participation and social justice and, above all, reestablishes the Estado docente (e.g., CBRV, 2000 Articles 102/103). Education should serve the full development of the personality in order to live a decent life. To ensure equal opportunities, state provided education now is obligatory from the nursery to the medium diversified level (age 18), and *free* up to the undergraduate HE level.

The construction of endogenous development[11] with the ultimate objective of a Socialism of the 21st century—i.e., a more egalitarian social structure, political sovereignty, and a higher grade of independence from the centers of the world system—has been following a 10-point strategic plan (MCI, 2004), of which we highlight seven objectives for whose achievement education assumes a critical role[12]: *to advance the configuration of the new social structure* which, among other conditions, requires universal access to all levels of education; *to rapidly advance the construction of the new popular participatory democratic model* through, for instance, participatory andragogical and emancipatory pedagogies, methodologies and practices; *to accelerate the creation of a new state apparatus institutionalism* where sustained student community project work aims to foster citizen participation and joint responsibility in the processes of design, implementation, and control of public policies; *to accelerate the construction of the new production model toward the creation of the new economic system*, i.e., endogenous development as the creation and consolidation of a diversified, efficient, and progressively self-sufficient national productive structure. Since spring 2006, *Misión Ciencia* (Mission Science)—an 'umbrella mission' that subsumes most of the other educational and social missions—provides local private and collective small and medium size producers with technical and scientific knowledge for their organization in Innovative Production Networks (*Redes Inovadoras de Producción*, RIPs). The 'new' Bolivarian professionals should be responsive to the needs of the impoverished communities and contribute to the diversification of production in order to counteract the country's oil dependency; *to continue installing the new territorial structure* in order to level out inherited territorial disparities, which involves the municipalisation of HE; and *to continue driving the new international multipolar system*, where an alternative educative cultural project is integral to the Bolivarian Alternative for the Americas (ALBA)—Venezuela's counter-hegemonic regional integration project which evolved in opposition to the US-promoted Free Trade Area of the Americas (FTAA) and has so far been joined by Cuba, Bolivia, and Nicaragua as full members.[13]

The explicit political positioning of Bolivarian education as a key instrument for societal transformation has unleashed ample criticism of an "excessive" ideologization of education and deteriorating quality, especially with regard to the substantial expansion of HE. Scrutiny of these middle/upper class opposition sector discourses, however, rather suggests that these fractions perceive themselves as increasingly deprived of one of the hitherto major distinguishing elements, namely the privilege of HE. Moreover, such sources ignore that the worldwide dominant education model is susceptible to similar criticism, disregarding that certain ideologies are becoming naturalized or more invisible due to the fact that they are hegemonic, which does not make them less ideological or more neutral (see Broccoli, 1977; Bowles & Gintis, 1998). As Robert Arnove (1986) notes, "some of those who object to political propagandizing [. . .] see the messages as indoctrination only when they are in conflict with their own personally held convictions or ideology." (p. 23)

The above allows the following suggestions: Firstly, the Bolivarian constitution unequivocally challenges the dominant World Bank discourse, where "basic education for all" has been perverted into poor children's access to minimalist four-to six-year primary schooling and functional basic skills acquisition for labor purposes (World Bank, 1995; 1999a; Torres, 1999). Simultaneously, while the globalized post-Jomtien Education For All (EFA) policies and programmes have been aligned to *"preserving* and *improving"* 'the traditional,' Venezuela has taken up the challenge of *"rethinking* and *transforming"* (cf Torres, 1999, p. 17; italics original). Secondly, although the legal tools for free state provided basic education also existed in the 1961 Constitution, they were inefficiently put into effect, as shortly before the inception of *Misión Robinson I*, 6.12 percent of Venezuelans were found illiterate. And, thirdly, Venezuelan education legislation transcends the MDGs, which normatively deprive the poor of HE (MDGs, Section III, Paragraph 19). Therefore, contemporary Venezuela does not only comply significantly more with human rights, but implicitly sets new international standards.

Contrary to World Bank-promoted focused education programs, which are firmly rooted in human capital and individualistic empowerment theories (Rambla et al., 2005), the Bolivarian Republic's objective to fight poverty through education first and foremost follows the logic of collective empowerment, to be realized through an educational process where individuals develop a critical understanding of their environment and get involved in the solution of the problems that affect them in an organized way. In other words, education becomes a means for organization in order to construct an inclusive society, rather than an instrument to include uncritical individuals into the status quo.

BREAKING WITH THE FATALISM OF MARKET DRIVEN REFORMS IN HE

Expansion of Free Public HE

The growing involvement of the private sector in HE worldwide since the 1990s has been facilitated through reduced government spending in conjunction with entry restricting policies and demand-side financing mechanisms that limit access to public universities (e.g., fees; replacement of grants with loans; graduate taxes), as well as direct and indirect (tax incentives) subsidy of education enterprises and private 'users.' (Carnoy, 1999; Johnes, 1995) This tendency is even more pronounced in the South, where budgetary constraints under structural adjustment in conjunction with the World Bank ideology of shifting public resources from the tertiary to lower levels of schooling have been accompanied by World Bank programs and companies that actively encourage private sector involvement (e.g., IFC, 1999). With public education investment in Latin America being eight times less than in the OECD countries (López Segrera, 2003), many formerly free public universities have turned toward models of mixed financing (Santos, 2004). The withdrawal of the state from HE as expressed in a pronounced proliferation of often government subsidized private HE providers in Latin America (World Bank, 1999b; Levy, 1998) has not necessarily increased the quality of HE and has further aggravated inequality (Carnoy, 1999).

Venezuela mirrors the worldwide trend, as between 1993 and 1999 private HE enrollment climbed from 34.5 percent of total enrolment to 43.9 percent,[14] which is considerably above the regional average. The recent reversal of this tendency is the product of the creation of four public universities since 1999, of which UBV is the most significant, alongside five technical university institutes (IUTs). Contrary to most other countries where the market ideology has remained unbroken, the municipalized UBV is a direct reply by the Venezuelan government to the previously unmet demand of HE *and* to the requirements of the new development model. The fundamental human right to HE is reflected in the HE budget, which has been raised 3.6 times since 2003, when the MES was founded, and in 2006 received 7.3 percent of the total national budget, as compared with 6.2 percent for security and defence (MF, 2007, pp. 364; 366).

DEMOCRATIZATION OF ACCESS

Although access to HE worldwide has increased over the past decade— most notably in Europe and North America, where gross enrolment approaches 60 percent, as compared with 28 percent in Latin America[15]— supply has not necessarily met the demand. In Venezuela, during the period 1984–98, public underfunding and privatization produced a gap of sixteen percentage points between rising applications and admission. Although total absolute intake climbed from 54,087 students in 1984 to 70,348 in 1998, the share of public universities decreased from 71 percent (1984) to 40 percent (1998) (derived from MES, 2005, p. 16).

In combination with a number of equality increasing mechanisms (e.g., the 'Initial Semester,' for key knowledge revision; scholarships; free public transport for students), the "democratization of access" to HE has meant that by 2006, 77 percent of the hitherto excluded 472,363 *bachilleres* of all ages, as nationally surveyed in 2003, exercised their right to HE in *Misión Sucre*, of which 57 percent were women (MES, 2007, p. 116). Together with UBV's 158,000 students, almost a third of all HE students in the state sector—at 1.8 million in early 2007—are enrolled in the two new institutions (see MES, 2007, p. 10). The problem of dropout is not reduced to 'student failure,' but takes into account the institution's responsibility of the phenomenon, which includes methodological and structural considerations (e.g., evening/weekend classes).

HE *For All* in contemporary Venezuela means that any *bachiller* who *wants* to enter and/or continue university studies is entitled and actively supported to doing so. In this sense, 'meritocracy'—i.e., education by aptitude, ability, and age (Brown, 1990) is put into effect. Ideologically, however, Bolivarian HE policies supersede Fourth Republic meritocracy (CRV, 1961, Article 78) in two respects: firstly, as stated, Fourth Republic meritocracy resembled a parentocracy where the poor, deprived of the means for 'choice,' were excluded. And, secondly, since 'merit' is commonly measured through examinations, in this case primarily internal university entry examinations, competitors from poor backgrounds were systematically excluded as they: a) came from 'second class' public schools with reduced chances to pass entry examinations compared to the wealthy from private institutions who b) could afford special preparatory classes.[16] 'Meritocracy' thus legitimized severe discrimination (Bourdieu & Passeron, 1977). Quite to the contrary, Bolivarian education policies explicitly aim to unite the two ethical and political imperatives of universality and equity in order to construct equity as an exercise of revolutionary governability (RBV/ PDVSA, 2005).

MUNICIPALIZACIÓN: A CHALLENGE TO FINANCE DRIVEN DECENTRALIZATION

Contrary to neoliberal decentralization, Bolivarian municipalization is a distinct, two-dimensional form of decentralization: Firstly, it democratizes HE as it geographically deconcentrates the traditional university infrastructure and takes the university to where the people are. In August 2007, all 335 municipalities had been reached, as well as factories and prisons. Expanding HE to all social environments contributes to the pursued territorial equilibrium, i.e., harmonic development across the entire territory at the demographic, productive, and environmental levels. Operationally, this is done through the creation of *aldeas universitarias* (university villages), i.e., integral and permanent municipal education spaces, currently often still located in existing infrastructure (schools, unused office buildings, etc.), but increasingly being transferred to newly constructed standardized and well-equipped aldeas. In this sense, *municipalización* counters the 'Plan Atcon' strategy of isolating universities from the rest of society (on remote campuses) in order to prevent student community interaction.[17]

Secondly, *municipalización* intends to immerse HE in concrete contextual geographies (geo-spatial, geo-historical, geo-social, geo-cultural, geo-economic) (MES, 2005). As Bolivarian HEFA aims to form critical and socially committed professionals for endogenous and sustainable development, transforming the "welfare culture" into a "local participatory culture" (Uzcátegui González, 2005) means breaking with the traditional university paradigm. For instance, students of Integral Community Medicine are educated directly in the community, where they work with the Cuban *Misión Barrio Adentro* doctors and become sensitized to the problems and needs of their environment.

CONTENTS, METHODOLOGY & METHODS

Bolivarian HE aspires to transcend the dominant 'global HE consensus'—an education agenda set by the global managerial elite and driven by discourses around 'lifelong learning,' 'skills,' and 'competencies,' where knowledge production and education policy are increasingly colonised by economic policy imperatives (Ball, 1998; Popkewitz, 1994). Rather than subordinating and marginalizing knowledges and contents not directly exploitable in the capitalist economy, the fundamental principle of holistic and integral education expresses itself in the transdisciplinary nature of the UBV study programs. Transdisciplinarity allows knowledge construction through opening up relationships between individual disciplines and therefore is sensitive to the complexity of the processes studied (Bolívar et al., 2003). The approach evidently counters the "fragmentation of knowledge" and narrow specialization inherent in the traditional faculty mode. For instance, the study program *Social Management for Local Development* combines elements of sociology, social work, psychology, economics, and geography. Methodologically, a pedagogy of horizontality is pursued, i.e., dialogical, democratic subject-subject relationships, both between students and university teachers as well as the university and the communities. In the Freirean sense, the (university) teacher becomes a motivator, facilitator and learner.

The process of "dialogical and transformatory education" includes 'dialogue with the self' (UBV, 2003), for instance students writing their autobiography in order to reconstruct internalized knowledge through a process of "learning through de-learning," i.e., liberating oneself from "old" knowledge in order to make space for "new" knowledge, accompanied by "learning through doing." Philosophically, this evokes Paulo Freire's social praxis or Habermasian emancipatory action, where "knowing and acting are fused in a single act" (Habermas, 1972: 212). The knowledge produced in these action-reflection-action processes is systematized through writing (article, theatre play, billboard) or video work and the like.

The theoretico-philosophical framework is put into practice through student community learning projects, which foster investigative capacities from a situated perspective. Transdisciplinary groups of UBV students— i.e., groups formed according to students' geographical origin rather than their respective programs of study—support their neighborhood throughout their entire period of study in resolving real community problems. Typically, projects are developed in marginalized communities, as it is there where most UBV students come from.[18] In that way, the university is at the service of the people rather than creating 'just another' elite alienated from society (Fernández Pereira, 2005). Additionally, the processes of analysis involve conscientization, which strengthens critical, non-positivistic problem solving. As a practice of participatory democracy, the popular sectors determine the research agenda and therefore gain partial control over the curriculum, thus challenging the "hegemony of the professional organisations." (Greenwood & Levin, 2000) With respect to participatory democracy, the projects further support the creation of community councils (*consejos comunales*), a form of participatory planning and budgeting at the community and municipality scales. Moreover, this element of Bolivarian pedagogy challenges positivistic notions of educational quality, as expressed in quantifiable standards, since the quality of education also manifests itself in "the possibility of improving the living conditions of the Venezuelan people." (Fernández Pereira, 2005, p. 9)

Ultimately, the Bolivarian pedagogies aim to support the subaltern's alienation from their own power of generating transformatory knowledge by their own initiative, to subsequently emancipate themselves from intellectual and economic dependence on privileged elites. In this sense, knowledge as a product of the work in situ, where the individual becomes a bearer of knowledge and a social subject, means a democratization of knowledge. The imperialist disqualification of knowledges alternative to the dominant western scientific knowledge equates with "epistemicides" (Santos cited in Dale & Robertson, 2004). However, alternative knowledges, or an "epistemology of the South," are a precondition for alternative sociabilities and societies. A "monoculture of knowledge," rather than an "ecology of knowledge" where scientific and lay knowledge can coexist, silences alternatives to the status quo (Santos, 2001).

INTERNATIONALIZING HE FROM A NONCOMMERCIAL PERSPECTIVE

Driven by a range of bi-/multilateral free trade agreements, most notably the World Trade Organization's GATS, the internationalisation of HE has since the mid-1990s onward been dissociated from cultural or cooperative motives (Larsen & Vincent-Lancrin, 2002), supplanted by a commercial rationale, as manifest in lucrative distance learning programs and the establishment of HE branches by Northern institutions in foreign countries.[19] Furthermore, it should be considered that the South's comparative advantage in the export of education services is minimal, if not nonexistent (Altbach, 2003). The Venezuelan case is paradigmatic for this disequilibrium: Even though our data are restricted to education service *consumption abroad* (as only one form of trade in services),[20] they demonstrate that Venezuela hardly exports any education services, whereas annually 9,957 Venezuelans study abroad, over half of which (5,333) is in the US.[21]

In stark contrast to Fourth Republic policy making, the Bolivarian government is one of the few (besides Argentina and Brazil) to overtly oppose the inclusion of education in commercial agreements due to the detrimental effect that a global education market, hegemonized by the education industry in the core countries, has on the fostering of national "cognitive sovereignty."

As much as the Venezuelan government objects to a market driven internationalization of education, it promotes an internationalization based on the logic of cooperativism, solidarity and complementarity. As established in the 10-point strategic plan, the Venezuelan approach forms an integral part of the broader counter-hegemonic ALBA proposal for regional integration. As an alternative to "free trade" and the accompanying inequalities—thus replacing liberal "comparative advantage" with a "co-operative advantage"—ALBA aspires to contribute to a multipolar global system embedded in international relations more adequate for the needs and potentials of developing countries. In education, the ALBA operates on various levels. With the objective to eradicate illiteracy in the entire region, Cuba and Venezuela have initiated *Misión Robinson* International in, for instance, Nicaragua and Bolivia. In HE, the University of the South is an incipient project that tries to construct a network between public Latin-American universities in order to promote South-South cooperation and the exchange of knowledge, technology, and culture. Via the internationalized *Misión Sucre*, students from the entire region receive studentships to study sports and medicine in Venezuela and Cuba (MES, 2006).

CONCLUSION

While the Fourth Republic education reforms did not take hold in the unequal and inequitable social context, the Bolivarian revolution in education is a true alternative to the contemporary hegemonic education paradigm. Conceiving of HE as an undeniable, universal social right, HE acquires a pivotal role in deepening all dimensions of the revolutionary process. This centrality expresses itself in a range of initiatives, which have a bearing on all areas of education policy: Firstly, public investment in HE has been dramatically expanded. Secondly, the Estado docente has been reestablished, where the new municipalized education spaces introduce significant innovations. With respect to regulation, new contents, methodologies and pedagogies have been introduced, guided by the principles of popular education and advancing an autonomous development model nevertheless tied into a counter-hegemonic regional integration strategy. Related to this is the open rejection of the commercial internationalization of education, while calling for an internationalization along cultural and cooperative lines. The challenge posed to the principal neoliberal axioms in education—as expressed trough discourses of "efficiency" and "competition" (understood as subordination to the prerogatives of capitalism)—allows us to argue that the fatalism which often accompanies (and legitimizes) neoliberal education policies can be stood up to under certain conditions. Some of these, as can be concluded from the Venezuelan case, are a strong political will and a clear conception of education as a public good and universal right.

> It is still early to evaluate with precision the impacts, potentialities or the limitations of the Venezuelan educational transformation. Undeniably, the challenges to be tackled are still many. Indeed, massifying HE can effect upon the quality, or access of the hitherto excluded may involve 'inclusion with segregation'—that is, the popular sectors participating in HE circuits different to those of the middle and upper classes. Nevertheless, some of these contradictions—heavily exploited by parts of the opposition—are not that different to those encountered in the "massified" levels of primary and secondary education in most countries marked by unequal social structures, not only in the South.[22]

Issues like these suggest that certain problems that manifest themselves in HE—in Venezuela and elsewhere—emerge in response to not only internal factors of the HE system (such as inadequate resources), but also to external factors. Such problems may be mitigated or resolved through, on one hand, improving the quality of education at the lower levels—as has been the case in Venezuela in the recent past through, for instance, substantial investment in infrastructure, teacher education, and via curricular innovations from the preschool to the HE levels—and, above all, advancement towards a more egalitarian society. The latter rests on the idea that in order for education policy to be effective with regard to improving equity and quality, it is indispensable to take the impact of poverty and other social determinants into account (Bonal et al., 2005). Therefore, education planning would have to transcend the sector concept and become sensitized to the potentially positive and/or negative impacts of noneducational public policies on the education sector. In this respect, the Bolivarian Republic's holistic approach to integral, endogenous development, where HE policy is firmly embedded in other revolutionized social, economic, and political policies—such as land and income redistribution, free health and state subsidized food, micro-credit and work creation programs—constitutes an example well worth studying further.

NOTES

1. The Venezuelan school system is structured thus: preschool/nursery (0–6 years of age); lower basic education (grades 1–6; 7–12 year-olds); upper basic education (grades 7–9; 13–15 year-olds); and medium diversified and technical education (years 1–3; 16–18 year-olds).
2. 'Min. Educación registra más de 13 milliones de personas en formación en el país.' *Agencia Bolivariana de Noticias.* Retrieved May 16, 2007 from http://www.abn.info.ve/go_news5.php?articulo=92060&lee=6
3. Basic education (i.e., 9 years) enrollment has been increased from 83 percent in 1998/99 to 92 percent in 2005/06 (RBV, 2007).
4. *Misión Sucre* may be considered a nonformal HE program for the hitherto excluded of all ages, and UBV as a formal university for secondary school leavers. In September 2005, *Misión Sucre* was academically integrated in the UBV, leaving the former with administrative responsibilities, such as coordinating the municipalized university spaces (*aldeas*), payment of municipalized UBV staff and allocation of students to study programs in collaborating non-Bolivarian universities.
5. The crisis of legitimacy was reflected in rising voter abstention in national elections. While between 1958–83 abstention had always been lower than 15 percent, it reached 20 percent in 1988 and 40 percent in 1993 (Mascareño 2000: 29).
6. 'Washington Consensus' refers to the set of World Bank and IMF-driven neoliberal adjustment policies, whose ten key features have been succinctly identified by John Williamson (1993): fiscal discipline, public expenditure priorities, tax reform, financial liberalization, exchange rates, trade liberalization, foreign direct investment, privatization, deregulation, and property rights.
7. Net primary enrollment (7–12 year-olds) steadily increased between 1970 and 1989, from 79.8 percent to 86.0 percent respectively, and then fell to 83.8 percent in 1996. Net secondary enrolment (13–19 years) decreased from 26.6 percent in 1970 to 18.3 percent in 1989, and climbed again to 22.3 percent in 1996 (UNESCO in CEPAL, 2008).
8. Statistics refer to *urban* population.
9. Contrary to traditional welfare programs, the missions circumvent bureaucratic resistance; as both a process and a system of inclusion, they combine short-term poverty alleviation and inclusion with long-term structural transformation (MED 2004). In addition to the educational missions, there are health (*Barrio Adentro*) and food missions (*Misión Alimentación/Mercal*), *Misión Cultura*, as well as cross-sector missions that promote the social economy, cooperativism (*Misión Vuelvan Caras, Misión Ciencia*), and (indigenous) rights.
10. Source: www.sisov.mpd.gov.ve
11. The neostructuralist 'development from within' model responded to both the failure of import substitution industrialization and the subsequent export oriented neoliberal 'mal-development' paradigm (see Sunkel, 1993).

12. For further details see Muhr & Verger, 2006.
13. The ALBA, however, is a transnational project and is not restricted to these for countries (see Muhr, forthcoming 2008).
14. Source: www.sisov.mpd.gov.ve
15. Data is from 2003. Source: UNESCO Institute of Statistics.
16. At the time of writing, abolishment of these examinations is being discussed.
17. Plan Atcon is named after U.S. State Department functionary Rudolph Atcon, whose 1961 landmark report "The Latin American University: a key for an integrated approach to the coordinated social, economic, and educational development of Latin America" advocated a redesigning of Latin American universities with the objective to demobilize the critical university.
18. To a limited extent, this policy has been universalized, as from autumn 2006 on, *all* Venezuelan undergraduate university students are obliged by law to community service in the form of a 120 (academic) hours, non-remunerated community placement over three months.
19. For a summary of the effects and criticisms of this commoditization, see García Guadilla (2003) or Knight (2002).
20. The others are: cross-border trade, commercial presence and movement of natural persons. See: GATS text at www.wto.org
21. Data from UNESCO Institute of Statistics.
22. A good example is the Spanish 'LOGSE' education law, implemented from 1993 on. This law expanded the compulsory education age from 14 to 16 years of age, implicitly targeting school-leavers from the most underprivileged sectors. Despite the fact that the reform was underfunded, it allowed a partial democratization of education. However, large parts of the education community and the conservative political class concluded that LOGSE preeminently diminished quality standards.

REFERENCES

Albornoz, O. (1999) *Del fraude a la estafa. La educación en Venezuela [From fraud to swindle. Education in Venezuela]*. Caracas: UCV.
Altbach, P.G. (2003) *The decline of the guru—the academic profession in developing and middle-income countries*. New York: Palgrave MacMillan.
Arnove, R.F. (1986) *Education and revolution in Nicaragua*. New York: Praeger.
Ball, S.J. (1998) Big policies/small world: An introduction to international perspectives in education policy. *Comparative Education*, 34 (2), pp. 119–130.
Battaglini, O. (2000) Consequencias socio-económicas y políticas del ajuste macroeconómico en Venezuela en la decada de los noventa [Socio-economic and political consequences of the macroeconomic adjustment in Venezuela in the nineties]. In A. Kon, C. Banko, D. Melcher, & M.C. Cacciamali (Eds), *Costos sociales de las reformas neoliberals en América Latina [Social costs of neoliberal reforms in Latin America]*. São Paulo: Pontifíca Universidade Católica de São Paulo.
Bolívar, O.; Goncalves, J. A.; Pérez, R.; Smeja, M.; Téllez, & M.; Vivas, J. (2003) *Bases, criterios y pautas para el diseño curricular de los programas de formación de la UBV [Bases, criteria and guidelines for the curricular design of the formation programmes at the UBV]*. Caracas: UBV.
Bonal, X.; Tarabini, A.; & Klickowski, F. (2005) ¿Puede la educación erradicar la pobreza? [Can education eradicate poverty?] *Cuadernos de Pedagogía*, 352.
Bourdieu, P. & Passeron, J.-C. (1977) *Reproduction: In education, society and culture*. London: Sage.
Bowles, S. & Gintis, H. (1998) Educación y desarrollo personal: la larga sombra del trabajo [Education and personal development: the long shadow of work]. In

M. Férnandez Enguita (Ed), *Sociología de la educación. Textos fundamentals [Sociology of Education: Fundamental Texts]*. Barcelona: Ariel.

Broccoli, A. (1977) *Antonio Gramsci y la educación como hegemonía [Antonio Gramsci and education as hegemony]*. México: Nueva Imagen.

Brown, P. (1990) The "Third Wave": Education and the ideology of parentocracy. In A.H. Halsey, H. Lauder, P. Brown, & A. Stuart Wells (Eds), *Education: Culture, Economy, Society*. Oxford: Oxford University Press.

Bruni Celli, J. (2004) Innovation and frustration: Education reform in Venezuela. In R.R. Kaufman & J.M. Nelson (Eds), *Crucial needs, weak incentives*. Washington, D.C.: Woodrow Wilson Center Press.

Carnoy, M. (1999) *Globalization and educational reform: What planners need to know*. Paris: UNESCO.

Casanova, R. (1999) Ese escurridizo curso de la descentralización: La dispersión de iniciativas [The slippery course of decentralization. The dispersion of initiatives]. In R. Casanova (Ed), *La reforma educativa [The educational reform]*. Caracas: CENDESUCV.

———. (2005) Venezuela después del liberalismo: De los consensos de la reforma de los años noventa a un nuevo contrato educativo? [Venezuela after liberalism. From the consensus of the nineties to a new educational deal] In CENDES *Venezuela Visión Plural*, 1. Caracas: CENDES-UCV.

CBRV. (2000) *Constitución de la República Bolivariana de Venezuela [Constitution of the Bolivarian Republic of Venezuela]*. Caracas: RBV.

CEPAL. (2008). *Social Indicators and Statistics (BADEINSO)*. Retrieved May 20, 2008 from http://websie.eclac.cl/sisgen/ConsultaIntegrada.asp

Chávez Frías, H. R. (2005) *Palabras inaugurales de la IV Cumbre de la Deuda Social [Inaugural speech of the IV Social Debt Summit]*. Caracas: MCI.

CRV. (1961) *Constitución República de Venezuela [Constitution of the Republic of Venezuela]*. Caracas: Republic of Venezuela.

Dale, R. & Robertson, S. (2004) Interview with Boaventura de Sousa Santos. *Globalisation, Societies and Education*, 2 (2), pp. 147–160.

Derham, M. (2002) Special section: contemporary politics in Venezuela. Introduction. *Bulletin of Latin American Research*, 21 (2), pp.191–198.

Ellner, S. (2003) Introduction: The search for explanations. In S. Ellner & D. Hellinger (Eds) Venezuelan politics in the Chávez era: Class, polarization and conflict. Boulder: Lynne Rienner.

Estaba B.E. (1999) La reorganización del Ministerio de Educación. Desconcentración, descentralización y transformación institucional [The re-organization of the Ministry of Education. Deconcentration, decentralization and institutional transformation]. In R. Casanova (Ed) (1999) *La reforma educativa [The educational reform]*. Caracas: CENDES-UCV.

Fernández Pereira, M. (2005) La lógica neoliberal excluyente para la educación Superior [The exclusive neoliberal logic for higher education]. In M. Fernández Pereira, *La municipalización de la educación superior [The municipalization of higher education]*. Caracas: UBV.

Gamus, E. (1999) La trayectoria de la descentralización educativa. Nuevos desafíos [The trajectory of education decentralization. New challenges]. In R. Casanova (Ed) *La reforma educativa*. Caracas: CENDES-UCV.

García, C.T., López, M., Aguilera, O., & Pargas, L. (1992) La educación en la crisis o crisis de la educación [The education of the crisis or the crisis of education]. *Fermentum*, 2 (5), pp. 3–8.

Greenwood, D.J. & Levin, M. (2000) Reconstructing the relationships between universities and society through action research. In N.K. Denzin & Y.S. Lincoln (Eds), Handbook of qualitative research (2nd ed.). London: Sage.

Habermas, J. (1972). *Knowledge and human interests*. London: Heinemann.

IFC (1999) Inversiones en educación privada en los países en desarrollo [Private education investment in developing countries]. *Corporación Financiera Internacional.*

Johnes, G. (1995) *Economía de la educación. Capital humano, rendimiento educativo y mercado de trabajo [Economy of Education. Human Capital, educational return and labour market].* Madrid: Ministerio de Trabajo y Seguridad Social.

Knight, J. (2002) *Trade in higher education services: The implications of GATS.* London: Observatory on Borderless Higher Education.

Larsen, K. & Vincent-Lancrin, S. (2002) International trade in educational services: good or bad? *Higher Education and Management Policy*, 14 (3).

Lauglo, J. (1995) Forms of decentralization and their implications for education. *Comparative Education*, 31 (1), pp. 5–29.

León Sanabria, J.C. (1992) El neoliberalismo y la educación venezolana [Neoliberalism and the Venezuelan education]. *Fermentum*, 2 (5), pp. 26–35.

Levy, D.C. (1998) *La educación superior dentro de las transformaciones políticas y económicas de los años noventa [Higher education within the political and economical transformations of the nineties]* Documento CEDES/98. Serie Educación Superior.

López Maya, M. & Lander, L. (2000) Fracaso y fatiga de los ajustes en Venezuela 1984–1998 [Failure and fatigue of the adjustment in Venezuela 1984–1998]. In A. Kon, C. Banko, D. Melcher, & M.C. Cacciamali (Eds), *Costos sociales de las reformas neoliberales en América Latina [Social costs of the neoliberal reforms in Latin America].* São Paulo: Pontifíca Universidade Católica de São Paulo.

López Segrera, F. (2003) El impacto de la globalización y las políticas educativas en los sistemas de educación superior de América Latina y el Caribe [The impact of globalization and the educational policies in the higher education systems in Latin American and the Caribbean]. In M. Mollis (Ed), *Las universidades en América Latina: ¿Reformadas o alteradas? [The universities in Latin America: reformed or altered?]* Buenos Aires: CLACSO.

Mascareño, C. (2000) *Balance de la descentralización en Venezuela [Evaluation of the decentralization in Venezuela].* Caracas: PNUD/Nueva Sociedad.

MCI. (2004) *Taller de Alto Nivel 'El Nuevo Mapa Estrategico.' [High level workshop: the new strategic map].* Caracas: MCI.

MED. (2004) *La educación bolivariana. Políticas, programas y acciones: 'Cumpliendo las metas del milenio.' [Bolivarian education. Policies, programmes and actions: achieving the millennium goals].* Caracas: MED.

MES. (2005) *Misión Sucre. Compendio documental básico [Sucre Mission. Basic Documents].* Caracas: MES.

———. (2006) *Memoria y Cuenta 2005. [Annual report and accounts 2005]* Caracas: MES.

———. (2007) *Memoria y Cuenta 2006. [Annual report and accounts 2006]* Caracas: MES.

MF. (2006) *Memoria y Cuenta 2005.* Caracas: Ministerio de Finanzas.

———. (2007) *Memoria y Cuenta 2006.* Caracas: Ministerio de Finanzas.

Morales Gil, E. (2003) *La exclusión de los pobres de la educación superior venezolana [The exclusion of the poor from Venezuelan higher education].* Caracas: OPSU.

Muhr, T. (2008) Nicaragua re-visited: from neoliberal 'ungovernability' to the Bolivarian Alternative for the Americas (ALBA). *Globalisation, Societies and Education* 6 (2), pp. 147–161.

Muhr, T. & Verger, A. (2006) Venezuela: Higher education for all. *Journal for Critical Education Policy Studies*, 4 (1).

Popkewitz, T.S. (1994) *Sociología política de las reformas educativas [Political Sociology of educational reforms].* Madrid: Morata.

Pucci, R. & Mundó, M. (1999) Escuelas: debilidad institucional, heterogeneidad y gestión descentralizada [Schools: institutional weakness, heterogeneity and decentralization]. In R. Casanova (Ed), *La reforma educativa [The educational reform]*. Caracas: CENDES-UCV.

Puerta, J. (1992) Dos líneas de modernización: Un esbozo histórico [Two modernization lines: A historical outline]. *Fermentum*, 2 (5), pp. 9–26.

Rambla, X., Valiente, O. & Verger, A. (2006) *Inducir a los Pobres a superar su propia adversidad: la fuerza de una idea sobre la educación y la pobreza en Chile [Leading the poor to overcome their adversity: the strength of an idea over education and poverty in Chile]* In X. Bonal, Globalización, Educación y Pobreza en América Latina: ¿hacia una nueva agenda política? [Globalization, Education and Poverty in Latin America: through a new political agenda?]. Barcelona: CIDOB.

RBV (2007) *Logros sociales [Social Achievements]*. Retrieved August, 27, 2007 from http://www.sisov.mpd.gob.ve/estudios/

RBV/PDVSA. (2005) La Misión Sucre [The Sucre Mission]. *Educere*, 28, pp.23–26. Caracas.

Riutort, M. (1999) *El costo de erradicar la pobreza [The cost of eradicating poverty]*. Retrieved November 13, 2005, from http://omega.manapro.com/editor-pobreza/index.asp?spg_id=5

Robinson, W. (1996) *Promoting polyarchy*. Cambridge: Cambridge University Press.

Santos, B.d.S. (2001) Nuestra America: Reinventing a subaltern paradigm of recognition and redistribution. *Theory, Culture & Society*, 18 (2–3), pp. 185–217.

———. (2004) *La Universidad del siglo XXI. Para una reforma democrática y emancipadora de la Universidad [The University of the XXI century. Towards a democratic and emancipatory reform of universities]*. Buenos Aires: Miño y Dávila—Laboratorio de Políticas Públicas.

Scherrer, C. (2007). GATS: commodifying education via trade treaties. In K. Martens, A. Rusconi and K. Leuze (Eds), *New Arenas of Education Governance: The Impact of International Organizations and Markets on Educational Policy Making*. London: Palgrave.

Social Watch. (2005) *Social watch report 2005*. Montevideo: Instituto del Tercer Mundo.

Sunkel, O. (ed) (1993) *Development from within*. London: Lynne Rienner.

Torres, R.M. (1999) *One decade of education for all: the challenge ahead*. Buenos Aires: IIEP UNESCO.

UBV. (2003) *Documento rector [Steering document]*. Caracas: UBV.

Uzcátegui González, Y. (2005) La municipalización de la educación superior como direccionamiento político de la revolución bolivariana [The municipalization of higher education as a political device of the bolivarian revolution]. In M. Fernández Pereira, *La municipalización de la educación superior [The municipalization of Higher Education]*. Caracas: UBV.

Verger, A. (2007). The Constitution of a New Global Regime: Higher Education in the GATS/WTO Framework. In D. Epstein, R. Boden, R. Deem, F. Rizvi, S. Wright (Eds), *World Yearbook of Education 2008: Geographies of Knowledge, Geometries of Power: Framing the Future of Higher Education*. London, Routledge.

Weisbrot, M. & Sandoval, L. (2007) *The Venezuelan economy in the Chávez years*. Washington, D.C.: Center for Economic and Policy Research (CEPR).

Williamson, J. (1993) Democracy and the "Washington consensus." *World Development*, 21 (8), pp. 1329–1336.

World Bank. (1979) *World development report 1979*. Washington, D.C.: World Bank.

———. (1995) *Priorities and strategies for education: A World Bank review*. Washington, D.C.: World Bank.

———. (1999a) *Education sector strategy*. Washington D.C.: World Bank.

———. (1999b) *Educational change in Latin America and the Caribbean*. Washington, D.C.: World Bank.

———. (2003) *World development report 2004*. Washington, D.C.: World Bank.

6 Legacy Against Possibility
Twenty-Five Years of Neoliberal Policy in Chile

Jill Pinkney Pastrana

INTRODUCTION

> The fundamental aim is to attend to the needs of the individual in the different stages of his life and to the communities in their struggle for development . . . ' 'For us every society must be a school and school must become an integrated element of that big school which is society. Schools must be open to pressures important to the community.
>
> (President Salvador Allende, Popular Unity government, 1970–1973)

> It is imperative that we change the Chilean's mentality . . . the government of the Armed Forces intends to open a new phase in our national destiny, giving way to new generations of Chileans who have been shaped in a school of healthy civic habits.' 'The political recess can only be ended when a new generation of Chileans formed in accordance with nationalist ideals is able to assume the direction of public life.
>
> (General Pinochet, Military Junta (1973–1989)

On December 10, 2006, former military dictator of Chile, Augusto Pinochet died. His passing marks an end to a chapter in Chilean history, and was met by celebration by many and tears by a few. Amidst the celebration of the crowds on the death of the dictator, the words of Mario Benedetti were scrawled poignantly on a building on the *Alameda*:

> "*La muerte le gano a la justicia*"[1]
>
> (Mario Benedetti, 12/10/2006)

Pinochet died never having served time in jail for the many crimes of which he was accused, namely treason, murder, and embezzlement.

The legacy of the dictatorship remains imprinted on Chilean culture and institutions in many ways. The economic reforms of the "Chicago Boys," put in place in the years directly following the military coup did effectively re-form the entire Chilean infrastructure. Chile was the first country in which the economic theory of neoliberalism was put firmly into place. We are now all too familiar with neoliberal economic policies; privatization and structural readjustment recommendations, almost anything that allows for 'free trade' and the ability of capital to flow unhindered between nations and corporate and personal financial interests to maximize profits. Accompanying these structural changes have been various austerity programs aimed at cutting public expenditures and opening the national economy to global capitalism. Within newly defined economic realities, the needs of various public sector services, such as health and education, struggle for survival amid muscular free market ideologies. Accompanying policies are driven by a strong faith in the private sector and a belief that democracy is best developed and supported by the "invisible hand of the market."

In the late 1970s, following a military coup, Chile, with its population brutally suppressed, became the first testing ground for the changes that now define the logic of neoliberal capitalism. The changes in Chile were dramatic and extensive. The Chilean people were violently denied their voice to negotiate the terms of change. Once the basic neoliberal economic framework was laid, the model was applied to all sectors of society—health, housing, social security, fisheries, agriculture, transportation and of course—education.

The following discussion will present a case study of the Chilean experience, the country where neoliberal reform—in all of its instantiations—was first systematically implemented.[2] Detailed examination of the Chilean legacy provides a unique opportunity for us to question and debate the plausibility and possibilities offered by neoliberal policy in education and elsewhere. Chile gives us a retrospective on policy implementation and its fallout, and can lend valuable insights to our current discussions concerning the potential of neoliberal policies. The case of Chile enables a series of detailed analyses of several important questions: Exactly what were the neoliberal education reforms initially put into place? How do these policies implemented in Chile compare with those we see throughout the world in both developing as well as industrialized nations? What are the results of these changes? And, what are some of the lingering challenges educators in Chile face as they continue to negotiate the subtle and not so subtle fallout of twenty-five years of neoliberal policy?

In the years since "re-democratization," following the plebiscite of 1989, successive center-left governments have attempted a series of education reforms in an effort to improve education in Chile. These reforms that formally began in 1997 and have continued to develop through the mid-2000s, arose out of and are also a reaction to, the logic of the neoliberal market that has become, in essence, the logic of schooling in Chile. However, despite such far-reaching and ongoing efforts to reinfuse resources into a decimated public system, and a reinvigorated national commitment to education, the system remains tied to the neoliberal structure that was put in place during the dictatorship. There is evidence to suggest that this remaining structure severely hampers even the most progressive and egalitarian reforms from breaking through organizational and ideological limitations that prevent Chilean education reform from realizing its potential for flexibility, creativity, and equal access for all Chilean students.

CHARACTERISTICS OF NEOLIBERAL REFORMS 1980–1989

Formal neoliberal restructuring of the Chilean economy and several public sector domains began during the 1980s when the ruling military junta directed the country and all of its institutions firmly toward the global marketplace. This mapping of "market logic" extended onto an educational system whose mandate had previously been firmly rooted in ideas of equity and opportunity rather than efficiency and competition (Puiggrós, 1996). Key ideologically weighted concepts used to promote and legitimate neoliberal reform fit into two categories:

1. Economic concern: "efficiency/decentralization" (can be linked to privatization as an option to attain efficiency), "accountability" (most easily tracked using standardized measures of 'excellence'), and "competition" (linked in interesting ways to the following point, but using market means with which to achieve desired results).
2. Public or popular concern: Often articulated in terms of individual rights, and/or freedom to choose and control private interests, i.e., "local control," "choice," etc. It is within the scope of these concepts that the seminal ideology of economic reforms such as those championed by Milton Friedman—excellence through competition, and the power of choice in the free market—find fertile ground in their translation into the realm of education.

In 1980, the military government passed two decrees that drastically changed the nature of Chilean education. Collectively known as the LOCE, *Ley Orgánica Constitucional de Ensenañca*, they remain a key element of popular discontent and continue to inspire public demonstrations of outrage from students and teachers across the country and educational spectrum. Decree #3,063 began the municipalization of K–12 schools, and #3,476 created government subsidies to private and public schools for each student enrolled, creating a "voucher" system for schools level K–12 (Collins & Lear 1995). The municipalization of kindergarten, primary, and secondary schools (Sometimes called *alcaldización* by Chilean educators, due to the power over educational decisions given to local mayors by this reform) was complete by 1986. The subsidies, or vouchers established in Chile effectively divided education options into three types of schools: 1) municipal ("public"), 2) "private subsidized," (semiprivate) and 3) "private paid," the first two types of institutions eligible to receive state subsidies.

Organizational streamlining based on neoliberal logic became a perceived panacea for low performing schools in Chile, a concept currently well known in the US and elsewhere. This logic points to the need for more "streamlined bureaucratic efficiency" and "choice/competition" as means to fix failing schools (Parry, 1997; Ramirez, 1994; Echeverria & Hevia, 1981; OAS, 1982).[3] With funding tied to student enrollment, and student enrollment influenced by test scores, and test score results influenced by multiple factors, and semiprivate and private schools able to cherry-pick high scoring students and deny entrance to others, Municipal schools faced (and continue to face) declining enrollments as the vicious cycle of marginalization plays itself out. As we are beginning to see in the United States, this "competition" widens the gaps between rich and poor as more affluent families and communities are better able to both negotiate the bureaucracy of the system and supplement limited government funding through individual family, local business, and other municipal revenues. Since the implementation of these reforms, schools in low income sectors and municipal schools in general have deteriorated. Many forced for economic reasons to adopt abbreviated school days and eliminate entire subjects from the curriculum. This, in turn, affects the morale of teachers within these institutions and in the profession as a whole. Wealthy schools have been better able to attract 'star' teachers with higher pay, making 'elite' schools more appealing and helping some private schools become profitable. Within the municipal schools, these changes led to great discrepancies in teacher pay between wealthy municipalities and working-class municipalities, further exacerbating problems of attracting strong teachers to low income areas of the country. Though we now have over thirty years of data from which to analyze these effects, many of these problems remain entrenched and many of the recent education reform efforts are attempting to reverse these negative consequences of neoliberal reform.[4]

CHANGING ROLE OF THE STATE

Ideologically and structurally, neoliberal reforms reduce the role of the state, or national government, leaving market mechanisms as sole regulators of goods and services. In education, as well as elsewhere, this is manifested through a steadily decreasing role for centralized/government oversight, control, and economic support. "Local control" has triumphed over centralized oversight, entrenching a popular concept that masks the realities of neoliberal structural changes. In Chile this took the form of an overall divestment in pubic education and a redefined government role in education to the narrow realms of setting national standards—linked to a fairly comprehensive national curriculum—and testing. In 1983, the

Chilean government initiated nationwide testing of fourth and eighth grade students. The results of this testing have consistently indicated significant gaps between student performance in the three types of schools: municipal, private subsidized, and private paid. However, test results reveal that the most significant differences are not between types of institutions—public vs. private subsidized or private paid—rather between these institutions in richer and poorer neighborhoods. In other words, the quality of primary and secondary schools depends more on the resources of the community, material and otherwise, than whether or not the school under question is public or private. Nonetheless, the perception of the superiority of private education, buoyed by slick advertising, cherry-picking the "good" students leading to comparatively higher test scores, and entrenched classism in Chile, has consistently led to a steady decrease in matriculation to public/ municipal schools. As funding follows individual students, the municipal sector sees a steady decrease in government subsidies, leaving the municipal system drastically underfunded, furthering the perception that the public sector is not capable of providing for the education of Chilean students.

These findings suggest several important issues regarding the relationship between education and neoliberal reforms. The first issue can de described as—the logic of the marketplace versus the logic of education: If the "invisible hand" is suppose to improve the quality of services provided—especially those freed from the oppressive bureaucracies which supposedly were constricting the effectiveness of their operations—then schools freed from these inefficient structures should respond to market pressures with increasing quality, a better product. The market should be providing effective, educational opportunities for those who are able to take advantage of them (either by means of cultural or economic resources—i.e., knowledge of and access to good quality education). Increasing excellence in one sector should spur all institutions on to higher returns. All schools should be improving, but after thirty years of neoliberal reform, quite the opposite has occurred.

Another key element in this discussion concerns the importance of financial resources in education. It seems that there have been various claims regarding efficiency—that it is not more money that is necessary, rather better organization. This claim reinforces a mythological faith in efficiency. If money is not the problem, it is easy to legitimate huge decreases in educational spending. Decreases that further exacerbate problems faced by schools serving low income communities (Puiggrós, 1996). Part of the struggle to improve educational quality and access to underserved populations requires that we face the myths of the market head-on. Arguments asserting the marginal link of funding to educational quality, as well as the dubious quality of some educational projects organized around pure business models, illuminate some of the problems encountered when a blind faith in the market is applied to schooling. Arguments made that negate the importance of money in creating good schools should be roundly critiqued on many levels, but it is highly suspect that the individuals whose political and economic interests tend to be represented by such claims also willingly pay high fees for the formal and extracurricular education of their own children.

FALLOUT FROM THE REFORMS, 1989–1996

Teaching

There is no arena in which the logic of the marketplace clashes with the ideals of education as dramatically as teaching. In Chile, we have extensive evidence that policy recommendations articulated in terms of economic efficiency, accountability, and excellence, when conceptualized away from the realities of classroom practice, create an aberration of all that schools have been envisioned to be. As one scholar put it recently, "It's very easy to become efficient and reduce overall educational costs if you simply cut teacher's salaries and increase class sizes" (Schugurensky, 1997). The drop in pay experienced in Chile as part of "efficiency" planning has created an environment where most teachers must work multiple jobs, usually at several different school sites, in order to make ends meet. The term "taxi teachers" has been coined referring to educators who travel from school to school by taxi to complete their working day.[5] Teachers continue to be paid in some sectors by the "chronological hour," for each 60 minutes of time spent in class, rather than the "pedagogical hour" which is equal to 45 minutes. This means that teaching four 45-minute classes is only worth three hours' pay with prep time and homework not considered worth financial compensation.

Though there are federal minimum limits for all teacher salaries, these are unacceptably low. Teachers now have become part of the "flexible" work force, often with "indefinite contracts," and they can be fired for no stated reason in most municipalities, though *La Reforma Educacional* has been trying to mediate and improve this condition. One example of an "efficient" use of these indefinite contracts occurred in 1987 when, to lower costs and compete against neighboring schools, some municipalities fired 8,000 teachers—most received zero severance pay, having been classified as recent hires because the schools where they taught had been recently municipalized.

Indeed, decentralizing and privatizing the educational system has significantly affected the professionalism of teaching. Teachers, once highly respected, remain yet another sector of workers lacking in job security and even such minimal guarantees (once enjoyed by all national employees) of due process and defense against accusation. Until the passage of the *Estatuto Docente*[6] by the Consertación government in 1990, teachers were not even regular municipal salaried employees (like school janitors), but "workers" under contract of the municipality's education corporation (Marin, 1990). As in the case of teacher pay, the security afforded teachers varies by type of school and municipality. Generally speaking, municipal schools offer marginally better job security and benefits followed by the semiprivate and private institutions. Teachers remain one of the more marginalized and exploited populations in the neoliberal Chilean workforce.

Dramatic evidence of market pressures destroying teaching and learning is also abundant when market measures of excellence are put into place. When excellence is measured only in terms of the results of standardized test scores, and a reward system—including job security, pay and other market "incentives"—is similarly linked, teachers have little apparent reason to explore the potential of student centered learning, constructivist methods, or critical thinking, practices that may appear to veer away from the focus of state exams. The focus becomes getting information that will appear on the test to the students as quickly as possible. This type of "efficiency" leads to a narrowed curriculum and teaching to the test, something now endemic to the schools of Chile.

Local Control

There seems to be a general consensus among educators that municipalization was one of the key factors responsible for the downfall of Chilean education. In workshops with teachers and principals from the 9th Region, a Region that is politically conservative and was the only Region in the country to support the dictatorship in the plebiscite of 1989, educators overwhelmingly expressed negative sentiments toward the decentralization of education in Chile (Pinkney Pastrana, 2000). Teachers and principals routinely referred to the municipalization of education in Chile as '*alcaldización*.' This refers to the transfer of authority in schooling away from the general national regulations coming from the National Ministry to the mayors—*alcaldes*—of each municipality. The mayors of these municipalities, perhaps without exception, are not educators and have a limited understanding of the lives of teachers or students and families in municipal schools. Despite this, they hold authority over many important educational decisions related to teachers, including pay scales, hiring, and tenure policies within each district. These drawbacks are over and above the obvious political conflicts that can arise when teachers or other staff members find themselves in differing political camps than their respective mayors. The complete breakdown of even the erroneous supposition of the 'neutrality' of schooling happened in Chile after the coup when the ruling military junta appointed every mayor in the country, giving them complete control over the nation's schools. Mayors were not democratically elected until 1992. Even with democratic elections, the legacy of direct political control over the schools manifests itself in the cultural realities of disempowered education communities.

Issues of 'local control' may hold emancipating potential when removed from an authoritarian context. Local control theoretically allows the possibility of creating democratic, oppositional spaces in which the socially reproductive aims of status quo educational organizations could be contested. The *Reforma Educacional* begun in 1997, coupled with the current entrepreneurial atmosphere, which is very much a part of neoliberal culture, has created an environment in Chile where geographically—and ideologically—different municipal plans may be allowed to proceed. The efficiency perceived in decentralized organizations and the faith that competition via parental choice will inspire schools toward 'excellence,' as measured on national standardized exams, has left educational establishments freed from the tedium of some controlling regulation. However, the time constraints on educators endemic in a system whose paramount organization stems from ideals of "efficiency," and the market mentality enhanced by funding mechanisms (vouchers/*subsidios*) that privilege competition among schools for the "best" students, has created an education ethos in which alternative visions are hard pressed to flourish, despite organizational opportunities to do so. Perhaps this potential for re-forming democratic spaces will be realized in some independently organized schools in Chile; thus far local control has not widely resulted in this.

We can see an interesting relationship between politics and education by contextualizing the processes and outcomes of the educational reforms of the past twenty-four years within the political and economic reality of Chile. Chile nicely illustrates the inextricable linkages and the complex interplay and interdependence between politics, economics, and education. This poses a challenge to research embedded in paradigms and methodologies that present positivistic, ahistorical research and policy decontextualized from social and cultural realities. Such investigation fails to adequately problematize the idea that the political system, the economic system, and the educational system somehow function autonomously.

EDUCATION IN "RE-DEMOCRATIZED" CHILE

Este Estado de carácter subsidiario ha modificado profundamente los objectivos mismos de la educación de nuestro país, concibiendo al educando básicamente como consumidor. De este modo, se ha ido transformando el concepto de calidad del educación, reduciéndose a una capacitación eficiente para generar los diversos tipos de capital humano que esta sociedad requiere para us desarrollo productivo, así como a la formación de un ser humano competente para ser buen consumidor en esta sociedad de mercado. (Colegio de Profesores, July 1999)[7]

Education policies favored by right wing political parties in Chile mirror those of the military government, and include none of the improvements (however small they may be) offered by *La Reforma Educacional*. During his tenure as Minister of Education, programs begun by former president

Ricardo Lagos contrasted dramatically with those of previous officials in the Ministry of Education.

> ... The solution of Maria Teresa Infante and Alfredo Prieto (super-intendent of education in 1979, and minister of education, December 1979–April 1982, respectively), and others before the plebiscite, to low performing schools was to close them down. Lagos comes into the Ministry and creates the program of 900 schools to improve the educational situation for the worst schools in the country. This represents a drastic change in policy and in national goals for education. It is also an indication of the differing impressions various government ideologies hold concerning Chilean students. (Ministry of Education presentation detailing the MECE Media to faculty from the Universidad de la Frontera, July, 1998)

In 1989 after the plebiscite symbolically removed General Pinochet from power and began the process of "re-democratization," the newly formed Consertación coalition of center and left-of-center representatives began the process of negotiating their ascendancy to the formal power structures in government. One of the concessions for "re-democratization" agreed upon by the fledgling Consertación coalition, was to respect the Constitution of 1980 (Flores & Varela, 1994; Martinez, 1993; Petras & Levia, 1994). The current Constitution was drawn up by the military government, and is designed to uphold the role of the military in Chile's development, and reinforce and support the current economic model as well as the socially conservative tenets of its authoritarian foundations (Collins & Lear, 1995).

In much the same way that political annalists portray the relationship between the actual policies of Third Way politicians and their "kinder, gentler" rhetoric, Chile's educational reforms post-re-democratization often appear to offer progressive potential without addressing the structural problems that are inherent to and responsible for the downfall of the Chilean education system. The policies regulating decentralization, vouchers, and privatization, called by some "post-welfare reforms" (Guari, 1998), are embedded in the Constitution and the *Ley Orgánica Constitucional de Ensenañca (LOCE)*. It is the neoliberal framework that supports the Chilean educational system that is ultimately responsible for the "crises in education" which recent reforms such as the *Reforma Educacional,* at once attempt to remedy and continue to aggravate. The neoliberal tenets that were put into place during the military regime have been facilitated by and are dependent on:

1. liberalization of labor practices, including the absence of standards regulating the working conditions of teachers.
2. continued encouragement and requirement of competition between schools for students in order that the subsidies not leave the site.

Reform initiatives post re-democratization have not significantly challenged or attempted to change any of these conditions. In fact, current reforms increase competition between schools through new market incentives such as "bonus" incentives recommended within the reform, i.e., merit pay, teaching awards for excellence, etc. One of the primary goals of *La Reforma Educacional* (1997–present), evident in all of its four major areas of concentration, is the creation of a professional teacher/ school culture better able to successfully administrate learning within the structural confines of the decentralized system (MINEDUC, 1998; Pinkney Pastrana, 2000).

LA REFORMA EDUCACIONAL

> ... las políticas educacionales iniciadas en 1990 han tenido dos grandes principios orientadores: el mejoramiento de la calidad de la educación y una mayor equidad en su distribución. El foco de las políticas respecto a la calidada ha estado en el mejoramiento de los procesos internos del sistema educacional y de sus resultados de aprendizaje. Asimismo, las políticas de equidad se han orientado de acuerdo al criterio de discriminación positiva, según el cual la igualdad de oportunidades educativas para grupos heterogéneos requiere asignar más recursos y prestar atención especial a los grupos más vulnerables del país. (MINEDUC, 1998, pg. 109)[8]

Given the political environment in which drastic neoliberal reforms in Chile were initially couched, questions of legitimacy or debate on the changes in education that took place pose a moot point, as any opposition to change during the dictatorship was met with violent oppression. Today Chile faces a different situation. Since 1989, the country has been on the road to "re-democratization," again holding political elections open to candidates from a variety of political parties. The past two presidential elections have resulted in Socialists running as part of the *Concertación* coalition.[9] The current education reform focuses its efforts on improving education in Chile by stressing the issues of excellence, equity, and participation, as well as an innovative and impressively progressive emphasis on learning— *Aprender de Aprender*.

The *Reforma Educacional Chilena* officially commenced in 1997. The reform was originally scheduled to be completed in 2002, but the scope of this initiative is enormous and the timeline for its implementation has been extended several times. As mentioned above, the three guiding tenets of the reform are *equidad, calidad, y participación* (equity, quality, and participation). Within these three central foci exist all of the contradictions between the underlying structure of neoliberal reform and many of the assumptions held within its logic, including paradoxically, approaches to schooling that draw our attention away from market incentives toward a focus on human development with arguably progressive elements embedded within.

When implementation of the *Reforma Educacional* began in 1987, four primary areas of focus defined the outline of the reform. These are:

1. The *Jornada Completa*—which extends the length of the school day to last from 8am to 4pm. This reform allows students three extra hours of classroom time per day, bringing the Chilean educational experience closer in line with that of most industrialized nations.
2. *Mejoramiento de la Calidad de la Educación (MECE)*—projects consist of various types of initiatives and can focus on rural or urban sectors, elementary or secondary institutions. They are usually written from within specific institutional sites depending on their unique needs. They can include government funding for projects of infrastructure improvements, projects that seek to develop curriculum for use in local populations, and projects aimed at making small rural and large urban schools more effective.[10]
3. *Desarrollo Profesional de los Decentes*—Universities across the country applied for and received funding from the Ministry to improve their teacher training programs.
4. *Aprender de Aprender*—This final aspect of the *Reforma Educacional* is specifically focused on diversification of the curriculum. These projects also include funding LN3 teacher professional development and in-service workshops throughout the country.

The following sections will detail how the *Reforma Educacional* articulated the three specific foci of the reform. It will also introduce some of the ways that the underlying neoliberal aspects of Chilean education infrastructure remain unchanged by these ongoing reforms and continue to frustrate any "progressive" potential present in ongoing reforms.

EQUIDAD REBORN

Virtually all Ministry publications detailing the *Reforma Educacional* express *equidad* as a primary aim (MINEDUC, 1998). Equity has again been placed firmly into the public conversation. Equity issues, whether conceptualized in terms of educational coverage or social justice, had been one of the major forces in driving expansion of the education system and change in education policy, as well as defining the role of the state in education in the years before the coup, (Farrell, 1986; Fisher, 1979; Martin et al., 1982). During the years of military rule, arguments for equity virtually disappeared from all discussions (Collins & Lear, 1995). Today, calls for greater equity can mean different things,[11] though with the advent of the current reform, they usually result in increased funding of public education and investment in the infrastructure and development of specific programs aimed at improving the educational attainment of low achieving, or traditionally marginalized populations, i.e., ethnic minorities, and poor/working class populations (as in the specific MECE programs, MINEDUC, 1998). Paradoxically, *La Reforma Educacional*, committed to equity, does not challenge in any way the institutionalized tracking system in Chile reinforced by the existence of *subvenciones*/vouchers.

The two-tiered system of *liceos humanístico-scientíficos* and *liceos técnico-professionales* is the means by which two sets of Chilean youth are formed, one college bound and the other destined for the blue-collar sector. These two types of schools serve different sectors of Chilean society. It is extremely rare to find middle or upper-class children in *escuelas técnico-profesionales*. They serve as the educational track for poor urban and rural students (MINEDUC, 1995, 1997; Guari, 1998). They also generally represent a significantly lower level of academic quality, or at least this is the general perception among teachers and parents (Pinkney Pastrana, 2000).

The system of *subvenciones* continues to encourage the development of *escuelas subvencionadas*, semiprivate schools that tend to exercise many of the flexible labor practices touted in the private sector and some degree of autonomy in curricular design. The subvention system and ease of opening schools in Chile has made education a profitable business for many Chilean entrepreneurs. Not all subventions are alike however, and the average per month/per student payment varies depending on the type of school. The highest subventions are paid for students enrolled in technical-professional high schools, increasing the attraction for entrepreneurs to establish and apply for status as this type of school (MINEDUC, 1995–1998). Virtually all semiprivate high schools fall under the technical-professional rubric. This situation in turn, decreases the pressure on these schools to become excellent academic sites, as their students are generally viewed as future workers, not college material. In Chile, even with the rebirth of equity in education reform discourse, neoliberal funding policies continue to support the formation of "two Chiles"—the workers and the "elite."

CALIDAD AND FUNCTIONALIST MEASURES

Educational quality is defined as education that is "pertinent and relevant" in terms of a "modern" curriculum (Pinkney Pastrana, 2000). Curricular objectives must meet the needs of a technologically changing world as well as take the initiative for renewing an emphasis on creativity in order that schools prepare students—"for a future they cannot imagine."[12] Thus, the need for quality schooling is readily tied to the requirements of boosting Chile's commitment to global capitalist development. Though quality has traditionally been defined in terms of continuing to improve system coverage, graduation and national literacy rates, since neoliberal reforms began, quality has been overwhelmingly conceptualized in terms of either increasing standardized test scores, and/or creating an illusion of improvement through global comparisons of educational achievement (such as recent and ongoing UNESCO studies used to compare educational attainment internationally [UNESCO, 1998]).

Global comparisons of education also imply that curricular objectives and achievement can be readily monitored by national testing measures. It is common practice in Chilean schools today that students use instructional time to prepare for the standardized exams. Criticisms of national testing point to the dubious nature of standardized measures, calling into question the class, gender, and race biases notoriously woven into the content and phrasing of standardized tests. Other criticisms point to the loss of instructional time for "real learning" that happens when weeks are dedicated to practice tests, aimed at making students feel comfortable and literate in the task of "filling in the bubble" (Fiske & Ladd, 2000; Colegio de profesores, 1999).

In Chile, the competitive backlash of *subvenciones*, as schools vie for student bodies in order to receive the funds needed for operation, furthers the complications related to standardized testing. "Choice" encourages parents to find the "best" schools for their children, but how does one judge the performance of one school over another? It is common in Chilean schools, as elsewhere, to find traditional authoritarian practices that create an environment where parents are virtually barred from the classroom—preventing parents from gaining a more intimate knowledge of classroom learning environments. Limited knowledge by many families leaves them without a critical understanding of issues regarding test scores—meaning possible contradictions between high test scores and effective learning environments are never questioned.

Standardized tests enable that readily comparable results be published in local papers. This is a font of information utilized by savvy parents to inform the choice of school for their children. Schools populated uniformly with students who fit neatly into the norms of traditional academic culture tend to score highly on standard measures. Similarly, there is evidence to suggest that often private and semiprivate schools spend more time on test preparation than some municipal schools (Pinkney Pastrana, 2000).

Over reliance on standardized measures can create an inaccurate picture of the academic quality found in different types of schools. Absent vigorous critique, standardized measures can serve to enhance the myths concerning the differences in quality between municipal and private schools. The problems that arise from a dependence and reliance on testing measures demand exploration in Chile as elsewhere. Clearly, indicators of success and vigor in educational settings go well beyond the limited scope of attainment measured by standardized tests. As the centerpiece of measures of excellence in models of neoliberal efficiency, the traditional problems inherent in testing

have become exacerbated. In fact, some prestigious schools promote themselves in very practical terms as being places where the entire focus of one's
studies is to prepare for the college exam.

PARTICIPATION, THE RADICAL POTENTIAL

The ideal of opening up Chilean educational communities to more
participatory practices represents the most radical element found in
the Chilean education reform. Participation implies the possibility of
agency, and agency implies that, "we can make history from the concrete conditions in which we find ourselves." (Marx, 1977) Participation
suggests that communities come together and join forces around common interests to realize and create new social formations. The concept
of participation follows logically in line with the tenets of curricular
reform as expressed by both MECE projects and curricular renovation
(MINEDUC, 1998). Namely, these reforms are founded on constructivist paradigms that point to the socially constructed nature of learning, and the importance of "communities of learners" in the learning
process. It is impossible by definition to create community without its
members engaged as participants.

In order that the educational communities in Chile take full advantage of the many material benefits of the reform, the full participation of
many actors within the education community is required. For example, in
the programs in MECE media, many projects make significant resources
and a considerable amount of prestige available to teachers and schools.
These market incentives provide the basis for justifying neoliberal education reform. The common sense view that 'competition creates a better
product' is held by many and vigorously promoted internationally, though
there is growing concern about its consequences (Fiske & Ladd, 2000;
McLaren, 2000; Puiggrós, 1996). In terms of the competitive nature of
the Chilean educational system, this makes the impact of national and
local recognition for outstanding work much higher. There are material
incentives to create participatory spaces in schools. In some cases, this
may have a positive result. However, as the reform continues to develop,
it is common to find school communities embittered and embattled over
failed projects due to:

- Distrust of administration
- Lack of information concerning the many new possibilities offered
  by the Reform
- Fear of the consequences of stepping out of traditional roles in school
  communities
- Lack of capacity to mount and design innovative programs reflecting
  the needs of the community

- Lack of practice in the democratic processes of opening discussions of innovation to voices and participants not traditionally included in these processes (Pinkney Pastrana, 2000)

Thus, democratizing incentives collide with the traditions of exclusion, and favoritism and participation become a product of and support for the current 'neoliberal' logics that drive the social reproduction of capitalist relations of power within schools and society.

In considering the radical potential for "participation" in Chilean education reform, we see a democratizing concept co-opted by the functional, market driven necessity of making decentralized schools independently autonomous. Again, participation at this level will make the mechanism of school organization run smoothly, but it does not challenge assumptions of social Darwinism. It privileges a position that holds competition and survival of the fittest—the assumptions that translate into market logic applied to the educational system, and that sees the goals of economic development through education based on enactments of human capital theory, rather than democratizing conceptualizations of education—necessary social precursors for countries that wish to articulate themselves in the global arena.

This is quite different from participation grounded in solidarity among school communities on the basis of an ethical commitment to education as a human right and necessary foundation for democracy. The project for transforming education into a site of emancipatory praxis involving the participation of a broad popular sector is the radical potential participation offers. In this ideal vision of education as facilitated by the *La Reforma Educacional*, the possibility of developing radical 'autonomous' schools exists, and so, too, the radical potential for counter-hegemonic, democratic social change.

Much of the impetus behind the current reforms is the recognition of the deterioration of the education system—especially the public sector that remains. *La Reforma Educacional* is in many ways an attempt to repair some of the damage that occurred prior to re-democratization. Yet, given the historical development of the reforms and the plurality of thought which once defined Chilean sociopolitical culture—what appears to now be the widespread contemporary acceptance and indeed the ideological hegemony of neoliberal reform (educational as well as otherwise)—may prompt one to explore other areas concerning the value and perception of reforms held by those both within the school system and the general population.

SCHOOLS, PRIVATIZATION, AND THE MARKET PLACE

The current reforms in education, though far-reaching and "progressive," do nothing to challenge the basic structural conditions that have created a free market mentality within the educational system of Chile. Within this neoliberal structural gridlock the debilitating effects of market- driven school policy collide with progressive curricular and pedagogical reform. Increased attention to professional development, a lengthened school day, and projects aimed at improving and democratizing the organization and management of schools and local ministry offices are restricted within the limitations they have inherited. Issues of local control and the right of parents to choose the best schools for their own children exacerbate the tensions between liberty and equity.

Education in Chile today is the scene of many contradictory visions and practices (Brunner, 2005). The 'progressive' vision of the ongoing *Reforma Educacional*, noteworthy for its emphasis on constructivist pedagogies, a return to a discourse of equity, and a commitment to gradually improving the conditions of teaching, collides with a legacy of authoritarian practices and the structural foundation of the education system that prohibits many of the very tenets of the reform.

In the 1980s, Chilean education became—and continues to be—a business of competition between educational institutions. The comparisons between these institutions are often based on the most superficial yet easily recognizable standards. Schooling in Chile is a business, and a very profitable one for entrepreneurs who play on the desperation of a destitute system to entice families into committing their children and economic resources to painfully overcrowded classrooms staffed by overworked and underpaid professionals. Meanwhile the public system, with its crumbling physical infrastructure left by years of neglect and no budget to invest in glossy ads, must also compete in this educational free market fiasco.

SIGNIFICANCE OF THE CHILEAN EXPERIENCE

Chile has twice followed an extraordinary path that has left a legacy of major importance to the world. History will always remember Salvador Allende, and the people who put him in power, as a remarkable example of democracy and *poder popular*. History will always remember Augusto Pinochet, and the people who put him in power, as an aberration of abuse and crushed dreams—the harbinger of an economic "miracle," capitalist development built on the bones and agony of a nation. History will decide what path of development reaps the greatest benefits for the people of Chile. Since the disaster of the military regime, Chile has firmly settled in a specific developmental direction the results of which, in education and elsewhere, are not quite as rosy as the hubris of shortsighted neoliberals would lead the world to believe. Resistance to neoliberal capitalist development and education policy grows (Compton and Weiner, 2008). In terms of education, Chile and the rest of the world would do well to heed the words of Iván Nuñez:[13] "I think the neoliberal policy makers did us a favor, now we know what definitely does not work in education."

NOTES

1. "Death vanquished justice."
2. For a detailed analysis of the nonformal underpinnings of the neoliberal reforms put in place immediately following the coup d'éta,t see: Pinkney Pastrana (2007).
3. It is doubtful that any of these debates took place in Chile in the early 1980's. There was little or no participation by any members of society on issues concerning the restructuring of the educational system. From all reports, the workings of the National Education Ministry and other governmental agencies during the military regime was clothed in secrecy and notably free from debate. It is even impossible to find documents pertaining to policy changes made during this period of time, as these were all destroyed before the transfer of power to the civilian government. Further, the restructuring of the educational system and all changes made by the military regime were never referred to as "Education Reform" by anyone encountered during the course of this research.
4. Attempts to minimize these conditions continue to be the focus of several aspects of the ongoing *Reforma Educacional* in recent years. Pay for municipal teachers has been increasing, a richer national curriculum has been developed, and the *Jornada Completa* remains a large part of Chilean education reform. The 900 schools program and some MECE rural programs have specifically focused on equity in low performing/low income areas as well.
5. Interestingly, the situation of teachers holding several jobs in different schools simultaneously poses a challenge for those who consistently maintain the superiority of private institutions. Many teachers in Chile today are teaching in both the public and private spheres. Lacking prep time, they often present the same lessons in both contexts, regardless of the material resources that exist at the specific site. One must question whether or not the advantages of abundant material resources sometimes found in private institutions (such as computers, didactic materials, extra texts, and perhaps even smaller class size) are realized when the actual human resources in both public and private sectors remain the same.
6. The *Estatuto Docente* is a law passed by the newly "democratized" Chilean government in 1990. It is a provision that creates an independent regulatory body in charge of teacher labor practices in municipal schools. Its passage was highly sought by the teacher *gremio*, the Colegio de Profesores, as it assured, for the first time in 17 years, a certain degree of job security and a minimum salary standard (See Guari, 1998 for a detailed discussion).
7. TRANSLATION: This state, and it subsidiary character has profoundly modified the very objectives of education in our country, conceiving of the student basically as a consumer. In this way it has transformed the concept of quality in education, reducing it to an efficient preparation that generates the diverse types of human capital that this society requires for its productive development, like so it has moved toward the formation of human beings competent to act as good consumers in the market society.
8. . . . the educational policies initiated in 1990 are defined by two principal orienting factors: improving the quality of education and improving the equity in its distribution. The focus of the policies with respect to quality has been improving the internal processes of the educational system and learning outcomes. At the same time, policies focused on equity have been oriented according to the criteria of positive discrimination, according to which the equality of educational opportunities within heterogeneous groups requires

increasing material resources and giving more attention to the most vulnerable groups in the country.

9. The *Consertación* coalition is made up of left-leaning Social and Christian Democrats from four different political parties: Socialist (*Partido Socialista*—PS), Christian Democrat (*Partido Demócrata Cristiana*—PDC), Radicals (*Partido Radical Social Demócrata*—PRSD), and Party for Democracy (*Partido por la Democracia*—PPD)

10. Some of these MECE projects are especially interesting in that they veer broadly away from traditional neoliberal approaches to education. The P-900 ("900 schools") project begun in 1990, for example, aimed extra funding for teacher training, curriculum development, materials, and infrastructure at the 900 poorest elementary schools in the country. This is an approach to education that is in sharp contrast to the "free-market" logic governing the majority of Chilean policy. If schools are not doing well, if students are failing, the free market in education enabled through choice should be able to take care of it, and failing schools unsupported will eventually succumb to the power of market forces and loose enrollment, perhaps closing down. In the P-900 project, the exact opposite occurred, with extraordinary results.

11. In one account, even the right wing political parties have attempted to co-opt the discourse of equity into their lexicon by calling on equity in schools in terms of rewards for performance. "Many private schools are actually doing a better job educating our children, if we want to be truly equitable in education policy, private schools should also be eligible for *subvenciones*/vouchers." (In Guari, 1998)

12. Gaston Sepulveda, conference presentation (November, 1998), "Desafios para la educación rural," Universidad Católica de Chile, Santiago.

13. Iván Nuñez served as Vice Minister of Education during the Popular Unity government, he was one of the primary policy makers responsible for Allende's ill-fated *Escuela Nacional Unificada*, the proposal for educational reform that was never implemented due to the coup. He currently works in the Ministry of Education in Santiago as Advisor to the ministry. He was interviewed on June 20, 1999.

REFERENCES

Brunner, J. J. (2005) Comparative research and public policy: from authoritarian to democracy. *Peabody Journal of Education*, 80 (1).

Colegio de Profesores de Chile A.G. (July, 1999) *Propuesta educacional del magisterio* A la ciudadanía y a los candidatos a la Presidencia de la República. Santiago, Chile.

Collins, J. & Lear, J. (1995) *Chile's free-market miracle: A second look.* Oakland, CA: Food First, The Institute for Food and Development Policy.

Compton, M. & Weiner, L. (Eds.) (2008) *The Global Assault on Teaching, Teachers, and their Unions: Stories for Resistance.* New York: Palgrave Macmillan

Echeverria, R. & Hevia, R. (1981) Cambios en el sistema educacional bajo el gobierno militar. *Araucaria de Chile* (No. 13): 39–56

Farrell, J. P. (1986) *The national unified school in Allende's Chile: The role of education in the destruction of a revolution.* Vancouver: University of British Columbia Press.

Fisher, K. (1979) *Political ideology and educational reform in Chile, 1964–1976.* Los Angeles: University of California Latin American Center Publications.

Fiske, E. & Ladd, H. (2000) *When schools compete: A cautionary tale*. Washington, D.C.: Brookings Institution Press.

Flores, F. & Varela, G. (1994) *Educación y transformación: Preparemos a Chile para el Siglo XXI*. S.A., Santiago de Chile, Redcom Chile.

Guari, V. (1998) *School choice in Chile: Two decades of educational reform*. Pittsburgh, PA: University of Pittsburgh Press.

Marin, C. (1990) El Estatuto Docente y la calidad de la educación. *Mensaje* (No. 395, December): 480–483.

Martin, P.; Cox, C.; and Edholm, F. (1982) *Education and Repression: Chile*. Edited by Felicity Edholm. London, United Kingdom: World University Service.

Martinez, M. (1993) Calidad de la educación y redefinición del rol del estado en Chile, en el contexto de los proyectos de modernización. *Estudios Sociales* (No. 77, trimestre 3): 171–196.

Marx, K. (1977) *Selected Writings*. Edited by David McLellan. Oxford University Press.

McLaren, P. (2000) *Che Guevara, Paulo Freire, and the Pedagogy of Revolution*. Rowman and Littlefield: Lanham.

Ministerio de Educación, (MINEDUC), División de planificación y presupuesto. (1995). *Compendio de Información Estadística, 1994*. Santiago, Chile

Ministerio de Educación, (MINEDUC), División de planificación y presupuesto. (1997). *Compendio de Información Estadística, 1996*. Santiago, Chile

Ministerio de Educación (MINEDUC), (1998). *Buena Educación para Todos*. República de Chile, Santiago

Nuñez, I. (1999) Personal Interview, Ministry of Education. Santiago, Chile. June.

OAS. (1982) La regionalización educativa en América Latina (II). *La Educación*, 26 (No. 88): 2–43.

Parry, T. R. (1997) Decentralization and privatization: Education policy in Chile. *Journal of Public Policy*. 17(I): 107–133.

Petras, J. & Levia, F. I. (1994) *Democracy and Poverty in Chile: The limits to electoral politics*. Boulder, CO: Westview Press.

Pinkney Pastrana, J. (2007) Subtle tortures of the neo-liberal age: Teachers, students, and the political economy of schooling in Chile. *Journal of Critical Education Policy Studies*. November.

———. (2000) *Subtle tortures of the neo-liberal age: The case of Chile*. Unpublished Dissertation. University of California, Los Angeles.

Puiggrós, A. (1996) World Bank education policy: market liberalism meets ideological conservatism. *NACLA report on the Americas XXIX* (No. 6, May/June): 26–31.

Ramirez, A. B. (1994) La privatización de la educación superior Chilena y la regulación a traves del Mercado. *Estudios Sociales* (No. 82, trimestre 4): 9–24.

Schugurensky, D. (1997) Personal interview. University of California, Los Angeles.

UNESCO, (1998). *Primer estudio internacional comparative sobre lenguaje, matemática y factores asociados, para alumnos del tercer y cuarto grado*. UNESCO—Santiago. Laboratorio Latinoamericano de Evaluación de la Calidad de la Educación.

7 A Class Perspective on the New Actors and Their Demands from the Turkish Education System

Fuat Ercan and Ferda Uzunyayla

INTRODUCTION

Today educational change is increasingly shaped by the demands of newly emerging actors besides the state. A structural/class analysis of these demands shows that they are articulated by national and transnational actors having different interests. In this context, the education system is going through a comprehensive and conflict ridden restructuring process.

When we look at the Turkish case in terms of the changing functions of the education system, we can see that the main function of education in the early phases of the formation of the Turkish nation state has been the development of citizen consciousness. By the 1980s, the restructuring of the capital accumulation process has led to the commodification of education and its redefinition as a semipublic service/commodity (Ercan, 1998 p. 163). From the late 1990s onward, the reconstitution of social relationships on the basis of internationalisation initiated a process in which the distinction between general and vocational education became increasingly blurred. In this process, representatives of various sections of capital, social sections other than capital, and the state (through its institutions such as the Higher Education Council, State Planning Organisation, Ministries of Education and Labour) have formulated various demands, policies, and projects concerning the link between education and employment.

Besides the demands of these internal actors and inner necessities of the accumulation process, the demands of international actors and institutions have also been influential in shaping the educational change in Turkey. In that sense, the policies of international actors such as the World Bank, GATS, OECD, and the EU on the link between education and employment are also important determinants of the process. In this study, we will discuss this process in terms of how the class actors mentioned above shape the restructuring of the Turkish education system as "the self-production of labour power."

DOMINANT CONCEPTS AND DISCOURSES

In recent years, various concepts and discourses have been developed to support the new educational policies that conceive knowledge production and education in terms of their functional relationship to employment, and students as the potential sources of labour power. The main concepts and discourses used for the realization, legitimization, and internalization of this transformation are: information society, lifelong learning, flexibility-standardization-evaluation, changing skills, and efficiency.

The concept of "information society," which is articulated by capital groups and their representatives to analyze educational change, serves to decontextualize the process of reconstitution of the content and functions of education, and the transformation of knowledge into a factor of competitiveness. When we contextualize these developments, we can say that the process defined as the "knowledge economy" or "globalisation" refers to the increasing internationalization of capital in response to the crisis of reproduction of the post-1970 capitalist accumulation regime. Mainstream approaches describe this process as the rise of the information society and accordingly redefine the concept of knowledge narrowly as *knowledge increasing employability.* While these approaches view *knowledge* as a requirement of economic growth and competitiveness, however, they exclude labour power from their analysis. They disregard the fact that it is labour power that produces and implements the knowledge seen as necessary for growth and competitiveness.

Brown and Lauder (2006) point out that the rhetoric of knowledge economy and knowledge workers contributes to the standardization of knowledge, which in turn leads to declining wages and rising control over labour power. Although there is more demand for highly qualified and educated workers, they argue, there are not that many opportunities to employ them, so what happens in practice is the decline of average costs of workers. Thus, the result is not an increase, but a decrease in wages. Brown argues that the increasing number of qualifications students are gaining in this process is a symptom of what he calls "credential inflation."

Another concept used to explain educational change is "lifelong learning," which is based on the idea that employees should continuously renew themselves in order to adapt to the rapidly changing social conditions and increasing competition. While the concept of lifelong learning has been used in the 1970s as the synonym for nonformal education of specific age groups not being covered by formal education, since the 1990s, it refers to the continuous education of employees in line with the requirements of the labour market. This understanding of education "from cradle to grave" implies that education is a lifelong process, but its content is limited to the training of individuals for more qualifications and flexibility in their working lives. In practice, the understanding of *lifelong learning* increases the tendency of employees to get various certificates and vocational documents, however the question of where the education is received loses its significance. The important thing becomes continuous upgrading of personal qualifications through school, workplace, or other means. This leads to a rise of interest in certificate and vocational programs rather than diplomas.

Certificates not only bring flexibility but also speed to the labor market, as it is much faster to receive them than diplomas. This has different implications for different capital groups. From the perspective of productive capitals, it means they can have quick access to labor power with the specific qualifications they need at a certain time. From the perspective of capital groups that invest in education, on the other hand, it means they can profit from marketing these education programs. Thus, "lifelong learning" leads to the intersection of different capital groups on the demand-supply axis in a complementary way. Furthermore, these certificate programs lead to the formation of a new source of income for public education institutions whose functions are defined by market mechanisms. Through the flexibility provided by lifelong learning, employees adapt themselves to the changes in the labour market. However, this also means that education institutions have to be restructured in line with the rapidly changing modern technology and labour markets, that is, schools are also made flexible.

In this process, education institutions are structured in response to two types of necessities. On the one hand, decentralization is needed so that education institutions as flexible structures can rapidly adapt to the requirements of local markets. On the other hand, centralization is needed to standardize the knowledge production in these institutions; in other words, a central system of control is required to determine the standards of the knowledge produced so that it can be marketed. Such a control system requires the standardization of the content of education and the transformation of education into something measurable, because "marketization (. . .) requires standard data production based on standardized processes and products, so that comparisons can be made and the customers can have access to the information they need to make their choices in the market" (Apple, 2004, p. 134). Marketization of education leads to the emergence of a central control system and a process of standardization in line with the criteria determined by this control system. Standardization of education is made possible through the education programs designed by the EU (Erasmus, Socrates, Tempus, etc.), which are extended to post-Soviet Union, Central, and East European countries, as well as countries in the process of entry to the EU. Ertl and Philips (2006) argue that these programs bring about similar changes in the education systems of all countries in which they are applied and lead to standardization through pilot projects, "best practice" models, or "benchmarks": "A standardizing effect of SOCRATES and LEONARDO on education and training in Europe is the consequence." (Ertl and Philips, 2006, 83). The European Commission uses the concept of *benchmark* to refer to the concrete goals for achieving development, and *benchmarking* to present comparative data on the relative performance levels of different countries (European Commission, 2002, p. 7). Fredrickson (2003) argues that concepts like *benchmark* and *benchmarking* are related to the "auditing society," and they are part of the attempts to control quality.

The main concept that incorporates all the other concepts such as *standardization, quality control,* and *evaluation,* on the other hand, is *accreditation.* This concept, which is one of the important topics in the Turkish agenda, is treated in terms of occupational competencies. Accreditation is seen as the process by which deficiencies in the occupational skills of university graduates can be determined, and their skills can be improved in line with the international standards. Even in critical circles, accreditation is discussed in relation to occupational competencies, but its relation to the requirements of the accumulation process is not taken into consideration. The question of what kind of requirements have made accreditation a structural necessity is answered by the Gazi University Department of Mechanical Engineering, the first department of mechanical engineering in Turkey accredited by MÜDEK (Association for the Evaluation and Accreditation of Engineering Education): "Globalization, international competition, lifelong learning requirement and changing expectations make accreditation necessary."[1] As capitalism is globalized, competition is intensified and the labour power is expected to have internationally recognized qualifications which must be constantly renewed in line with the changing needs of capital. In this context, accreditation forms a new component of accumulation in the field of education, leading to a process by which occupational skills are constantly renewed in line with the demands of capital, and the *costs of this process are assumed by individuals/students themselves* through certificate programs or similar documents, thereby contributing to the commodification of education and the self-production of labour power.

NATIONAL ACTORS OF THE EDUCATIONAL CHANGE

1. Capital Groups: In periods of restructuring of the accumulation process, inner components of capital are affected differently from the restructuring, so they formulate different demands and policies. The analysis of these policies before making generalizations about capital as a whole allows us to understand the process better by revealing the relations of conflict and complementariness among inner components of capital.

Capital groups that see education as an area of investment demand the state's withdrawal from education and a decrease in public expenditures. On the other hand, capital groups which have reached a certain adequacy and had been internationalized in the 1980s on the basis of using cheap labour power, changed their strategies in the 1990s, stating that this is not a sustainable situation, and reoriented themselves toward production of more surplus value through competition on the basis of a qualified labour power. Therefore, from the perspective of these productive capital groups, the function of education in the training of qualified labour power has gained a new importance. It is for these reasons that they demanded an increase in public expenditures toward education, as opposed to capital groups which see education as an area of investment.

The conflict between capitals marketing education and productive capitals on the issue of public expenditures has at the same time formed a relationship of complementariness, especially with respect to lifelong learning. The development of lifelong learning has increased the interest in certificate and vocational programs that follow formal education, making it possible for employees to gain occupational competencies or improve their skills in various fields through certificates that can be received more quickly than diplomas. From the perspective of productive capitals, this is an opportunity to have a better employment structure in terms of speed and flexibility without having to assume its costs. From the perspective of capitals marketing education, on the other hand, it is an opportunity to market certificate or vocational programs to students and employees who assume the costs themselves. Thus, a relationship of complementariness is established between productive capitals and education marketing capitals on the axis of demand and supply.

For capital groups, education has always been a vital issue in terms of its function in training the required labour power. From the 1990s onward, this function has gained even more importance as capital groups have started to compete with international capital on the basis of qualified labour power supplied by education. In this process, the concepts used by capital such as *efficiency*, *quality*, and *flexibility* have been incorporated into curriculua starting with primary education, and they have been presented as the key elements of social change that will bring the same positive results for everyone.

In the Turkish case, TÜSİAD (Turkish Industrialists and Businessmen's Association), the key association representing big capital groups in Turkey, focused its demands on the commodification of education in its 1994 report, whereas it has shifted its priority to "human capital" in its 2006 report, articulating a series of demands concerning the link between education and employment on the axis of education qualified labour power competitiveness. The report argues that conventional production factors like labour power, capital, and land cannot form the dynamics of growth as they have diminishing returns, however, knowledge can be the triggering factor of growth. ". . . Skills gained through education and other learning devices make the individual more efficient. (. . .) While education increases the mobility (adaptation capacity) of the labour power, on the one hand, it also contributes to the mobility of capital by increasing the amount of qualified labour power." (TUSİAD, 2006, p. 24) According to the report, the increasing access to information and technology resulting from the outward oriented policies can only be used for the transition to a high value-added economy through qualified labour power. Thus, education is assigned a functional status in terms of both providing flexibility to capital and training the qualified labour power in a way to increase surplus value, thereby the link between education and employment policies is established.

TÜRKONFED (Turkish Enterprise and Businessmen's Confederation), another business association founded recently by the regionally and sectorally organized business associations, believes that, on the road to joining the European Union, the country's education system should be structured in such a way that utilizes its young population to get ahead in international competition, promotes youth's involvement in the labour power, and fulfills businesses' needs. "In the forthcoming period, education will be the only common factor that will help Turkey utilize its young population and its current demographic change, and promote its human development and competitiveness, therefore it is of strategic importance." (TÜRKONFED, 2006, p. 7) One of the significant observations of TÜRKONFED on education is that the relationship between vocational training and the employment market is being transformed to incorporate the general education system as a whole. "The transformation of the economy and the labour power gradually reduces differences between general and occupational skills of the individual worker. In parallel to this, the rigid boundaries between general and vocational training, and differences between their structure and content are being softened in many countries. The influence of this transformation is especially felt in secondary education." (TÜRKONFED, 2006, p. 9)

In its report submitted to the 17. National Education Council, TİSK (Turkish Confederation of Employers' Associations), a business association focusing on wage bargaining issues vis-a-vis labour unions, also points out the need for educational change and explains the rationale for this change as follows: the adaptation of the country to the process of a globalization and information society, improvement of international competitiveness, struggle against unemployment, rise in the level of social welfare, training of the labour power in accordance with the qualities and quantities demanded by the labour market. One of the important points in TİSK's report is the legitimization of "lifelong learning" by the expression "lifelong employment guarantee." In the current economic conditions, it is argued, lifelong employment guarantee can only be achieved through having the qualifications demanded by the labour market, which necessitates the formation of a highly skilled, efficient and creative labour power capable of improving these skills.

In its 2006 Economic Report, MÜSİAD (Independent Industrialists and Businessmen Association), a business association representing capital groups with an Islamic orientation, has come up with a demand reflecting the most crystallized form of the link between education and employment. It demands that the Ministry of Education be renamed as the "Ministry of Education and Human Resources." MÜSİAD expects this new ministry to change the education system so as to transform students into global entrepreneurs, technicians, and researchers. This expectation is a clear indication of the content of the educational change demanded, but more importantly, it is an indication of how students are seen as part of the potential labour power.

The question at this point is, will the transformation demanded by capital groups, as exemplified above, *have the same implications for everyone, or, will different social classes be affected differently by this transformation?* We can say that the increasing flexibility of labour power which results from "lifelong learning" has led to a process by which both students and employees are put under more control, and find themselves in an extremely competitive environment in which they have to constantly equip themselves with certificate or vocational programs after their formal education. Furthermore, the costs of this *lifelong learning* process are assumed by the individuals themselves, thereby decreasing the cost of labour training for capital. Students and employees feel themselves obligated to buy these programs in order to become more competitive. The effects of this process on students and employees are not only financial but also psychological. Faced with the necessity to make themselves more flexible in line with the demands of capital, and to constantly renew themselves through courses and certificates programs in their spare time, students and employees find that their social activities are increasingly limited and feel like they turn into robots. The implication of all these transformations for capital, on the other hand, is the declining costs of labour training and the ability to adapt to the changing conditions of the accumulation process through a more qualified and flexible labour power. Thus, if we go back to the question posed above, it is possible to say that the educational transformation process has different implications for labour and capital. Not all sections of society are affected in the same manner by the transformation process, so we should talk of "conflicting interests" rather than "common interests."

Another important discourse used by capital groups to legitimize the transformation based on the linking of education and employment is the argument that it will decrease unemployment. At this point, we need to ask two important questions. First, *is it education policies or the content of education that causes unemployment?* Second, *if the structure of education institutions and the content of education programs are changed, will the problem of unemployment be solved?*

We can say that the search for the reasons and the solution of unemployment solely in education is a sign of the inability to see the functioning of the system as a whole. The explanation of social reality on the basis of a single factor obstructs the understanding of it. Unemployment is a phenomenon caused by a number of factors that emerge necessarily in the functioning of the capitalist system. Among these factors are the employment of a single worker for a job that can be done by more than one worker and the extension of working hours with the rationale of efficiency and flexibility, the orientation of productive capital to speculative gains rather than investments as a result of the liberalization of capital movements, the narrowing down of the domestic employment opportunities due to the import of intermediate goods by productive capital groups because of their lower costs, the liquidification of the assets of productive capital and its transformation into money capital in response to the 1970 crisis, the movement of productive capital of advanced capitalist countries to places where the labor is cheaper, transition from labor-intensive sectors to technology-intensive sectors as a result of technological development, and the liberalization of agricultural production. Thus, it is not only education but all these other social factors, their interrelationships, and their relationships to the system as a whole, which causes unemployment.

2. Labour Unions: The changing demands about education are not only articulated by representatives of capital, but also by social sections other than capital. In the following sections, we will examine the discourses of two major public employee unions in the education sector (Türk Eğitim-Sen and Eğitim-Sen) and the major confederation of workers' unions, Türk-İş, on educational change. We will see that the demands made by these organizations are not homogenous. While Türk-İş and Türk Eğitim-Sen focus their demands on *qualified labour power* in parallel to business groups, Eğitim-Sen focuses on the *right to education* and criticises privatization of education, but it does not address the new policies of labour power training in detail.

Türk Eğitim-Sen points out that there has been a transition from industrial to information society that has brought new opportunities, but this situation demands a mentality change that can only be achieved by a parallel transformation in education. In their book named *Turkish National Education in the 21st Century*, they demand that education and other sectoral policies should be integrated, the youth should be given such a training that they can be employed not only in Turkey but also in the EU and elsewhere, and each step of education should be directly related to the working life. The rationale of all these demands is explained as the necessity to have the capacity for competitiveness in the information society (Türk Eğitim-Sen, 2001, p. 218–226). Thus, Türk Eğitim-Sen emphasizes the need for educational change, but it does not question the structural characteristics of this change, which will put the social sections it represents under more control and force them into a pragmatic and functionalist education process.

In its report submitted to the 17. National Education Council (2006), where the latest changes in education and preparations for the process of integration with the EU were discussed, Eğitim-Sen has focused on the "right to education" and those who cannot use this right due to the regional inequalities in preschool, primary, and secondary education. Eğitim-Sen also criticizes the Ministry of National Education's approach to the problem for not being comprehensive, that is, for exclusively focusing on the quantitative aspect and disregarding the qualitative aspect. However, although Eğitim-Sen criticizes the Ministry of National Education's approach for not being comprehensive, its own approach also suffers from the same problem. It only addresses the quantitative aspect of the issue, such as the number of children who cannot use their right to education, the insufficiency of the number of schools and teachers in certain regions, etc. Eğitim-Sen's explanation of educational change does not go beyond the analysis of commodification of education, that is, "privatisation." Therefore, it does not address the next step of the process, that is, the linking of education and employment policies, and the redefinition of the function of education as the training of labour power in line with the needs of the labour market.

In its "4. Democratic Education Congress" in 2005, Eğitim-Sen made important demands about the individuals' needs to improve themselves and their productive skills in a democratic society (p. 460 and 576). However, these demands about the integrity of individual development inevitably require a critical analysis of the policies and discourses on the function of education in the post-1990 period. Otherwise, Eğitim-Sen's demands cannot be differentiated from the demands of capital groups, and their proposals become contradictory with their own understanding of education. In their brochure evaluating the four years of AKP government, they demand that "the Ministry of National Education, Labour Ministry and labour unions must cooperate for making the necessary regulations to link the certificates provided by education, employment and working life." (Eğitim-Sen, 2007, 39) However, these demands form the backbone of the structural transformation in education in the post-1990 period. The inclusion of the Labour Ministry in the process of the formation of educational standards in line with occupational standards, the orientation toward certificate programs which bring speed and flexibility to the labour markets, are demands made by capital groups and the World Bank.

Lastly, we will discuss the "TİSK-TÜRK İŞ Pilot Project for Increasing Effectiveness of Education and Employment," an EU-financed project jointly prepared by the employer confederation TİSK, and the workers confederation, TÜRK İŞ. This is a project where the demands for linking education to employment policies are made concrete. An interesting point about the project is the presentation of the contradicting interests of two different unions representing labour and capital as compatible under the name of "social dialogue." It is important at this point to reiterate the fact that labour and capital will be affected differently by the education and employment policies described in the project. While the restructuring of education in line with the needs of the labour market will put labour under more control through an instrumentalist process of training which obstructs the development of critical thinking skills, it will benefit capital by providing the qualified labour power it needs. Thus, what is involved here is not a compatibility but rather a conflict of interests.

INTERNATIONAL ACTORS OF THE EDUCATIONAL CHANGE

Capital accumulation is a dynamic process that brings various changes in social relationships, and the Turkish case is not an exception. The social changes in Turkey emerge as a result of the interaction between the demands of internal actors and inner necessities of the accumulation process, with the demands of international actors and institutions. Thus, the ongoing changes cannot be explained with exclusive reference to internal or external actors; rather they need to be assessed in the context of the reciprocal interactions between internal and external actors. In what follows, we will examine the process of change with reference to the demands of the EU, WB, OECD and ILO.

In the European Union, education has been increasingly linked to the economy in the post-1970 period, and it has become a factor of competitiveness in the 1990s.

> Education issues traditionally have not played a central role within the European Union (EU). This has gradually started to change in recent years. At the March 2000 Lisbon European Council, the heads of states and governments of the EU member countries, in response to the challenges of globalisation and the information society, set out a new strategic objective for the coming decade: 'Becoming the most competitive and dynamic knowledge based economy in the world capable of sustainable economic growth with more and better jobs and greater social cohesion.' This implies major changes, and education will be among the areas affected." (Fredrickson, 2003, p. 522)

Thus, starting with the Lisbon process, education has been defined as a factor of competitiveness and a strategic field for achieving the goals of the EU. This has led to a qualitative transformation of education. "Throughout the 1990s education and training policy became increasingly mired in the belief that simply boosting the outputs of the vocational education and training system by expanding the supply of educated and skilled employees, would be sufficient to transform national economic competitiveness and realize the vision of high skill, high value-added capitalism." (Payne, 2000, 359) The fact that it is education institutions that can provide the formation of a more qualified and skilled labour power and the knowledge production necessary for competitiveness and a high value-added economy has led education institutions to be directly exposed to the demands for "flexibility." The White Paper states that in an ever-changing economy, the employment problem can only be solved by changes in the education system. Accordingly, the important question is how such flexibility that answers people's demands can be established. "These institutions are too rigid to provide the education of citizens and employees for continuous employment. (. . .) To better fulfil various demands, more flexibility must be guaranteed." (European Commission, 1995, 24) The proposed solution is lifting the barriers between school and work, and granting more autonomy to schools, in other words, decentralization. " . . . Decentralised systems are the most flexible and quick to adapt, and this makes them most capable of developing new social partnership forms." (European Commission, 1995, 26) As noted, a decentralized education system is expected to adapt to changes more easily and respond to the requirements of the local markets more quickly.

The World Bank calls the recent accumulation process information economy. Using the data it has gathered from its research on various countries, it concludes that, in the context of information economy and globalization, there is an increasing demand for qualified labour power, especially in countries with opening economies. This qualified labour power is expected to adapt to technological change, and implement it as well. It is also expected to be creative, flexible, and competitive not only at the domestic but also at the international level (WB, 2002).

Another international actor that advocates the linking of education and employment, and emphasizes the change in the required qualities of labour power is the OECD. The OECD believes that information economy has transformed the requirements of the labour market. According to the OECD, as information based industries grow rapidly in the industrialized countries, the labour market requires more qualified workers; workers who have information and communication technology skills in particular. These observations point to the direction of the transformation in the labour market, and they also provide some ideas for how employment policies should be as well. "As the reciprocal links between education, economy, and welfare of nations get stronger, the fundamental policy will be providing the youth hands-on experience during their education, and successfully transferring them from the education environment to working life." (OECD, 2005)

In November 2003, the ILO decided to discuss the issue of youth unemployment during the 2005 International Employment Conference. Here it has indicated that maximization of young workers' potentials is central to economic growth and development that reduces poverty. In its 2005 report named "Youth: Pathways to Decent Work," the ILO advocates education as a means for increasing employability. It points out the fact that in many countries reforms are structured to build a bridge between formal education and occupational training.

The reason why international organizations give education this much importance and demand common education standards is the internationalization of capital. As capital is internationalized, it wants to invest not only domestically but also in any part of the globe where it profits the most. As a result, it wants to find qualified labour power wherever it invests. This can only be achieved by education, and international organizations are therefore expected to ensure that the same educational standards are met in any part of the world.

THE ROLE OF THE STATE IN LINKING EDUCATION AND EMPLOYMENT

Educational policies articulated by representatives of capital and labour are reflected upon the state as conflicting or intersecting demands. The state is then in a position to meet these demands through new laws and projects.

Thus we will discuss the state under a separate subheading, not because it is a third actor besides labour and capital, but because of this specific position.

State and social classes are not externally related. The state is directly involved in the formation of the conditions of capital accumulation. The recent process of restructuring of the education system is no exception in this regard. The definition of education as a strategic field in the post-1990 accumulation process has led the state to become a part of the process of formation of the laws and projects that link education and employment more closely. The Turkish state has formed these policies through the Ministry of National Education, State Planning Organisation, and Higher Education Council.

The approach of the Ministry of National Education to education and employment policies is shaped by the requirements of integration with the EU, and particularly by the EU's emphasis on the training of qualified labour power for increasing competitiveness. According to the Ministry, lifelong learning based on the vocational training of individuals at school and workplace in line with the changing nature of occupations is the backbone of contemporary education. In his speech at the 17. National Education Council, Hüseyin Çelik, the Minister of National Education stated that the aim of education in the globalized world is to train individuals in such a way that they can be competitive not only at the domestic but also at the international level. The most striking development in terms of the linking of education and employment is the protocol signed by Minister of National Education and Minister of Labour and Social Security Murat Başesgioğlu on the improvement of the effectiveness of the vocational training programs of the Turkish Employment Agency (İŞKUR), and the strengthening of the links between vocational training and employment. In his speech at the ceremony for the signing of this protocol, Başesgioğlu stated that the stronger the link between education and employment is, the higher Turkey's performance will be in fighting unemployment. "... Occupational standards will be determined through a process in which actors of the business world will be involved, and education programs will be prepared in line with these standards. In this way, the content of education will be determined by the labour market (...)." (Başesgioğlu, 2006, p. 22)

On this issue, the State Planning Organisation stated: "Development of knowledge-intensive industries and enhancement of opportunities to benefit from the labour power located in other geographical areas are increasing the importance of qualified labour, especially in developing countries, on a global basis. Within this context, enhancing opportunities for the training of qualified labour power has become the main topic, which is emphasized by the entire world." (SPO, 2006, p. 5) Thus, it stresses that education should be restructured toward the training of a qualified labour power in line with the labour markets. The 9. Development Plan, which is the latest one, also emphasizes the link between education and employment.

The Higher Education Council reports defined strategies that aim to link education and industry and integrate concepts such as quality, efficiency, and standardization into the university education structure so as to place universities in a competitive process in the context of free market economy. These strategies have been the determining factor in the formation of the university structure. This is reflected in the 2006 draft report of the Higher Education Council as follows: ". . . in the underdeveloped areas (. . .) universities are expected to guide the local development and have a major role in it. This is a nongovernmental organization or entrepreneurship function that is expected from the university." (ibid. p. 154) This demand summarizes the approach of the Higher Education Council to universities. If this demand is met, universities will lose their role as education institutions improving the individuals' potentials to realize their life projects; their critical thinking skills; and consciousness about human rights, democracy, environmental, cultural, and aesthetic values, which are stated in the vision part of the report, and turn into development agencies that provide knowledge, technology, and labour power to capital.

There are two projects initiated by the Ministry of National Education for the strengthening of the link between education and employment. One is called "Strengthening the System of Vocational Education in Turkey" (MEGEP), and the other is called "Modernization of the Vocational and Technical Education" (MTEM). The most frequently emphasized themes in these projects are "standardisation" and "social dialogue." Both projects have led to the development of occupational standards in line with the needs of the labour market, and the formation of educational standards in line with these occupational standards.

Lastly, we should mention the new legal regulations made by the state to provide the legal framework for the linking of education and employment policies. One of the new legal regulations on this issue is the Law No. 2547, which concerns the formation and functions of Vocational and Technical Education Regions. According to the Ministry of National Education, this law aims at the integration of the vocational and technical secondary school programs, *the training of the qualified labour power necessary for the business world*, and the participation of social partners (government, employers, and employees) in the vocational and technical education process. Another legal regulation is the Law No. 3308, which aims for the participation of the business world in the planning, development, and evaluation of vocational training processes, the initiation of development and adaptation programs to increase the efficiency of the labour power and its adaptation to new technologies. The same law also involves the establishment of Provincial Vocational Education Institutions, and the work of these institutions in cooperation with the Provincial Employment Councils toward the linking of education and employment at the local level. Among all of the legal regulations, the Law No. 5544 on the Establishment of the Authority for Vocational Competencies, which aims at the formation of education programs in line with occupational standards, has been endorsed by all social sections (both capital groups and labour unions). The Minister of National

Education, Hüseyin Çelik described this law as a revolution: "*The estab-lishment of the Authority for Vocational Competencies is a revolution in terms of occupational standards. In this way, vocational training will be integrated with the labour market in every sense.*" And Minister of Labour, Murat Başesgioğlu, stated: "*It is very difficult for those who haven't gained the necessary occupational qualifications during their education, or those whose previously learned skills are not valid in the labour market, to find jobs in their own occupation. In that sense, the Law on the Authority for Vocational Competencies is crucial in terms of establishing the optimum relationship between vocational training and employment.*" This statement is an indication of the intermingling of education and working life and the reduction of education to a technical phenomenon.

CONCLUSION

From the 1990s onward, the main determinant of education policies has been the training of a labour power with the ability to compete in the labour mar-kets, to continuously renew itself in the face of rapid technological changes, to produce and implement the new technological knowledge, and to learn how to learn in order to adapt to rapid changes. The clearest expression of this trans-formation is the change in the discourse from *employment* to *employability*. This discursive change has led to the argument that the reason for unemploy-ment is not the structural inability to create employment in various fields, but the individual's lack of necessary knowledge, skills, and qualifications. This argument has paved the way for the educational changes ahead. It has been argued that education institutions have weak links with the labour market and as such cannot produce labour power with the necessary qualifications, and that this problem can only be solved by the strengthening of the link between education and employment. Accordingly, demands have been raised by vari-ous social sections in this direction. In this way, education has been exposed to an instrumentalist mentality reducing it to occupational training, and disre-garding its broader functions of improving critical thinking skills, cultural and aesthetic capacities of individuals. The understanding of lifelong learning has initiated a process whereby both students and employees have been put under more control, their lives have been reduced to the occupational sphere, and they have felt themselves obligated to purchase the knowledge that will make them more efficient and flexible, leading to the process we call self-production of the labour power. As education and knowledge are defined as the main ele-ments of competitiveness, they have gained a new strategic significance. The exposition of the content of education to evaluations has initiated competi-tion among education institutions. The marketing of certificate and similar programs by the private sector and universities in the name of upgrading indi-viduals' occupational qualifications and efficiencies has intensified the process of commodification of education. Students are seen as potential sources of labour power even when they are still in the middle of their education process. Thus, students as outputs of education are defined as inputs for the labour market. The current transformation of the Turkish education system is a process whereby this definition increasingly is dominating educational practices.

NOTES

1. www.mmf.gazi.edu.tr/makina/akreditasyon, 06.27.07

REFERENCES

Apple, M. (2004) Eğitimde Denetim Kültürü, Rekabet ve Sınıf Stratejileri (Culture of Auditing, Competition and Class Strategies in Education). *4.Demokratik Eğitim Kurultayı* Cilt: I. Eğitim Sen Yayınları: Ankara.
Brown, P. & Lauder, H. (2006) *Globalisation, Societies and Education*, vol. 4, March pp. 25–27.
Başesgioğlu, M. (2006) The Education will be determined by the Private Sector. *Isveren Dergisi*, vol. 4, no: 1, October.
Çelik, H. (2006) Speech made at the 17. National Education Council. Retrieved from: http://www.meb.gov.tr/haberler
EĞİTİM SEN. (2005) 4. Demokratik Eğitim Kurultayı (4.Democratic Education Congress). Cilt:I. Eğitim Sen Yayınları: Ankara.
———. (2006) *Report submitted by Eğitim Sen to the 17.* National Education Council, http://www.sendika.org/yazi.php?yazi_no=8342
———. (2007) *Milli Eğitim Bakanlığı'nda AKP'nin 4 Yılı (4 Years of AKP in the Ministry of National Education)*. Eğitim Sen Yayınları: Mart 2007.
Ercan, F. (1998) *Eğitim ve Kapitalizm: Neo-Liberal Eğitim Ekonomisinin Eleştirisi (Education and capitalism:The critique of neo-liberal economy of education)*. Bilim Yayıncılık: İstanbul.
Ertl, H. & Phillips, D. (2006) Standardization in EU education and trainign Policy: findings from a European research network, *Comparative Education*, vol. 42, no. 1, February, pp. 77–91.
European Commission. (2002) *Communication from the commission: European benchmarks in education and training—Follow up to the Lisbon European Council*. Commission of the European Communities: Brussels.
———. (1995) *White paper on education and training, teaching and learning, towards the learning society*. Commission of the European Communities: Brussels.
Fredriksson, U. (2003) Changes of education policies within the European Union in the light of globalisation. *European Educational Research Journal*, 2, (4).
ILO. (2005) *Youth: Pathways to decent work*. International Labour Conference.
MÜSİAD. (2006) *Turkish economy 2006*. Müsiad Yayınları: İstanbul.
OECD. (2005) *From education to work: a difficult transition for young adults with low levels of education*. OECD.
Payne, J. (2000) The unbearable lightness of skill: the changing meaning of skill in UK policy discourses and some implications for education and training. *Journal of Education Policy*, 15 (3), 353–369.
SPO. (2006) 9. Development plan. http://plan9.dpt.gov.tr/
TISK. (2006) 17.*Milli Eğitim Şurası'na Sunduğu Görüş ve Öneriler (Views and suggestions submitted to the 17. National Education Council)*. Retrieved from: http://www.tisk.org.tr/duyurular.asp?ayrinti=True&id=2047

TÜRK EĞİTİM SEN. (2001) *Turkish national education in the 21st century*. Türk Eğitim Sen Yayınları: Ankara.

TÜRKONFED. (2006) Beceriler, Yeterlilikler ve Meslek Eğitimi: Politika Analizi ve Öneriler (Skills, competencies and vocational training: Policy analysis and recommendations).

TÜSİAD. (2006) *Eğitim ve Sürdürülebilir Büyüme (Education and sustainable growth)*. Lebib Yalkın Yayımları: İstanbul.

World Bank. (2002) *Constructing knowledge societies: new challenges for tertiary education*. Washington, D.C.: The World Bank Publication.

YÖK. (2006) "Türkiye'nin Yükseköğretim Stratejisi (The higher education strategy of Turkey)." (Draft Report).

8 The Neoliberalization of Education Services (Not Including Higher Education)

Impacts on Workers' Socioeconomic Security, Access to Services, Democratic Accountability, and Equity—A Case Study of Pakistan

Ahmad Mukhtar

INTRODUCTION

There is a clear sense of "forced liberalization" within the education sector in Pakistan, with external and internal actors playing their roles without recognizing the impact of such neo-liberal "reforms." The waves of globalization and liberalization appear to be inevitable as resistance by civil society and users of education services is negligible.

The recent wave of unbridled privatization in Pakistan is spread over all Sectors, including education. The Task Force Report on the improvement of higher education in Pakistan (2002) expressed 'strong skepticism about the realization of change and improvement in the quality of higher education provided in the public universities and colleges.' (p: 27)

There are certain "levers" facilitating the liberalization of educational services in Pakistan. The wave of liberalization started in the early 80s when the previous nationalization policy was deemed unfit for long-term growth. At the same time, the World Bank and IMF started their "prescriptions" of liberalization and deregulation in all sectors including education. The WTO General Agreement on Trade in Services (GATS) covers educational services, but Pakistan did not commit any type of educational services in the Uruguay Round (GATS Schedule submitted in 1995). However, during more recent negotiations on GATS, most countries involved have requested Pakistan to "open up" educational services to free market trade. It is not simple for a developing country to disregard such "requests" made by countries and organizations such as the U.S.A., Japan, and the EU. Autonomous liberalization is very much present, and the number of private schools (both with local and foreign ownership) is increasing exponentially.

The dark side of such "forced" and "voluntary" liberalization is the lucid deterioration of educational quality and the unprecedented rise in cost (school fees, etc.). In Pakistan the most important parameter of adjudicating quality schooling is analyzing the number of students getting into the Central Superior Services (CSS) and the Pakistan Army, because entry requires passing the most competitive exams. From 1973 to 2002, the candidates with public sector schooling constituted 67.8 percent of all those who qualified with the CSS and were accepted into the Civil Services while the share of private schools was 24.3 percent. Candidates from other types of schools, (including foreign and unconventional schools) accounted for 7.9 percent of the share. In the case of Army induction, 79 percent had received public sector schooling during the period 1973–2002, while the share of candidates coming from private schools was 14.8 percent and others (predominantly madrassa schools) were 6.2 percent (FPSC, annual report 2002–03). Attendance at public sector schools costs an average of Rs. 50 per month from grade 6 onward, while grades 1–5 are free. The average private school in a rural area costs Rs. 200 per month from grade 1 onward while the average school in an urban area cost Rs. 800 per month (ranging from Rs. 500–8000) (Haq, 2004). The average pay for a middle class worker is Rs. 5000 per month while the average family size in Pakistan is seven heads. In this scenario, private education has been made "selective" rather than "education for all."

A primary school teacher in the public sector earns on average Rs. 4000 per month while a secondary school teacher's average pay is Rs. 8000 per month. The private sector has deteriorated the teaching standards by offering substandard salaries which are, on average, Rs. 2500 for primary schools and Rs. 5000 for secondary school teachers (Haq, 2004). There are, of course, certain exceptions where the elite schools offer hefty salaries, of course by charging proportionate fees. There is no concept of on the job training nor of retirement benefits, etc., in private schools. About 16 percent of the private school teachers are part-time workers (Haq, 2004).

One of the main reasons teachers are attracted to by jobs in private schools is the easy switching option. Due to economic stagnation for the last 2–3 decades, very few professions are considered to offer employment security, or "stable careers," and therefore competition is very high. People resort to one profession and always think of changing if a better option comes along. School teaching in Pakistan is losing its attraction as a career. Rather it is considered as the best stopover and one of the easiest jobs to get. The enrollment in formal education for school teacher training is reducing, evidenced by the Primary Teaching Course (PTC) exam that used to be the first choice of approximately 68 percent of the women passing graduation exams between 1975–1995. However, between 1996–2003, the first choice of going for PTC was given by merely 13 percent of the women passing graduation (Mahmood, 2003). Secretarial, air ticketing, and allied, computer-based jobs, as well as in other social services are taking over as the top choices of women graduates. Male graduates rarely opt for teaching as a career; rather they would take it as a stopgap arrangement while searching for a better one. This situation is leading to a vacuity in the school teaching profession, as public schools are no longer the first choice due to teachers' easy entry and exit in private schools. On the other hand, these "transitory" teachers found in private schools are not able to meet the required standards of teaching and dedicated efforts thus leading toward a clear deterioration of the quality of education of private schools. At the same time, private schools as employers typically do not pay attention to employment security, on the job training, good working conditions, long-term growth options, or other basic rewuirements of social and economic security. The reasons private school employers give for this short-sighted vision that they are not sure how long their employees will stay. Public schools, on the other hand, are also not very forthcoming in getting the best of the skill base since regular appointments by the federal and provincial governments stopped about fifteen years ago. Candidates are offered contract jobs which they prefer in the private sector where they can get at least a better salary. In the private sector, there are only two well-established institutes (in Karachi and Lahore) imparting education and training for school teaching. These training institutes are preparing a crop for the top-notch private schools, which offer better education to students and better working conditions to teachers, although these schools constitute less than 1 percent of the school population in Pakistan (Mahmood, 2003).

The Education Sector Reforms Action Plan (ESR) (2001–4) and its off-shoot the Task Force Report, propose to 'enhance the role of the private sector through a package of incentives and a liberal policy of private participation.' The ESR ambitiously sets out to increase the enrollment of private institutions from 15 percent to 40 percent by 2010 (GOP, Education Sector Reform Action Plan 2001–04, pp 34). While the issue of privatization raises many questions with regard to equity and accessibility, there is another dimension which deserves equal attention: the drive for privatization is also about preparing the ground for the next stop: "Globalization."

Primary education faces far-reaching challenges, particularly from the thrust toward globalization. Globalization is not uncontested. The deeply rooted concepts of communities based on cultural, spiritual, and historical identities are still embedded in the fabric of societies, and most assuredly in Pakistan society. Societal values and identities are in contradiction with the businessman's view of communities as customers, clients, contractors, and producers.

Three key and related themes characterize the impacts of globalization. The first is the destructive effects of a globalized competition that increasingly operates without restraint. The second is the restriction of democracy—limits on the capacity of the government to carry out the wishes of its citizens to put restraints on the excesses of globalization. The third is the distortion of the social purposes of education when education becomes too centered on its relationship to the economy. For developing economies such as Pakistan, the rapid cross-national flow of people, goods, capital, and information will dissolve the National State, and push institutions— with schools being one of the affected institutions—into a common mold. In contrast, for advanced economies, societies that are stable in their political, social, and institutional makeup, globalization promises dramatic—and rewarding—changes to their higher education systems.

Globalization has left economies like Pakistan's vulnerable to many desired and undesired adjustments in its economic and social institutions. For example, schools could become a purely commercial activity serving the investors and venture capitalists. The entrepreneurs behind these schools would be able to get the best of talent, both in student and teaching bodies, instructional facilities, and infrastructure, thus leaving public sectors far behind. These schools then would try to get down to the middle class and the surrounding segments of society affecting the school choice behavior of the general public. Public schools would never be able to provide an equal level of infrastructure, teaching resources, state of the art curriculum, and above all, affiliations with international schools, and so on.

On the other hand, developed economies like the USA stand to gain a deal in this arena. Their markets would be able to "export" education in the countries who pledge to liberalize education services through GATS or otherwise. Privatized the higher education from the USA and Europe is already being "exported" through all four modes of supply as defined in the WTO agreement on GATS. The liberalizations that are envisaged would place developed countries in a better position to take over the education services sector in developing countries such as Pakistan.

Knowledge has always been power as well as a public good. Access to knowledge and information and their roles in innovation determine both the place of nations in the world order and of individuals in society. But commodification, that is, the use of knowledge as a good which can be purchased and sold, displaces the creation and passing on of knowledge from the social sphere to the sphere of production. Displacing and reinterpreting knowledge under these conditions raises fundamental questions about academic freedom and the 'ownership' of knowledge. They also pose questions about the ethical obligation to make knowledge freely available to those who seek it.

Defining schools simply as 'service providers'—bending in front of the rewarding contract—is an unacceptable constriction upon their responsibility to society.

Trade agreements historically have been mainly about reducing tariffs and eliminating other barriers to trade. Social services like education and health care generally have been too place-specific to be tradable. In the last round of international trade negotiations that established the WTO, an enormous first step was made toward a comprehensive agreement on international trade in services. This occurred through a document called the General Agreement on Trade in Services (GATS). This agreement is a multilateral, legally enforceable agreement covering international trade in services. Education services, including higher education, are one of the 12 broad sectors included in the agreement.

Only when a service is provided entirely by the government does it fall outside the GATS rules. Because most education systems have some private providers or have some commercial aspect, virtually all systems could be affected by the GATS in some ways. Some argue that institutions that require the payment of fees (even public institutions) could be deemed as 'commercial activity' and brought under the ambit of the GATS as it currently exists.

If education were to become fully covered by the GATS, measures that would be put at risk include:

- Local hiring preferences (e.g., preference given to local school teachers)
- Minimum wages for education sector workers
- Local content requirements (e.g., required use of local textbooks)
- Restriction of 'consumption subsidies' (i.e., student loans and scholarships) and research subsidies to local citizens
- Restriction of degree granting authority to local universities only
- Restriction of public subsidies to local and not-for-profit institutions only

PRIVATIZATION—PREPARING THE GROUND FOR GLOBALIZATION

The underlying philosophy of trade liberalization in international trade agreements is that whenever something can be provided by the private sector, conditions should exist so that this can occur. These agreements are about creating and expanding private markets and, whenever possible, identifying and eliminating government actions which hinder the growth of the private sector.

One specific 'barrier' in the WTO background paper on education and the GATS that is particularly alarming is the identification of 'the existence of government monopolies'. How would the elimination of government monopolies in education be carried out? This is an important question as it is highly unlikely that any country would agree to direct attacks on their public education systems, if only because of the political risks involved. Something more subtle than a direct attack will need to occur at the bargaining table. The international corporate world has had considerable experience in honing effective, gradual steps to secure a firm base in undermining services in the public sector.

The first step is usually an overall attack on the funding of public institutions, by claiming that taxpayers can no longer afford to support overblown public institutions. As public institutions buckle under financial pressure, they seek out other funding sources like increasing user fees or introducing self-finance schemes. These public-private initiatives steer schools toward corporate approaches to education, bringing them under the rules of private trading structures.

Another effective maneuver which the private sector frequently resorts to is to make sure that it can tap into the money the government spends on a service like education. The private sector certainly has no objection to the government paying for services. What it wants, however, is to have that spending diverted to them. The trade agreements are a crucial step in this direction because they can enable the private sector to insist on a 'level playing field' in the education market.

Generally, when the private sector begins identifying a specific area for privatization that has long been in the public sector, it gets a foothold in the area through some marginal activity in the industry. The strategy subsequently is to complain about the existence of government monopolies and the difficulties of trying to maintain a business. The usual charge is that the public sector can provide the service cheaper than private providers can under normal commercial conditions because the public sector is subsidized by tax money.

When this reasoning is established, that is, that the government funded institutions have an unfair advantage, the trade agreements can support the private sectors' claim to access to money in distinct ways. The most obvious way is to ensure that the private sector be eligible for 'like' treatment when it comes to government subsidies.

Private Sector Involvement in Education

Private sector involvement in education was prevalent in Pakistan in the past, and some of the most reputable institutions were privately run. In fact, prior to 1972, private institutions constituted a sizable portion of the total educational system. Most of these institutions were at the primary through to college levels. In 1972, the government nationalized all 19,432 private institutions (Niazi & Hameed, 2002). By 1979, the government reviewed the consequences of nationalization and concluded that it could not carry the burden of the whole educational process alone, and the National Policy once again called for private community involvement. Since the mid-1990s, a major shift has occurred in the government's approach to the country's education sector. The government has formally acknowledged that the public sector on its own lacks the necessary resources and expertise to effectively address and rectify low education indicators. Moreover, public policy has been amended to mobilize private sector and civil society organizations (CSOs) in the financing, management, and delivery of education services in Pakistan.

Among other initiatives, the GOP has undertaken policy reforms and provided incentives for Public Private Partnerships (PPPs) to flourish in the education sector. The government has also stepped up its efforts to include the NGOs and various other stakeholders in the delivery of education policy measures designed to encourage new private involvement. First Punjab, then NWFP and Sindh promulgated Private Educational Institutions Ordinances.

These Ordinances were designed to:

- Provide for the registration of all private schools with a Registration Authority.
- Spell out conditions of registration and provide for the establishment of a managing body for each institution.

The Ordinances also made mandatory government approval for the adoption of a fee structure by private institutions. However, it did prevent the setting of high fees.

These Ordinances gave rise to a second wave of private involvement in education. The current status of this involvement is that there has been a mushrooming of private schools from preschool to postgraduate studies. There are an estimated 56,000 private educational institutions currently operating in Pakistan, providing education at all levels, to approximately 6 million students (GOP, Federal Bureau of Statistics 2004, Annexed Table 1). Of particular note is activity at the higher education level. Most recently 12 new private universities and 6 degree awarding institutes have been created (GOP, higher education commission, annual report 2003–04).

A few general characteristics of private institutions are:

- Most are "English medium" schools.
- They can be community based or privately owned.
- They are concentrated in urban areas.
- Their fee structures are usually high.

It is clear that the private sector has a role to play in the tremendous tasks of improving quality and expanding the educational system, and efforts are generally seen as burden-sharing with the government in the development process. However, there are several issues of concern with private institutions, which to date existing regulatory controls have been unable to address. As the number of private institutions continues to grow, these issues will have to be addressed and rectified. The main issues are fees, language, and whether the proliferation of private primary schools can be seen as a contribution toward the achievement of universal primary education.

a. Fees: Private education fees have been severely criticized by society as being too high. As a result, these schools, whether they are English medium or not, are not developing as institutions of equal opportunity. The high fees make them inaccessible to poor but talented students. Although the laws regulating these institutions provide government approval of the fee structures, they contain no preventative measures on charging high fees. As such there is no legal control over establishing a fair fee structure that would allow for access by students from lower–income families. Another difficulty is the fact that most of these institutions are being established as commercial or for–profit ventures, so their fees reflect business rather than altruistic considerations. However, the institutions argue that in the absence of grant–in–aid from the government, fees have to be high because they are the only source of income for the maintenance and quality of the institution, and of quality.

b. Universalization of Primary Education: The government argues that, due to the immense resource requirements of achieving universal primary education, it considers the opening of private primary schools as meeting that goal (Haq, 2004). This decision has been widely criticized because many argue that these institutions make no real contribution to expanding access to basic education for those that need it the most, namely the rural poor. Furthermore, by including these schools as part of the program, the government has found a loophole that allows it to fall short of its responsibility to educate the rural poor, while pointing to increasing number of schools being created (Haq, 2004). It is argued by some that the proliferation of private primary schools should not be included in the data on universal education goals for the following reasons:

- Private primary schools are concentrated in urban areas, and participation rates in these areas are already high. More schools are needed in rural areas, therefore these schools should not be counted.
- Students going to these schools would participate in education regardless, so these schools are not expanding the reach of education to include those that did not previously have access. Their role in universalization efforts is therefore marginal at best.
- Because of their use of English as a medium of instruction and their high fee structure, these schools cater to the elite, which runs counter to the concept of developing an egalitarian society—a premise which is central to the importance and aim of universal education.

One of the main reasons why private schools are impeding access to poor children is the fact that the government is implicitly putting the onus of primary education on the private sector and thus absolving itself from one of its core social responsibilities. In the last few years, the increase in number of public sector primary schools has never been proportionate to demand. With a population increase of 2.8 percent per annum, the number of primary schools is not even increasing by 2 percent per year (Niazi & Hameed, 2002).

The government has resolved to increase enrollment in private schools from the current 15 percent to 40 percent by 2010 under the education sector reforms (ESR) project (GOP, Education Sector Reforms Action Plan 2001–04, pp 34). However, this move is more like "eat cake if you don't have bread." In the rural areas particularly, the income level of households would impede them from sending their children to private schools. Above all, teachers rarely like to go to rural areas even if they are offered comparatively better salaries, resulting in low quality teaching staff employment in rural areas. Recently, the government offered 100 percent better salaries to doctors for serving in rural areas, but the results have been dismal to date. After three years since this scheme was introduced, 54 percent of the rural health centers are still waiting for doctors while in urban areas the doctors are working on smaller salaries and some are even unemployed.

The education sector reforms have developed a conceptual framework for public-private partnership. The strategies in the current model under implementation include: engaging the private sector for improving access and quality of education; enhancing managerial performance, entrepreneurial spirit through capacity building; access to proven leading knowledge technologies, and support for local knowledge and employment generation at local levels. Traditionally private institutions and individuals have played an important role in the delivery of education in Pakistan. In order to create a conducive environment for private sector involvement in the education sector, the Cabinet has passed a decision to facilitate the entry and participation of nongovernmental entities in the sector. These concessions are in addition to several existing incentives, which are detailed below:

Existing Educational Incentives (GOP, Education sector Reforms Action Plan 2001–2004)

1. Income tax exemption for the teaching faculty and researchers are in place on a sliding scale whereby income higher than Rs 1,000,000 receives a tax reduction of 5 percent all the way down to annual income of Rs 60,000 receiving a tax reduction of 80 percent.
2. Exemption of custom duties and other taxes on the import of education equipment/material is granted to institutions that are recognized, aided, or run by the government.

New Concessions (GOP, Education Policy 2004)

1. Provision of land free or on concessional rates in rural areas and urban areas, respective departments/organizations shall undertake appropriate zoning for educational institutions in residential areas.

2. Electricity shall be provided on domestic tariff rates.
3. Provision of concessional financing for establishing rural schools, through respective education foundations and credit, through Khushali Bank and other such financial institutions.

However the achievements to date of such drive by the government of Pakistan warrant a rational analysis and review of such a liberalization policy in the education sector. The quality of education has reduced coupled with an increase in the cost of education. Higher fees charged by private schools have a negative correlation with wages of the workers in the education sector. Primary education has become one of the most profitable businesses and a good way to evade taxes.

GATS and Education

Pakistan has not made any commitment for its educational services under GATS, however there is definitely an existence of autonomous liberalization. In the current round of GATS negotiations Pakistan received requests for liberalization in its education sector from the USA and Norway. The following observations are speculative in nature because there is no existing GATS commitment in the education sector.

1. Commitment to cover fully educational services under the existing GATS rules would require that foreign educational service providers be guaranteed access to the educational market. This includes the right to invest within the country (establish a commercial presence), to provide services from abroad through distance education or internet, etc. (cross- border supply), to provide services to foreign students (consumption abroad), the right of service providers to move between countries to provide educational services (movement of natural persons).
2. Governments will be required to give degree granting authority to foreign educational service providers.
3. Governments also will be required to provide foreign educational service providers with the same grants, financial assistance, and other advantages that they provide to like educational service providers. In the same vein, any preferential tax treatment for like schools, universities, colleges, and other educational institutions would either have to be eliminated, or also given to foreign educational service providers. However some of these areas are still under negotiation.
4. These requirements that 'like' institutions be treated the same would appear to protect the public system because governments would only need to support 'like,' that is private, educational providers. With increased commercialization of public institutions, they come into

competition with private ones, and hence 'like' treatment can be claimed by foreign competitors as well.

5. Public grants or tax incentives for research and development by educational institutions would be problematic, as would any requirement that people within the country be given preferential access to the benefits of publicly supported research and development. Any residency requirements that stipulate first preference for teaching positions be given to national or immigrants would need to be eliminated. Also any government provided student loans, bursaries, and other financial aid to students attending foreign educational institutions or taking courses from such institutions would need to be provided on the same basis as students attending public institutions.

6. Signing on the existing GATS will also substantially affect the public nature of education as once the issues are codified in the GATS, changes can only be made through a tough negotiation process that may involve giving some preferences in other areas.

7. The good news about GATS is that it is a voluntary agreement. Now is the time to take a long hard look at where we are. Pakistan should try to not commit anything within the education services because the results from autonomous liberalization are not sufficiently encouraging. The United States and Norway have requested that Pakistan open up its education services at all levels. Their offers (and subsequently commitments) by Pakistan have not yet been made to date, so we are not sure of the result of such requests.

Key Findings and Observations:

There are certain levers working implicitly and explicitly for liberalization in the educational sector.

- The World Bank and IMF are predominantly following the U.S. interests in developing countries like Pakistan. These institutions prescribe whatever U.S. firms strategize as long-term goals in Pakistan. The educational sector reforms (ESR) project is being funded by all major donors including the World Bank and the ESR Fund, and these go mainly for privatization and liberalization (thus commercialization) of primary and secondary education. Now under the GATS negotiations, the USA has requested that Pakistan liberalize its educational services, and based on the previous Pakistani policy response to U.S. requests, it seems likely that at least something in this regard is likely to happen. This wave of privatization, liberalization, and commercialization has made education a commodity for those who can afford it, rather than education for all.

- The workforce employed in the education sector is inevitably facing a "corporate" rather than a "social" employer. The private schools are mostly profit seeking entities, thus ignoring the workers' rights to a great extent, as in Pakistan's private sector employment lacks the international benchmarks of workers' socioeconomic security. Private schools offer 35–80 percent less salary while employment security and career prospects are the missing elements in mostly short term/temporary assignments. Pensions, medical, and other facilities and group insurance, etc., are not taken care of by most of the schools in the private sector.

- The students and parents of these students are suffering from low quality education mainly due to untrained and less motivated teachers. It is hard to find any teacher who has spent the whole of his/her career in school teaching, thus leaving students with new and experimenting teachers. Fees, on the other hand, are rising day by day and high fees are considered to be one of the indicators of a good private school irrespective of the quality of education that is imparted there. The facts given in the introductory part of this chapter, such as the low share of students from private schools entering CSS and Army exams is one indicator of quality of education imparted while the increase in fees is unchecked because there is no government regulation in place to assess the appropriate fee. Moreover, these schools are exempt from income tax, therefore making the schools' commercial earning hubs the name of the game.

The ownership structure of private schools in Pakistan is an interesting case in point.

- Three of the largest school chains are owned by political families who are most of the times in the corridors of power. These political giants invariably influence public policy and never allow policies to be framed which would take care of employees in the private education system. The World Bank has recently been supporting the largest private school chain in Pakistan which is owned by a renowned political family (Niazi & Hameed, 2002). The financial institutions are financing such types of schools on terms better than offered to any industrial undertaking. This has led to a race among the rich and powerful to open these types of schools and "educate" students belonging to a privileged social class. There is no regulatory mechanism in place to check all of these loopholes. Most of the small private schools are owned by entrepreneurs who are or have been in the education field, thus lacking a real commercial or even social management style. This also leaves the workforce employed under them astray.
- There is no existence at all of trade unions or groups in the private school workforce. However, there is a small voice in the public sector workforce employed in schools. The private schools have owners' associations but are never encouraged to participate in employees'

Table 8.1 Summary of Main Findings of Private Sector Survey in Education

VARIABLES	YEAR 2005	VARIABLES	YEAR 2005
Institutions		*Registration Status*	
Total	76.047	**Registered**	59,040
Rural	35,438	Recognized	9,856
Urban	40,609	Affiliated	5,594
i. General Education	57,505	Others	43,590
ii. Technical/Professional	898	**Unregistered**	17,007
iii. Vocational	2,143	Affiliated	16,437
		Recognized	570
		Ownership of Institutions	
		Self-owned	59,236
		NGO	5,247
		Trust	2,598
		Foundation	1,678
		Others	7,288
Enrollment		*Ownership of Buildings*	
Total	12,121,394	Owned	32,524
Rural	4,536,690	Rented	32,747
Urban	7,584,704	Rent Free	8,815
Male	6,784,361	Govt Provided	1,012
Female	5,337,033	No Building	949
Teaching Staff		*Enrolment by type*	
Total	632,926	i. General Education	10,150,246
Rural	211,892	ii. Technical/Professional	
Urban	421,034		189,365
Male	213,258	iii. Vocational	134,935
Female	419,688	iv. Madrassas	1,504,462

Source: National Education Census, Federal Bureau of Statistics (2005)

Table 8.2 Participation Rate in Private Education: Pakistan (**In percentage**)

Stage	Both	Male	Female
Primary	19.93	22.16	17.71
Middle	9.05	9.56	8.61
High	4.67	5.01	4.34

Source: Federal Bureau of Statistics (2004)

associations. One of the main reasons could be a short stay by most of employees and taking their job as a transition to better ones.

- The government should take serious note of the situation instead of using private schools as a means of escaping its responsibility. It should come forward and put in place a strong regulatory mechanism to get the optimum results out of such privatization and liberalization.
- The current pattern of school system and the investment and ownership structure indicates the "Americanization" of education services, especially at the primary school level. We must, however, keep in mind the huge gap in the American and Pakistani education and social system. We cannot afford to follow the American model of services delivery in education due to various factors, some of which are discussed above.

REFERENCES

Alderman, H.; Orazem, P.F. ; & Paterno, E.M. (2001) School quality, school cost, and the public/private school choices of low-income households in Pakistan. *Journal of Human Resources* 36 (2), 304–326.

Alderman, H. ; Behrman, J.; Khan, S.; Ross, D.; & Sabot, R. (1997) The income gap in cognitive skills in rural pakistan. *Economic Development and Cultural Change*, 44.

Arrow, K. (1997) *The benefits of education and the formation of preferences.* (Chapter 2) In Jere Behrman and Nevzer Stacey, ed., The social benefits of education. Ann Arbor: University of Michigan Press, Ann Arbor.

Banerjee, A. (2000) Educational policy and economics of the family. *Mimeo*, December. Cambridge:Massachusetts Institute of Technology.

Behrman, J.; Khan, S.; Ross, D.; & Sabot, R. (1997) School quality and cognitive achievement production: A case study for rural Pakistan, *Economics of Education Review* 16(2), 127–142.

Curle, A. (1966) *Planning for education in Pakistan: A personal case study.* Cambridge, MA: Harvard University Press.

Gazdar. (1999) Universal basic education in Pakistan: commentary on strategy and results of a survey. SDPI Working Paper Series # 39. SDPI: Islamabad.

Government of Pakistan. (1959) *Report of the Commission on National Education*, January–August. Government of Pakistan: Islamabad.

———. (1960) *Second five-year plan 1960–65.* Pakistan Planning Council. Government of Pakistan: Islamabad.

———. (1983) *Sixth five-year plan 1983–88.* Planning Commission. Government of Pakistan: Islamabad.

———. (1997) *Report on the PIHS 1995–96.* Islamabad.

———. (2002) *Education Sector Reform Action Plan 2001–04*, Government of Pakistan: Islamabad, pp. 34.

———. (2002) *Task Force Report on improvement of higher education in Pakistan.* Government of Pakistan: Islamabad.

———. (2003) *Annual report of Federal Public Services Commission* (FPSC) *2002–03.* Government of Pakistan: Islamabad.

———. (2004) *Economic survey of Pakistan 2003–04*. Government of Pakistan: Islamabad.

———. (2004) *Annual report 2003–04*. Higher Education Commission. Government of Pakistan: Islamabad.

———. (2004) *Statistical year book 2004*. Federal Bureau of Statistics. Government of Pakistan: Islamabad.

Hanushek, E.A. (1995) Interpreting recent research on schooling in developing countries. *The World Bank Research Observer*, 10 (2), August.

Haq, R. (2004) Causal link of illiteracy with poverty in Punjab. *Pakistan Development Review*. August.

Hoodbhoy, Pervez, ed. (1999) *Education and the state: fifty years of Pakistan*. Pakistan: Oxford University Press.

Hsieh, C. & Urquiola, M. (2002) When schools compete, how do they compete? Assessing Chile's nationwide school voucher program. *Mimeo*. January.

Khan, S.; Kazmi, S.; and Latif, Z. (1999) The state of basic education in Pakistan:A qualitative, comparative, institutional analysis. SDPI Working Paper Series # 47. SDPI: Islamabad.

Kremer, M.R. (1995) Research on schooling:What we know and what we don't. A comment on Hanushek. *The World Bank Research Observer*, 10(2). August.

Krueger, A. & Lindahl, M. (2001) Education for growth: Why and for whom? *Journal of Economic Literature*, Vol. XXXIX. December.

Mahmood, K. (2003) Career choice amongst urban women: shift in industry due to wage levels. *Economic Review*, 23(7). The University of Agriculture: Pakistan. July.

Naqvi, S.S. & Javed, T. (2002) All for education. *The Dawn*. Karachi. February 28.

Niazi, Z. & Hameed, S. (2002) *Privatisation in basic education: Pakistan case study, Raasta marketing research*. Paper for Save the Children Alliance in South Asia, June.

Qureshi, A.K. (2001) Mushroom growth of public schools in Hazara. *The Nation*, *Internet Edition*. November 24.

Warwick, D.P. and Reimers, F. (1995) *Hope or despair? Learning in Pakistan's primary schools*. Westport, CT: Praeger.

9 State, Inequality, and Politics of Capital

The Neoliberal Scourge in Education

Ravi Kumar

INTRODUCTION

The Indian 'education sector'[1] has become a site of fresh activities since the beginning of the 21st century—the 86th Constitutional Amendment making education a fundamental right was passed in 2002[2]; many versions of the Right to Education Bill[3] meant to operationalize the Amendment have come up; and finally, the writing of the formation of the Central Advisory Board of Education (CABE), the highest advisory body on education for around a decade. Seven committees[4] were constituted within CABE to look at some of the most fundamental issues confronting education in contemporary India. There has also been a host of activities after loans for Sarva Shiksha Abhiyan (SSA, the Programme to Universalise Elementary Education) were sanctioned by the external financing agencies like the World Bank and the DFID. Despite such efforts, the problems of equality and quality in Indian education persist. This paper delves into how the trajectory of capital across different stages of capitalist development becomes an important tool to understand the nature of changes in Indian education policy making.

The current historical conjuncture defined by the onslaught of insatiable capital is not limited only to particular countries. Marx wrote that "the need of constantly expanding market for its products chases the bourgeoisie over the whole surface of the globe. It must nestle everywhere, settle everywhere, establish connections everywhere." (Marx and Engels, 1984, p.34) India, being touted as the emerging economic power, is an innate part of this global expansion of capital.

Located within a space where capital marches unbridled, modifying all possible spheres into commodified zones, the education system in India is under tremendous attack. This attack emanates out of the subservience of the State to neoliberal capital. This new phase, located at a particular moment in the trajectory of the march of capital, signifies the death of welfarism in policy making. Dismal, inegalitarian, and discriminatory convey the essence of the present state of the educational scenario in India. Though the situation persists across elementary education (Grade I–VIII), secondary education (Grade IX–XII) and higher education (above Grade XII), this paper will largely reflect on elementary schooling, which has been the focus of attention recently. The roots of inequality and discrimination that we witness today so acutely are not new, but date back to the time when India got independence from British colonialism. The much celebrated Indian Constitution did not include the Right to Education as a fundamental right, which would have been justiciable (can be challenged in the court of law in case of its violation), but rather as a Directive Principle that the state should have educated all children up to the age of fourteen years within ten years of implementation of the Constitution (see Dhagamwar, 2006). Year 2002 marked a departure from this position with Parliament passing the 86th Constitutional Amendment, making elementary education a fundamental right. Though rife with problems, the Amendment is still to be operationalized through an Act in Parliament.

In this moment of crisis, discourses and actions about alternatives as well as corrective measures have emerged. Certain institutions have emerged as saviors in this time of crisis—advocating use of legal means to ensure 'equity' in schools. Their initiatives fish out clauses in documents to ensure equality and quality as if those policies are shorn of class character. What kind of alternatives do these groups call for? They are organizations that are driven by the idea that improvements can be brought about within this system; issues of equality can be resolved without addressing the sources of inequality; schools, therefore, can become autonomous agencies of change and transformation rather than centers which reproduce already existing inequality. Capital is not the issue for them. In other words, the world can be changed without challenging capitalism, which is considered as the given, immutable, inevitable reality. This has been perhaps a general problem with liberals across the globe. One can, in fact, replicate what McLaren says about the US to the Indian situation to a great extent. Like American liberals, the Indian counterparts also call for capital controls, controls in foreign exchange, better wages, the end to informalization, the safeguard of the public sector companies, etc., however, they are the few who would demand the abolition of capital itself (McLaren, 2005, p.23). Their activities have not only redefined the notion of equality but they have also helped establish that there is no alternative to capitalism. Hence, changes in the education system will have to be located within a framework where private capital governs and determines the rules of the game.

THE ABSENCE OF CLASS AND THE TERRAIN OF STRUGGLE

One of the much frequently visited debates in the Indian context has been that of the non-significance of 'class' and the significance of 'caste' as the most momentous category of social division or form of social relation.

However, it has also being argued that changes are taking place within the caste structure (Gupta, 2001; Singh, 1996). The discourse on caste located within the realm of capitalism is almost negligible in India, and therefore it remains the autonomous basic structure of society to many, divorced from the capitalist mode of production. It also emerges as a powerful identity, which determines and influences the development of theory as well as practice.

With the growing visibility and prominence of caste identity in national politics, it has become easier to decipher the actual form of changes that have taken place. The emergence of the elite among all castes (which could very well be identified with parallel class positions), especially among the so-called Backward Castes and Dalits (literally meaning 'oppressed'), has shown how capital uses the existing identities to sustain and expand itself. The direction in which Dalit politics has moved recently has been that of co-optation into the larger system of capitalism. In the context of 'inclusion' of hitherto unrepresented social categories into the dominant forms of capital accumulation, it can be said that there has been a democratization of opportunities to access the realm of competition. In other words, it is ultimately the expansion of capital that happens as more and more people, hitherto excluded, become a part of it. However, it would also mean that the assertion of Dalits and Backward Castes should be read as emancipatory or liberation from drudgery only up to a certain level or in a certain sense. It only substitutes one form of drudgery by another.

The educational debates in India have been reading too much into the identities, taking them as the actual social relations. Consequently, there is an overwhelming dominance of multiple subjectivities in their discourse, wherein class is just one of them. And as many of the subjectivities also come to be identified as noncapitalist, the idea of discrimination and exclusion developed seldom indicates the correlation between capital and knowledge. Consequently, class never appears in such a discourse as the determining category of educational policies and systems. Even if class is talked about, they are not grounded in, as McLaren says, "the labour-capital dialectic, surplus value extraction, or the structure of property ownership, but instead refer to consumption, or job, income, and cultural prestige." (McLaren, 2005, p. 19). Kelsh and Hill (2006) identify such a trend with the predominance of the Weberian notion of class. They argue that

> in the place of the Marxist theory of class, the revisionist left has installed a Weberian-derived notion of class as a tool of classification useful only to describe strata of people, as they appear at the level of culture and in terms of status derived from various possessions, economic, political or cultural. (Kelsh and Hill, 2006)

These tendencies have been fatal for the struggle to develop and create a revolutionary critical pedagogy as the opposition to capital gets reduced to a liberal, social democratic position that wants to live within capitalism with minor modifications.

GLOBALIZATION AND NEOLIBERALISM— WHAT IS IN STORE FOR THE MASSES

Globalization has been interpreted in different ways. It has been argued that presently globalization is altering the character of the economy the world over, and therefore it is a departure from the past, but Nayyar argues that "Globalisation is not new." (Nayyar, 2006, p. 71; Sen, 2002). If it has been seen as the phenomenon that has connected people globally through markets, then it is also seen as a process of homogenization of choices (Kumar and Paul, 2006a). Strong defences of globalization and capitalism have also emerged in the recent past. Norberg argues that capitalism is the only option for development because it gives one liberty to chose and even the poor will benefit if the true agenda of global capitalism is pursued. The need is for 'free capitalism, which exists "when politicians pursue liberal policies and entrepreneurs do business."' (Norberg, 2005, p. 29) In the Indian context, the scholars, 'in defence of global capitalism,' believe that "there has been no attempt to sell reforms to the poor, the beneficiaries. Consequently, reforms have been perceived to be top down, with a pro-urban, pro-rich bias. Myopic governments at the Centre and the State have been driven by populist considerations. Major beneficiaries of true reforms will be unorganized labour, small farmers, efficient trade and industry and consumers . . ." (Debroy, 2005, p. 14) Like other committed soldiers of free markets and capitalism who, while claiming to be poetic, humane, pro-poor, rationally try to bring the benefits of market to everybody, Norberg powerfully expresses his fascination for the potential miracles that market can do (Norberg, 2005). The examples of the way the BPOs brought jobs and high salaries are often cited in this context.

On the other hand, there are scholars trying to humanize the market and the rule of capital when they argue for an open society where trade and exchange benefits can accrue to the poor as well (Sen, 2002). Markets are not the culprits for inequality, Sen argues, because they have their own potential for development. The pool of scholars who speak in favor of humanizing the rule of market/capital has increased in the recent past. Another such scholar advocates strongly the cause of the market when he overtly pronounces support for the market, "but only if it helps companies become more efficient and lowers prices for consumers. This is more likely to happen if markets are competitive, which is one of the reasons I support strong competition policies." (Stiglitz, 2006, p.xi).

However, it is extremely difficult to believe that the market would provide 'fair share and fair opportunity' to the poor. We also have evidence which indicate that, in an economy where markets have an uncontrolled freedom, it becomes difficult to control the accumulation of wealth and ensure that the public expenditure on education, health, etc., is maintained and improved. The recent developments in the education sector in the USA (Farahmandpur, 2006; Gibson, 2006), Britain (Hill, 2006), and in Latin America show how markets have compelled the States to curb expenditure on education.

Capital, despite its relentless march, is also facing stiff resistance. And this emanates from the kind of uneven developmental consequences that flow out of it. The last quarter of the 20th century "witnessed a divergence, rather than convergence, in levels of income between countries and between people. Economic inequalities increased during the last quarter of a century as the income gap between rich and poor countries, between rich and poor people within countries, as also between the rich and the poor in the world's population, widened. And income distribution widened." (Nayyar, 2006, p. 91) In the case of India, the changing character of economy has resulted in the informalization and the casualization of the workforce on a mass scale. The government is disinvesting in the public sector enterprises and the State institutions, handing them over to private companies. There is an ever inflating informal sector, scarcely governed by any labor laws that safeguard the worker's interests. A recent study by the UNDP's Human Development Resource Centre estimates that the percentage of informal employment among total workers is a whopping 91.7 percent—in the case of males it is 90.1 percent and among females it is 95.3 percent (Sastry, 2004, p. 28). All this has only made the majority of Indians more vulnerable.

Such developments have far-reaching consequences when the issue of educating children, for instance, comes up. While the majority remains deprived of education, the state, rather than working for such children, starts making it more and more inaccessible by converting it into a commodity. Today the Indian government, rather, argues for an enhanced role of private capital in the secondary education sector (Kumar, 2006a) given the widely known fact that the economic difficulties do not allow a great number of children to proceed with education, even when the education provided by the government, though termed free, involves a great deal of investment (Tilak, 1996).

The current phase of globalization is characterized by the neoliberal capital's assault. It excludes the vast mass of people from the basic facilities that they require for survival. Schooling gets privatized; the state fails to make any commitment to educate the children; and water, land, forests, and other resources are thrown open for sale and purchase in the market. How will the issue of accessibility be addressed in a society and economy that is dominated by the market? How will the problems of ownership and sharing be resolved in a society where the collectives and collective symbols are being broken up into fragments? Neoliberalism has brought forth before us such pertinent questions, and unless education is located within this larger context of how the policies of the State change as per the desires and designs of the capital, one will be at a loss of explanation to understand why the state which promised and saw the Common School System (even in its incomplete form) as an equalizing instrument in education up to 1986 not only begins a wholesale delegitimization process of the full-fledged government schools, but also refuses to pass legislations to make elementary education free and compulsory.

Neoliberal globalization has brought along with itself a package that is against those who lack the purchasing power. On the other hand, it also concentrates this purchasing power in the hands of a few. In the name of globalization, it is the interests of the capital that occupy the center stage, whether it is the debate on technology, availability of new facilities [read 'products'], or the economic growth and the climbing of Sensex. Ultimately, who benefit are obviously those who invest and those who can buy. The fact that, in the age of globalization, solidarity of the marginalized and workers is curtailed, not allowing any mobilization for transformation, is never even acknowledged. Their rights are trampled as the owners of capital demand deregulation and liberalization of labor laws and the labor market. More than holding spears at each other's heart the antiglobalization activists need to understand that capital is responsible for the systemic deformations that we experience today, and it is ultimately the private capital which dictates the rules of living according to its own motive of profiteering.

The debate between the 'market fundamentalists' and the liberal welfarist scholars, who want globalization with a human face, has the danger of getting our discourses trapped in the viciousness of a reproductive logic, which fails to transcend the 'given' context of capitalism. It does not try to critically evaluate the role and the rule of capital, which by its natural logic of evolution takes such a vicious form in the age of neoliberalism. To put it squarely, capital has always been on the lookout for surplus generation, only the forms change or the intensity differs. Rather, historically, one needs to look at the "continuities in capitalist mentality and practices" if one is to understand the dynamics of capitalism and the current phase of so-called globalization (Tabb, 1997).

But then the obvious question is how to curb the offensive of capital? Many would argue that in the current phase of capitalism it has become extremely difficult to counter the power of capital. Tabb argues that the idea of state's powerlessness is "a powerful tool of capital." It is not powerless but rather collaborative. The state wants to protect the money fleeing to the tax havens and to offshore banking centers when it can very well penalize the banks for not providing information on tax capital transfers. "It is the governments of the advanced nations, especially the United States and Britain, which have encouraged deregulation. This was a political choice and not a technical necessity." In fact, "it is time for greater clarity in our critique of the basic workings of what are called 'free markets' but are in reality class power." (Tabb, 1997)

The Neoliberal Offensive

As indicated above, the current phase of globalization is represented by the offensive of the neoliberal capital. It has been argued that it is "impossible" to conceptualize neoliberalism theoretically because: (a) it "is not a mode of production," (b) it is "inseparable from imperialism and globalization," and (c) its roots are "long and varied." (Saad-Filho and Johnston, 2005, p. 02). It is seen as "part of a hegemonic project concentrating power and wealth in elite groups around the world, benefiting especially the financial interests within each country, and US capital internationally. Therefore, globalization and imperialism cannot be analyzed separately from neoliberalism." (ibid, p. 01) Globalization is nothing more than the "international face of neoliberalism: a world wide strategy of accumulation and social discipline that doubles up as an imperialist project, spearheaded by the alliance between the US ruling class and locally dominated capitalist conditions." (ibid, p.02) As its most basic feature, it uses quite systematically the State power to "impose (financial) market imperatives, in a domestic process that is replicated internationally by globalization." (ibid, p.03) McLaren and Farahamandpur (2005) put it very succinctly when they define neoliberalism as

> a corporate domination of society that supports state enforcement of the unregulated market, engages in the oppression of non-market forces and antimarket policies, guts free public services, eliminates social subsidies, offers limitless concessions to transnational corporations, enthrones a neomercantilist public policy agenda, establishes the market as the patron of educational reform, and permits private interests to control most of social life in the pursuit of profits for the few . . . It is undeniably one of the most dangerous politics that we face today. (p.15–16)

Education and Neoliberalism: State as Agent of Capital

The current avatar of capital, in fact the current politics of capital, is manifested in neoliberalism, and it becomes important for us to understand what it does to the social sector and society at large in India. The phase of making education available to all children never came here, and with neoliberal capital in offensive, it has become impossible now. The education system is being hierarchized through a variety of mechanisms—from making educational facilities coterminous with purchasing power to depriving a vast mass of that required purchasing power.

Giroux argues that

> neo-liberalism attempts to eliminate an engaged critique about its most basic principles and social consequences by embracing the 'market as

the arbiter of social destiny.' Not only does neoliberalism bankrupt public funds, hollow out public services, limit the vocabulary and imagery available to recognize antidemocratic forms of power, and produce narrow models of individual agency, it also undermines the critical functions of any viable democracy by undercutting the ability of individuals to engage in the continuous translation between public considerations and private interests by collapsing the public into the realm of the private. (Giroux, 2004, p. 494)

Even the postmodern scholars like Zygmut Bauman argue that it is no longer the colonization of the 'private' by the 'public,' rather it is the 'private' that is colonizing the 'public.' "The opposite is the case: it is the private that colonizes the public space, squeezing out and chasing away everything which cannot be fully, without residue, translated into the vocabulary of private interests and pursuits." (Bauman quoted in Giroux, p. 494).

Within this new space, defined by an ever increasing domination of a hegemonizing meta-discourse that uses all possible instruments of state apparatus and the strength of capital to diminish the presence of alternative discourses, education has become one of the most significant sites of contest and struggle. It needs to be noted here that neoliberalism is different from the classic liberalism of the mid-19th century in the sense that the latter "wanted to roll back the state, to let private enterprise make profits relatively unhindered by legislation" whereas the former "demands a strong state to promote its interest." (Hill, 2004) It is this difference that makes the activities of the State resemble the interests of private capital. What can explain the situation much better than the fact that the legislations which the central government formulates "promote privatization and 'corporatisation' of school education" and franchises parts of the education infrastructure to corporate or religious bodies (Sadgopal, 2004a, p. 38), leave aside the fact that it closes down its own schools, sells its assets, and deliberately allows the government schools to deteriorate, which then get replaced by the fee charging private schools (Kumar, 2005; Sadgopal, 2006b, p. 23).

Today neoliberalism is creating a common sense that "education should be divorced from politics and that politics should be removed from the imperatives of democracy" (Giroux, 2004, p.495). And if we try to locate this in Indian context we find that education is seen largely as an isolated governance issue which has no place in the political priorities of the state. Hence, questions such as finance crunch and the feasibility/viability argument dominate the discourse on education, though we have examples of countries poorer and/or bigger than India having tackled their educational issues in a much better way. The tragedy of this country has been that, though a great hullabaloo is created at the rising growth rate of the Indian economy, the State is not able to contribute anything substantial to the education sector. This basic need remains a perpetual need because the state says it is still 'strapped' of basic resources. In fact, the state, in its neoliberal phase, has decided to keep the education system the way it is. Consequently, the majority of Indians are faced primarily with the question of whether they can avail the school education that they want or not. Then comes the question of what kind of education is being served in schools. Neoliberalism has only accentuated this crisis. Neoliberalism in India has resulted in the following:

1. It has commodified education at a much faster pace, for it must be noted that education in the form of private and state run schools were already present in India.
2. It has established, through mobilizing and creating new centers of knowledge, that the State cannot provide quality education of comparable quality to all children, hence, new options need to be explored.
3. It has curtailed whatever ethos characterized the state institutions such as Parliament, the Central Advisory Board on Education, etc., to serve the interests of private capital directly.
4. It has managed to transform the nature of discourse on education and equated it with literacy, making its attainment the only goal of elementary education.
5. It has successfully tied the alternative discourses on education within a framework that inevitably turns to the state for concessions, despite knowing that it caters to the interests of private capital;
6. The possibilities of social movements of a larger scale have been diminished due to the boom in economy and the effective use of state apparatuses (though everyday resistances have increased over the years, but without the ability to take the shape of larger political resistance).

Thus, the impact of neoliberalism has not been much different in India. It has gradually diminished the differences between the market and the State in the sense that both are pursuing similar kinds of policies/politics. Consequently, the State withdraws in order to let the market flourish. There has been either a reduction in the amount spent on the social sector as a whole or a very marginal increase which does not contribute much to salvage the situation (Table No.1).

This decline, stagnancy, or nearly negligible improvement in expenditure has not been because the government suddenly became poor or because the requirements of schooling outstrip its financial capabilities (as it often tries to convey). This decline has been in consonance with the demands of the private capital as well as the larger conglomeration of the ruling elite. Therefore, the need to educate all children in a schooling system that is nondiscriminatory and offers equal educational

Table 9.1 Trends of Social Sector Expenditure by General Govt. (Centre and State Govt. Combined).

Items	2000–01	2001–02	2002–03	2003–04	2004–05	2005–06
	Actual	*Actual*	*Actual*	*Actual*	*RE*	*BE*
As a proportion of GDP: (In percent)						
Total expenditure	28.05	28.26	28.77	32.27	28.97	27.76
Expenditure on social sector	6.25	6.04	5.92	5.68	5.98	5.81
Education	3.17	2.98	2.95	2.78	2.87	2.81
Health	1.32	1.25	1.28	1.26	1.32	1.35
Others	1.74	1.8	1.68	1.63	1.78	1.64
As a proportion of total expenditure:						
Expenditure on social sector	22.3	21.4	20.6	19.7	20.7	20.9
Education	11.3	10.6	10.3	9.7	9.9	10.1
Health	4.7	4.4	4.5	4.4	4.6	4.9
Others	6.2	6.4	5.8	5.7	6.1	5.9

Note: RE: Revised Expenditure; BE: Budgeted Expenditure
Source: GOI (2006a)

opportunities of uniform quality never emerged as a political priority in India, even when the Constitution was being framed. And there is a need to understand and acknowledge it in order to understand the political economy of education. Though many scholars try to understand it, they always see it as an alienated discourse divorced from class interest, politics class relationship, or ignore the trajectory/movement of capital, its corresponding interests over different periods of time and the changes in education policy. And the consequences are there when one sees the massive increase in the budget heads of sectors such as military and defense and the decline in the budget head of education. For instance, the All India percentage of expenditure on education to the total budget went down from 14.1 percent in 1970–71 to 11.3 percent in 2000–01 (Tilak, 2003). With the arrival of the neoliberal avatar of capital, the principle of public private partnership has come to dominate the development strategy of the state (Kumar, 2006b). The funding, for example, by international funding agencies has increased over the years (see Table 9.2). This does not indicate so much toward the increased commitment among the external funding agencies for alleviating the educational problems of the country as toward fomenting a trend of state withdrawal from funding the education sector.

Table 9.2 Foreign Aid for Elementary Education in India

Rs. in crore.

Projects	1993–94	1994–95	1995–96	1996–97	1997–98	1998–99	1999–00	2000–01	2001–02[B]
Shiksha Karmi	5.00	5.00	8.00	9.00	13.85	5.20	19.28	24.46	30.00
Mahila Samakhya	6.71	3.68	4.08	4.64	3.73	5.00	6.00	8.73	11.00
Bihar Education Project	16.00	10.00	—	—	—	—	—	—	—
Lok Jumbish	6.26	9.30	15.00	22.20	32.66	37.50	20.98	56.10	59.00
DPEP	3.50	94.00	201.14	183.16	559.58	549.75	682.80	858.29	1100.00
GOI-UN Prog.								0.00	10.00
Total	37.47	121.98	228.22	219.00	609.82	597.45	729.06	947.58	1210.00
As a % of Central Government Budget									
Total Elementary Education (Plan)	9.60	22.29	19.00	14.00	27.30	21.73	25.56	30.40	31.84
Total Education (Plan)	3.08	7.38	10.40	8.77	18.65	14.97	16.63	17.39	20.44
Total Elementary*	388.80	547.15	1201.80	1560.59	2234.94	2749.82	2851.97	3117.38	3800.00
Total Education*	1217.37	1653.87	2193.41	2496.75	3269.50	3990.60	4384.96	5449.00	5920.00

Note: *Central Budget plan account only (Department of Education). B: Budget Estimates.
Source: Analysis of Budgeted Expenditure on Education, Working Group Report on Elementary and Adult Education: Tenth Five-Year Plan 2002–2007, and Annual Report 2002–03.
Source: Tilak (2003)

The direct repercussion of such policies can be seen in the status of education in India. The posts of teachers are lying vacant and the teaching learning infrastructure is insufficient even today. Though a large-scale macro-picture can be constructed only through the data provided by the government, we have to assume that the situations are worse than this. There are still 16,777 schools without buildings in the country according to the figures provided by the State (NCERT, 2002). Though the number is much higher, as we saw during visits to some schools in the state of Bihar, which are shown as having buildings, but in reality do not have even a room. There are still around 553,179 primary schools in the country with less than five teachers, which means that there is not even one teacher per class, so the question of administrative staff in the schools does not even arise.[5]

Although the teachers, the buildings, and the teaching learning materials are insufficient, one finds that these government schools are generally used by people who cannot afford the private schools. Hence, it is the girl children, the poor, and the Scheduled Castes who mostly access the government schools. National Sample Survey illustrates the relation between low income and low level of education (Kumar, 2006b). The economic and social factors combined produce high dropouts, and this is truer of girls and the Scheduled Castes (SCs), who are mostly landless and poor. While around 53.5 percent of all girls enrolled in Class I drop out by time they reach Class VIII, the figure for the SCs is 59.4 percent, and among the SC girls it is 62.2 percent (see Kumar 2006b for details).

The most recent survey by Government of India shows that there is a direct correlation between the capacity to spend and the attendance of children in schools. The attendance percentage in schools improves as the monthly per capita consumption expenditure increases (see Table 9.3).

The need is to democratize the accessibility to education in real terms. Despite the rhetoric of people's participation in education management, the system remains hierarchized. It would remain so also because the knowledge production and the education process are not contextualized in the processes of production and social relations emerging out of them. Quite evidently, it cannot even be expected out of a capitalist system. Once education gets commodified, the interest of capital remains in only maximizing its surplus through it. While schools become centers of reproducing existing social relations and producing uncritical mechanical beings who serve the system, the democratization of access remains a non-agendam for capital till it does not directly affect its aim of profit maximization.

One of the obvious developments due to the situation described above has been the burgeoning of private schools in urban as well as rural areas. Some studies have pointed out that "access to school in urban areas is largely through private schools" and "even in rural areas, poorly monitored government schools have created a good field for the new private schools.

Table 9.3 Current Attendance Rates in Educational Institutions by Age Group and Household Monthly per Capita Consumer Expenditure Class

MPCE* class (Rs.)	5–14 (Urban)			5–14 (Rural)		
	Male	Female	Person	Male	Female	Person
less than 335	68	68.5	68.3	65.7	57.5	61.7
335–395	71.1	73.7	72.4	71.6	67.1	69.3
395–485	80.3	79.4	79.9	76.3	68.3	72.4
485–580	89.3	87	88.2	77.1	69.3	73.4
580–675	90.3	88	89.2	81.6	75.2	78.5
675–790	90.6	90	90.3	83.3	77.1	80.4
790–930	94.5	94.6	94.6	86	78.3	82.4
930–1100	97.3	96.2	96.8	87.9	81.8	85.1
1100–1380	98.3	97.9	98.1	91.1	86.5	89
1380–1880	98.7	99.1	98.9	93.9	89.4	91.9
1880–2540	98.6	98.4	98.5	94.9	93.8	94.4
2540 & above	97.7	98.3	98	96.4	95.2	95.9
all classes	89	87.9	88.5	83.5	76.7	80.3

*Monthly Per Capita Consumption Expenditure
Source: GOI (2006b), p. A-27.

However, cost remains an excluding factor for private schooling. The very poor are dependent on government schools and in fact can generally access only the government primary schools seen to be the worst in the sector" (De, Noronha and Samson, 2002, p. 5235). What one comes across then is that students access private schools even though they are not only poor in infrastructure (poorer than the government schools in most of the cases) but even the teaching learning is worse. In states such as Bihar one finds nearly every village having some sort of private school or 'tuition centre' where the students, who can afford to pay the fees (which are not very high compared to the urban private schools, but are definitely higher than the local government schools), flock in great numbers.

Many analysts and scholars have treated these developments as indicators of a general 'hunger for education' among people. Everybody wants to send their children to school because education is seen primarily as a source of upward mobility (Kumar, 2006d), and if it fails to deliver that (due to various reasons, such as bad quality of education or the larger logic of the capitalist economic system that flourishes on minimizing its costs of production) by employing less people and at lower costs to maximize profiteering, a sense of disenchantment also seeps in the general psyche, which gets reflected in the relapse in illiteracy among other things.

Capital Wants Machines, Not Critical Beings

Recent developments in the education sector have seen an emphasis on skill development as a means of enhancing human capital. This emphasis has a major bearing on the conceptualization of education, its aims and goals. Direction to the discourse tends to show that (1) education must also help in finding livelihood, (2) critical consciousness is secondary to information generation, and (3) knowledge can be seen as two distinct possibilities of 'practical' and 'theoretical' knowledge. Literature generated with these orientations in education has been innumerable, being produced by UN agencies, the World Bank and the Indian government alike. For instance, one of them argues that "most human capital is built up through education or training that increases a person's economic productivity—that is, enables him or her to earn a higher income ... Governments spend public funds on education because they believe that a better educated population will contribute to faster development. Employers pay for employee training because they expect to cover their costs and gain additional profits from increased productivity. And individuals are often prepared to spend time and money to get education and training, because in most countries people with better education and skills earn more. Educated and skilled people are usually able to deliver more output or output that is more valuable in the marketplace, and their employers tend to recognize that fact with higher wages" (Soubbotina and Sheram, 2000, p. 35). Education, thus, is losing its critical edge as it becomes nothing more than a mechanistic process as well as an instrument of producing 'professional' beings geared to sell their labor as and when required. However, the idea of education as a tool to enhance productivity has its own inner contradictions, such as what if the economy is not able to absorb the new productive workforce that is generated as shown by the increasing unemployment in the country?

NEGLECT OF EDUCATION FLOWS FROM THE LOGIC OF CAPITAL

At such a juncture, it becomes crucial to understand and conceptualize the reality which may appear to be located at two different levels, but are in fact united as a part of the larger system. For our conceptual clarity, let us look at these two different levels taken in abstraction: (1) The discrimination within society reflected in the school and the education system at large bears semblance of the unequal social relations such as in the case of girl children (Chanana, 2006); (2) the policies of the state, which, during the era of the Welfare State were supposed to rectify many of such maladies, have rather been perpetuating the inequality in education in the age of globalization dictated by the neoliberal capital. In fact, discrimination is being institutionalized (Kumar and Paul, 2006b, p. 253–289). Therefore, what one comes across is a system where the poor, SCs, STs and girl children are deprived of education because they are the most marginalized in the larger society outside the school as well. Similarly, at the macro-level the policies of the state have very clearly spelled out that, for the out of school children, 'other' methods of education will be followed. Hence, comes the nonformal methods and the recent government program of Sarva Shiksha Abhiyan. Why can't the formal schooling system that already exists be strengthened so that every child gets education of comparable quality?

These two levels also unite because they are components of the same reality. If one brings down the abstracted conceptual categories to reality, it becomes clear that the Indian State has always lacked interest in implementing the paradigm of equal educational opportunities of comparable quality for every child. Though scholars have tried to explain this failure as 'lack of political will,' 'problem of financial crunch,' 'low growth rate,' etc., what one finds is that many nations in the world, despite their low growth rate, effected laws of compulsory and free education for all. Secondly, 'lack of political will' is not something that is constituted in isolation, but there are interests that constitute a 'strong' or a 'weak' will. Why does it happen that the Central Government takes half a century to enact education as a Fundamental Right and then decides not to pass a central legislation in Parliament for free and compulsory education (Goswami, 2006), but takes decisions about investments in construction of infrastructure for Asian Games or Commonwealth Games in the blink of an eye? Before liberalization, the logic of resource crunch many a times emanated from the fact that the growth rate of Indian economy was too low, but now when the growth rate is being touted to be above eight percent, even then the same situation persists.

Education in Historical Location of Capital

Coming back to the frequent references to past committees and policies, as principles taken out of a particular concrete historical situation and placed in another completely different historical conjuncture, we need to pay some attention to the fact that the education policies and discourses are products of their own historical milieu. Scholars argue about the positive aspects of the Kothari Commission and the NPE-1986 and they demand that many of their recommendations be implemented, but what skips their attention is a very basic principle—the education system serves the need of the ruling elite in every society. It is never an anti-systemic force. It becomes so because of the larger political economic reasons. The transplantation of the welfare state principles in a neoliberal state is an impossibility, but then that does not mean that we stop fighting for the spaces that develop criticality. However, unless a larger political perspective is put forth, it will be difficult to have any social movement that can force the State, at this particular historical conjuncture to expand itself when the private capital wants the complete, limitless freedom to expand.

While the National Policy on Education 1986, considered to be the last of the National Policies that had retained the flavor of equality through its emphasis on the CSS (Common School System), also acknowledged that the elementary school education of comparable quality will not become available to all children of India in the 6–14 age group (Sadgopal, 2006a) and recommended strongly the nonformal education techniques. These two sides of the same document are not essentially contradictions, but we need to locate it in a context when the Indian economy was in transition. And the twin principles in the policy represented that transition. The new age of a modern economic system based on professionalism, and a strengthening voice against what used to be called the license raj was strengthening as the new generation of political rulers in form of Rajiv Gandhi had occupied the throne at Delhi. Even if he cannot be taken as a success story (though the picture might have been different had he not been assassinated), he was the political leader who had set the tone for expansion of the capital as we see today. He introduced reforms in certain sectors, such as electronics and telecommunications, automobiles, etc., and eased tax rates. From this point of view his 1985/86 budget was a landmark. Thereafter, he exempted a number of industries from licensing, "large business houses regulated by the MRTP (Monopoly and Restrictive Trade Practices) and FERA (Foreign Exchange Regulation Act) legislations were encouraged to participate in a number of high technology industries; limits on foreign exchange for import of raw materials were raised, and tax concessions for the corporate and urban upper-middle classes were introduced." (Frankel, 2005, p. 586). It needs to be understood that what appears as 'contradiction' is not necessarily a 'conflict,' but it also, in many cases, shows the 'transition.' Hence, what becomes important for the analysis of the education policy is the relevance of the larger political economy which makes us understand why the Kothari Commission, the Parliamentary Committee of 1967, the NPE-1986, the Ramamurti Committee, or the post-liberalization State policies have their own particular characteristics. They are, after all, not so much an exercise of individual craftsmanship, but rather documents emerging out of respective historical needs.

Pauperization and the Neoliberal Model of Growth: Who Can Afford this Education?

The much touted above eight percent growth of the Indian economy has not resulted in any major benefits accruing to the majority. The landless agricultural laborers, the small and marginal farmers, and the daily wage workers, as well as the section striving to meet their basic needs through employment in this age of globalized world order, none of them have gained from the new economy that has come into existence. The Government of India estimates that "the unemployment rate went up between 1993–94 to 2004. On the basis of the current daily status (unemployed on an average in the reference week), during the reference period, the unemployment rate for males increased from 5.6 percent to 9.0 percent in rural areas, and from 6.7 percent to 8.1 percent in urban areas. Similarly, unemployment rate for females increased from 5.6 percent in 1993–94 to 9.3 percent in 2004 in rural areas, and from 10.5 percent to 11.7 percent in urban areas" (GOI, 2006a, 208). On the other hand, there has been tremendous commercialization of the agriculture sector. The stress on growing cash crops led the farmers to opt for loans from a variety of moneylenders—from banks to pesticide shopkeepers. However, it has had tragic consequences, as the agricultural productivity did not match the amount invested in agriculture and the farmers were compelled to commit suicide. The investments in agriculture have substantially gone up while the rate of return has come down. For instance, in Andhra Pradesh, where thousands of farmers committed suicide, the share of agriculture in the gross state domestic product has come down from 53 percent in 1960–61 to about 13 percent in 2002–03, but the workforce in agriculture declined only marginally. Thus, the population has been sharing the declining income from agriculture. On the other hand, the area under cash crop cultivation has grown, but the yield has gone down. "With a high cost of cultivation, diminishing productivity and low returns, it becomes difficult for farmers to withstand crop failures."[6] (Rao & Suri, 2006, p. 1547) The result has been suicides on mass scale in states of Andhra Pradesh, Uttar Pradesh, Punjab, Maharashtra, and Karnataka as well. The agricultural models of the post-Green Revolution have crumbled under the heavy weight of the neoliberal attack (see Kumar, 2006c).

The market is there, everywhere, meeting one in every nook and corner. Now one need not go to the designated geographical location of exchange to experience it, it has penetrated deep inside every household. Education, considered to be the State's responsibility, is being thrown open to the market. But can the majority of Indians buy it? The answer is obviously a big *no* given that: farmers have been committing suicide (Sainath, 2005), workers are beaten mercilessly when they protest against their employers (Kumar, 2005), the Government of India's Economic Survey shows that unemployment is rising (GOI, 2006a), there are still a great number of people trapped in the viciousness of poverty (Sastry, 2004), the Mushars in Bihar remain stagnantly trapped in the viciousness of their educational deprivation (Kumar, 2006d), there is the ever serious problem of hunger facing the poor people (Patnaik, 2007), and 21.8 percent of Indians live below the poverty line, as per the Planning Commission estimates[7] in March 2007 (based on the 2004–05 survey). With this situation, it is not at all surprising that a large section of people do not attend schools due to direct economic reasons (Table 9.4). In this context, when the educational status of the masses is being determined by their economic status, the situation would alter only with a new framework where surplus maximizing interest of capital is not the key determinant of educational accessibility.

Table 9.4 Distribution of Persons of Age Group 5–29 Years Who Were Currently Not Attending Any Educational Institution, by Status and Broad Reason for Nonattendance for Each Age-Group

All India	*School too far*	*Has to supplement household income*	*Education not considered necessary*	*Has to attend to domestic chores*	*Others*	*All*
		Reason for not Attending Educational Institution				
Male	1.7	54.7	10.8	2.5	30.3	100
Female	2.7	10.8	20.1	30.0	36.5	100
Total	2.2	32.0	15.6	16.7	33.5	100

Source: GOI (2006b)

On Resistance to the Neoliberal Assault

In the current phase of capitalist development, even those who stand in opposition to the market and the privatization of education are not able to locate the causes of such a system. 'Capital' as the determinant of inequity in education is, therefore, missed out. To understand the State's refusal to legislate a central law, or implement the Common School System must be seen in context of a State driven by an ever powerful and dehumanizing capital. Hence, any effort to change the system would entail: (1) understanding the transforming character of education policies in context of the changing forms, needs, and requirements of the capital; and (2) developing an understanding that such a system can be reformed only if there is a strong resistance based on this understanding. The possibilities of 'entering the system' to bring about change are not only bleak but inconceivable at the current juncture. It is also impossible because firstly, the State has full control over its apparatuses and becoming a part of it to radically transform it will be unacceptable to it; secondly, the 'pressure' on the State can be exerted only through a powerful popular mobilization on the issues; thirdly, the mobilization as well as the work by the representatives working within the State structure need to have a clear understanding about the character of the State and the origins of a dehumanizing and inegalitarian education system.

Within this larger framework, as a counter resistance to the tendencies of objectification of knowledge and shrinking critical spaces of engagement, it is important to reclaim even the social and cultural politics as the site of "dialogue, critique, and public engagement" so that in "a democratically configured space of the social . . . the political is actually taken up and lived out through a variety of intimate relations and social formations." Culture becomes even more important as a site of new pedagogical possibilities to create new spaces of resistance under neoliberalism, which destroys the ethos of dialogicity and therefore criticality by dissolving the "public issues into utterly privatized and individualistic concerns." (Giroux, 2004, p.499) However, while culture becomes an important site of resistance, it needs to be carefully treated due to the fear of relapsing into the graveyard of postmodern phantasms. This can be done if we locate different sites of the struggle as components of a singular system, where the economic, social, political, and cultural coalesce into one singular mode of production.

NOTES

1. The term 'sector' is used primarily in terms of a locale that has been assigned to education nowadays. It is relevant to recall that there are a host of players active in this locale now such as the government, nongovernmental institutions (NGOs), independent academics and some 'activists.' It is also important to mention that this locale functions within a paradigmatic framework, which largely treats education as an agency capable of effecting radical changes on its own (which I have argued elsewhere [Kumar, 2004] and does not link education to the larger framework of development [which largely excludes the critical engagements with the development plans and strategies]), and thus education becomes, what the State wants, another field where the 'apparent' contests do not question its own policies and politics. It is interesting to note that such problems have been part of the international organizations as well (Tomasevski, 2005).

2. It has been argued that the Constitutional Amendment failed to clearly define the responsibilities of the State and also excluded the 0–6 age group children as well [see Sadgopal, 2004b].

3. The Right to Education Bill was first drafted by the right-wing National Democratic Alliance but was never put to a vote in Parliament. Thereafter, the United Progressive Alliance (UPA) government constituted a committee under the aegis of the Central Advisory Board on Education to prepare a draft bill, which was changed many times in an undemocratic way, without the consent of the members of the committee. The bill is yet to be tabled in Parliament. The UPA government decided, after looking at the financial commitments involved, to ask the different state governments to pass their own respective bills and circulated a pro-privatization model bill to be followed in case the States did not want reduction in Central Government grants. The government's claim of resource crunch and therefore consequent withdrawal from its responsibilities is a sham as evidences show that money is spent and invested for building the infrastructure for the Commonwealth Games, to beautify the city of Delhi, or pay subsidies to the private power distribution companies so that their losses are compensated.

4. The following seven committees were constituted via the Government of India notification dated September 8th, 2004: (1) Free and Compulsory Education Bill and other issues related to Elementary Education, (2) Girls' education and the Common School System, (3) Universalization of Secondary Education, (4) Autonomy of Higher Education Institutions, (5) Integration of Culture Education in the School Curriculum, (6) Regulation Mechanism for the textbooks and parallel textbooks taught in schools outside the government system, and (7) Financing of Higher and Technical Education.

5. As per the NCERT Seventh Survey (NCERT 2002) the situation of pupil-teacher ratio in 2002 was as follows:

Area	Primary Schools	Upper Primary Schools	Secondary Schools
Rural	44	35	31
Urban	36	32	29
Total	42	34	30

In States like Bihar there were 85 students per teacher in rural primary schools, in Chattisgarh the same figure was 43, in Jharkhand 59, Haryana 42, Madhya Pradesh 38, Orissa 41, Punjab 39, Rajasthan 42, Uttar Pradesh 61, West Bengal 55, etc.

6. For a detailed account on the suicides in Andhra Pradesh and Maharashtra, please refer to the series of articles by P. Sainath that appeared in *The Hindu*. One may also look at them to understand the gendered dimension of the agrarian crisis (Sainath, 2004c), the growing commercialization and how the government relaxed rules and controls for the MNCs. After such dropping of controls, the rate of the germination of seeds has gone down, farmers are made to sign papers by shopkeepers who also act as moneylenders when the farmers need loans for agriculture (seeds, pesticides, etc.). (Sainath, 2004a, 2004b)

7. The estimation of poverty undertaken by the Government of India has come under serious criticism from economists (see Patnaik, 2007, p.137–147). The government has been trying to show the reduction in poverty by reducing the amount needed to spend for basic necessities. Firstly, the amount shown is highly insufficient, for instance, as an all India average it says that Rs. 356 per month is sufficient to survive. Can those who prepare the estimates live on that amount?

REFERENCES

Chanana, K. (2006) Educate girls, prepare them for life. In Kumar, Ravi (ed.), *The crises of elementary education in India*. New Delhi: Sage Publications, pp. 200–224.

De, A.; Noronha, C.; and Samson, M. (2002) Private schools for less privileged: some insights from a case study. *Economic and Political Weekly*, December 28, pp. 5230–5236.

Debroy, B. (2005) In defence of this book. Foreword to Norberg, Johan. *In defence of global capitalism*. New Delhi: Academic Foundation.

Dhagamwar, V. (2006) Child Rights to Elementary Education: National and International Provisions. In R. Kumar (Ed.), *The Crisis of Elementary Education in India*. New Delhi: Sage Publications, pp. 57–91.

Farahmandpur, R. (2006, September). A critical pedagogy of hope in times of despair: teaching against global capitalism and the new imperialism. *Social Change*, 36(3), pp. 77–91.

Frankel, F.R. (2005) *India's political economy 1947–2004*. New Delhi: Oxford University Press.

Gibson, R. (2006) The rule of capital, imperialism, and its opposition: radical education for revolution and justice. *Social Change*, 36(3), pp. 92–120.

Giroux, H.A. (2004) Public pedagogy and the politics of neo-liberalism: Making the political more pedagogical. *Policy Futures in Education*, 2(3 & 4), pp. 494–503.

Goswami, U. (2006, May 15) Guaranteeing right to education: Centre to pass the bill to states. *The Economic Times*.

Government of India (GOI). (2006a) *Economic survey 2005–2006*, Economic Division, New Delhi: Ministry of Finance.

———. (2006b). *Status of Education and Training in India 2004–2005.* Report No. 517 (61/10/3), NSS, 61st Round (July 2004–June 2005). National Sample Survey Organisation, Ministry of Statistics & Programme Implementation. New Delhi: Government of India.

Gupta, D. (2001, December). Caste, race, politics. *Seminar,* No.508, pp. 33–40.

Hill, Dave. (2006, September) Class, neoliberal global capital, education and resistance. *Social Change,* 36(3), pp.47–76.

———. (2004) Educational perversion and global neo-liberalism: A Marxist critique. *Cultural Logic,* 7, Retrieved July 14, 2006, from: *http://clogic.eserver. org/2004/hill.html.*

Kelsh, D. & Hill, D. (March 2006) The culturalisation of class and the occluding of class consciousness: The knowledge industry in/of education. *Journal of Educational Policy Studies,* 4(1), Retrieved January 22, 2007 from: *http://www. jceps.com/index.php?pageID=article&articleID=59*

Kumar, R. (November 2006a) State, class and critical framework of Praxis: The missing link in Indian educational debates. *Journal of Educational Policy Studies,* 4(2). Retrieved January 12, 2007, from *http://www.jceps.com/index. php?pageID=article&articleID=68*

———. (2006b) Introduction: equality, quality, and quantity—mapping the challenges before elementary education in India. In Kumar, Ravi (ed.), *The crisis of elementary education in India.* New Delhi: Sage Publications.

———. (2006c) When *Gandhi's Talisman* no longer guides policy considerations: Market, deprivation and education in the age of globalization. *Social Change,* 36(3) pp. 1–46.

———. (2006d) Educational deprivation of the marginalized:A village study of Mushar Community in Bihar. In Kumar, Ravi (ed.), *The crisis of elementary education in India.* New Delhi: Sage Publications.

———. (2005, September 17) Education, state and class in India: towards a critical framework of praxis. *Mainstream,* XLIII(39), pp.19–26.

———. (2005) Farewell to class struggle in name of secularism. *Mainstream.* July 29–August 4, pp. 4–5.

———. (2004) Nationalism and education in India: the rise of the BJP. *Eurasia Bulletin.* Brussels: European Institute for Asian Studies. July & August, pp. 6–8.

Kumar, R. and Paul, R. (2006a) Transforming spaces or refashioning hierarchies? Some preliminary reflections on gender relations, media and globalisation. In Somayaji, Sakarama and Somayaji, Ganesha (ed.), *Sociology of globalisation: perspectives from India.* New Delhi and Jaipur: Rawat Publications. pp. 377–390.

Kumar, R. and Paul, R. (2006b) Institutionalising discrimination:Challenges of educating urban poor in neo-liberal era. In Ali, Sabir (ed.), *Managing urban poverty.* New Delhi: Council for Social Development and Uppal Publishing House. pp. 253–289.

Marx, K. & Engels, F. (1984) *Manifesto of the Communist Party.* Calcutta: Pearl Publishers.

McLaren, P. (2005) *Capitalists and conquerors: A critical pedagogy against empire.* Lanham, MD: Rowman & Littlefield Publishers, Inc.

McLaren, P. and Farahmandpur, R. (2005) *Teaching against global capitalism and the new imperialism:A critical pedagogy.* Lanham, MD: Rowman & Littlefield Publishers, Inc.

Nayyar, D. (2006) Globalisation and development in the long twentieth century. In S., J.K. (ed.), *Globalization under hegemony: The changing world economy.* New Delhi: Oxford University Press.

NCERT. (2002) *Seventh educational survey.* New Delhi: National Council for Educational Research. Retrieved May 10, 2007, from http://www.7thsurvey. ncert.nic.in/national/fs10.asp

Norberg, J. (2005) *In defence of global capitalism.* New Delhi: Academic Foundation.

Patnaik, U. (2007) *The republic of hunger and other essays.* New Delhi: Three Essays Collective.

Rao, N.P. & Suri, K.C. (April 22, 2006) Dimensions of agrarian distress in Andhra Pradesh. *Economic and Political Weekly,* pp. 1546–1552.

Saad-Filho, A. & Johnston, D. (2005) Introduction. In Saad-Filho, Alfredo & Johnston, Deborah (eds.). *Neoliberalism:Acritical reader.* London: Pluto Press. pp. 1–6.

Sadgopal, A. (2006a) Dilution, distortion and diversion: A post-Jomtien reflection on education policy. In Kumar, Ravi (ed.), *The crisis of elementary education in India.* New Delhi: Sage Publications. pp. 92–136.

———. (2006b) Privatisation of education: an agenda of the global market. *Combat Law,* 5(1). February–March, pp. 22–27.

———. (2004a) *Globalisation: Demystifying its knowledge agenda for India's education policy.* Durgabai Deshmukh Memorial Lecture. July 15, 2004. New Delhi: Council for Social Development and India International Centre.

———. (2004b) Elementary, it's education. In Bharat Jan Vigyan Jatha, *India's education policy:Creating political space for social intervention.* September. Ghaziabad: Bharat Jan Vigyan Jatha.

Sainath, P. (2005) The swelling "register of deaths" *The Hindu.* 12/29/2005.

———. (2004a) Seeds of suicide I. Retrieved July 10, 2006 from http://www.indiatogether.org/2004/jul/psa-seeds1.htm

———. (2004b) Seeds of suicide II, Retrieved July 10, 2006 from http://www.indiatogether.org/2004/jul/psa-seeds2.htm

———. (2004c) How the better half dies. Retrieved July 10, 2006 from http://www.indiatogether.org/2004/aug/psa-womenfarm.htm

Sastry, N.S. (2004). *Estimating informal employment and poverty in India.* Discussion Paper Series-7. Human Resource Development Centre, New Delhi: United Nations Development Program, December.

Sen, A. (2002) How to judge globalism. *The American Prospect,* 13(1), January 1–14. Retrieved June 21, 2006 from http://www.prospect.org/cs.article=how_to_judge_globalism

Singh, Y. (1996) *Modernization of Indian tradition.* New Delhi and Jaipur: Rawat Publishers.

Soubbotina, T.P. & Sheram, K. A. (2000) *Beyond economic growth: Meeting the challenges of global development.* Washington, D.C.: World Bank.

Stiglitz, J.E. (2006) *Making globalization work.* London: Allen Lane (an imprint of Penguin Books).

Tabb, W.K. (1997) Globalisation is *an* issue: The power of capital is *the* issue," *Monthly Review,* 49(2).

Tilak, JBG. (2003) Public expenditure on education in India:Areview of trends & emerging issues. In Tilak, JBG (ed.) *Financing education in India.* New Delhi: NIEPA and Ravi Books.

———. (1996) How free is "free" primary education in India?" *Economic and Political Weekly* 31(4–5), February 3 & 10.

Tomasevski, K. (2005). Has the right to education a future within the United Nations? A behind-the-scenes account by the special rapporteur on the right to education 1998—2004. *Human Rights Law Review* (5)2, pp. 205–237.

10 Global and Neoliberal Forces at Work in Education in Burkina Faso
The Resistance of Education Workers

Touorouzou Hervé Somé

INTRODUCTION: GLOBAL AND NEOLIBERAL FORCES AT WORK IN BURKINA FASO—THE CRUSADE OF WORKERS FOR EDUCATION FOR ALL

If education is historically heavily centralized in Burkina Faso with the European Ministry of Education model as a result of the French colonization, Burkina Faso, "... like many countries, is transforming its educational system within the context of the changing global economic system." (Hursh & Martina, 2003, p. 3) Carnoy and Rhoten (2002) contend that the combination of economic restructuring in the world economy and the powerful ideological conceptions of how educational delivery needs to be changed, spread by international institutions as a consequence of the globalization process, is having a significant impact on educational systems worldwide. (p.2)

Also, the contradictions that inherent in international assistance and the lack of control of the private sector have imparted to education no precise direction, thus reinforcing the dependence on external donors.

EDUCATION IN BURKINA FASO: STATUS OF THE ART

In Burkina Faso, the colonial past and private and global forces are nongovernmental arrangements impinging on a fast fading state. According to Hill (2003), "The privatisation of public services, the capitalisation and commodification of humanity and global demands of the agencies of international capital . . . have resulted in the near-global (if not universal) establishment of competitive markets in public services such as education." (p. 3)

Burkina Faso belongs to the Highly Indebted Poor Countries (HIPCs). The Human Development Index (HDI), an indicator of the level of life expectancy, education, and real income reached by a country, places Burkina at the 172nd position out of 175 with a GDP of $300 per year

Table 10.1 Schooling in 2001–2002.

	Boys	%	Girls	%	Total
Primary	550, 504	58.40 %	392,108	41.59 %	942,612
Secondary	130,485	60.08 %	86,691	39. 91 %	217,176
Postsecondary	11,530	74.59 %	3,946	25.40 %	15,535

Source: Kedrebeogo, G. (2002); in African Gender and Development Index; Guissou (2003).

(Nama, 2004). Although illiteracy is decreasing, the net enrollment ratios are very low with 1 percent in the preschool, 42 percent in the primary, and 9 percent in the secondary. There has been an explosion of enrollment in the higher education level. However, only 1 percent of the age cohort has access to a postsecondary education.

This table, a synopsis of the situation in 2002, shows a stark imbalance in gender schooling. Girls are still left behind (Some, 2006). The enrollment in basic education is beneath the average in Sub-Saharan Africa. In 1999, the net enrollments in Burkina Faso were 34.6 percent against 57 percent, the mean in Sub-Saharan Africa.

Schooling entails an important opportunity cost for an economy relying basically on human force, raising the burning issue of the worst forms of child labor. School in its current state corrupts and disrupts the stability of the community: the educated ones despise farm work and the many dropouts of the school system find sanctuary, or at least in the big cities, magnifying the already squalid living conditions in urban areas. This has led Hagberg (2002) to wonder pertinently whether education in Burkina Faso is learning to live or to leave.

Private secondary schools constitute 49.40 percent of all secondary schools in the country. Private secondary education is very noticeable in the secondary school system with 35.64 percent of the classes in the grammar schools and 31 percent of the student population in 1994. Private technical education accounts for 82.76 percent of all the technical schools and 73 percent of the total technical school student population. The secondary school level is also characterized by a severe lack of teachers. Dipama (2003) reports that in 2001–2002, the gap was 950 teachers, and an estimate for 2003 set the figure as a deficit of 1100 teachers.

For-Profit Providers in Education

There is an increasing number of private institutions in the primary, secondary, and tertiary educational institutions, all operating like for-profit ventures with tremendous fiscal advantages. During the People's Democratic Revolution (RDP), started in August 1983, the private schools were told in no uncertain terms to charge only moderate tuition fees to allow the maximum of children to access education. Tuition fees were topped at 40,000 FCFA ($80.00) for the middle school of the secondary education and 45,000 FCFA ($90.00) for the high school, irrespective of the standing of the institution. In the private primary schools, the maximum was 20,000 FCFA ($45.00). Today, with the Structural Adjustments Programs (SAPs) accompanied by deregulation, providers are raising the tuition fees as they see fit. In October 2006, private schools agreed that the tuition should be raised between 5,000 and 10,000 cfa, only after the government had given a subsidy to the tune of $50,000 to be shared among them. The amount may be insignificant, but this has instituted the precedent that private ventures in education could be funded with public monies.

Since the liberalization of the economy, tuition fees have soared, generally to no proportion with the purchasing power of the average citizens. Struggling with a monthly minimum wage barely at the level of 30,000 FCFA ($60), they find it hard to ensure the education of their children. It is little wonder that institutions are polarized. There are those of the well-to-do such as Belemtisé, Les Oisillons, L' Aurore, l' Ecole Primaire Théa, St Viateur, Universalis, l' Ecole Bilingue de Ouaga 2000, Le Lycée de la Jeunesse, and the low quality ones left to the populace. The government regards the (for-profit) private providers as unavoidable partners and allows a "land grant" for the expansion of private provision. This is in accord with the demands of the SAPs that encourage the charge of user fees in public education that used to be free, and privatization altogether whenever possible, in the true spirit of the Washington Consensus. "It [the Washington Consensus] argued that the keys to success in developing countries were three things: macro-stability, liberalization (lowering tariff barriers and market deregulation) and privatization." (Stiglitz, 2000, p. 1)

Structural Adjustments and Education

In the 1990s, when the government was seeking World Bank and IMF assistance, it bragged that, unlike other countries, Burkina Faso was going to these institutions standing on its two feet, not on a stretcher (Diabré, 1998). Guenda (2003), in fact, shows that there was no Burkinabé exception as

> Burkina Faso has suffered from the deterioration of international economic conditions, which has brought about such problems as the drop in the price of raw material, the increase of interest rates and national debt, and the subsequent devaluation of the CFA franc by 50 percent in 1994. (p. 195)

The structural adjustment policies have ushered in extreme hardships (CNPS, 2001). The devaluation of the CFA franc was the last straw that broke the camel's back. This contradicts the rosy analysis of Diabré (1998) who contends that structural adjustments have worked wonders. In his view,

> Unions for the most part strongly opposed the process [privatization], mainly for ideological reasons. They claimed privatization was a subordination of the common good to private interests. They also blamed privatization for leading to layoffs, which was not true in the Burkinabé context. (Diabré, 1998, p. 70)

Forgetting that SAPs are not free from "ideological reasons" either, Diabré—he was the Minister of Economy and Finance in 1992—produced a discourse that smacks of the official mantra. Egulu observes that with structural adjustment programs, "[e]ducation and health budgets have been drastically reduced, depriving a majority of people of access to basic

Table 10.2 Corporations Whose Privatization Was Authorized in July 1994

Enterprises Phase 1	Date of Privatization	Industry	Buyer
BRAKINA	05/21/92	Brewery	BGI
SOBBRA	05/21/92	Brewery	BGI
SBCP	06/05/92	Leather	Ouedraogo Alizèta
SBMC	06/05/92	Leather	Ouedraogo Alizèta
SIFA	03/09/93	Bicycles	CFAO
SOBCA	03/29/93	Credit, leasing	Local Investors
SONAR	09/09/93	Insurance	Local Investors
Zama Publicité	09/30/93	Advertising	Yaméogo Louis de Gonzaques
FASO PLAST	11/02/93	Plastic	Barro Djanguinaba
GMB	11/26/93	Wheat mill	Barro Djanguinaba
CIMAT	12/28/93	Cement	UMAR
SONAPHARM	08/10/94	Pharmacy	CFAO
SCFB	12/12/94	Railway	SITARAIL
FLEXFASO	03/25/95	Fruit, vegetables	Ismael Ouedraogo
Phase 2			
RNTC X9	06/11/96	Transport	Appolinaire Compaoré
SHSB-CITEC	06/30/96	Oil & Soap	CFDT
Burkina & Shell	12/31/96		

Source: Zéphirin Diabré, 1998, The political economy of adjustment in Burkina, p. 72. http://pdf.usaid.gov/pdfdocs/Pnacj920.pdf. Retrieved 01/20/2007.

public services." (2001, p. 21) This state of pervasive poverty has also taken its heavy toll on education. The National Council for the Strategic Planning (2001), or CNPS, graphically depicts the social decay that started in 1990 with the first tide of layoffs affecting workers. During demonstrations of former workers whose severance pay have not been paid, it is usual to read words emblazoned on a banner illustrating the fate of thousands of anonymous ex-workers whose children go hungry at night in bed and who cannot afford to go to school nor benefit from health care. Out of nearly all the companies—around fifty—operating in the country, a great many have been slated for privatization. Bonal (2002) captures the social costs of SAPs so well. For him, structural adjustments have been devastating with "a number of negative effects that [they] have had on several educational indicators: the falling of educational expenditure, increase in educational absenteeism and school failure, a contraction in access to primary and secondary education, and so on." (Bonal, 2002, p. 7) Thus, teachers themselves have seen their conditions plummet. Guenda (2003) remarks that "[t]he material and social conditions of teachers in Burkina Faso have declined" because of "cost-cutting measures." (p. 202)

Nongovernmental Forces or Incentives in Education: Closing the Stable Doors with the Wolf

In Burkina Faso, the for-profit basic and secondary institutions seem to be laws unto themselves. As admitted by the Permanent Secretary for Private Education, Koueta Fla, most private providers are flouting the terms of references governing the opening of private schools. Several private schools would have to close down were these terms of references strictly enforced by government (Zongo, L'Evénement, October 15, 2007). A private school, before being authorized to open, must have qualified personnel available as well as latrines, sports grounds, etc. The reality is very different. What is more, many unscrupulous owners of private institutions do not refrain from 'bloating' the results of their students in the national exams for marketing purposes. During the 2002–2003 year exam, Mrs. Drabo, the owner of le Collège Saint-Joseph and le Collège Saint-Laurent, alongside another private school owner, was arraigned in court for masterminding the leaking of exam scripts leading to the resumption of math and physics in the capital city (Angola Press, August 3, 2005).

Le Village Scolaire (a pseudonym) which opened in the 1990s provides another example of how privatization is destroying education. This private school, with a prohibitive tuition fee, provided transport to the students, adopted a school uniform, and marketed to parents a disciplinarian approach to learning. It experienced an expansion that the owner was little prepared to deal with. Teachers were constantly under the fear of being fired by their unpredictable boss and were only paid when he thought it fit. The national government Labor Department as an institution was too pusillanimous to bring the owner to book. As a rule, the overwhelming majority of teachers in the private sector are denied social welfare benefits such as retirement pensions, social security, housing, healthcare, etc.

Teachers themselves are part of the problem. Many of them who are tenured in the civil service embark on moonlighting in the private institutions, and in private tutoring. As they teach too many classes, this lessens their efficiency, damages their health, and makes them "baby-sitters." If educators join the bandwagon of laxity, graft, and corruption, we might as well start chanting the requiem of morals in Burkina Faso.

The Agony of Morals: Corruption Running Wild in Education

Burkina Faso means the Land of Integrity and Dignity. However, it begs another name in the face of wanton corruption today. Spanning a decade or so, a spate of scandals has smeared the government. Millions of francs hoarded in ministers' homes have been stolen by their dependents and squandered in nightclubs. In its 2005 classification, Transparency International (TI) ranked Burkina Faso as a country where corruption warrants public concern (TI, 2005). The Groupe National de Réflexion sur le Développement Durable (GNR-DHD)[1] in its Human Development Report-2003 also worries that corruption is pervading education, a vital and sensitive sector. It traces the explosion of corruption in Burkina Faso to the period corresponding to the implementation of the SAPs in 1991.

SAPs have lowered the living conditions of the people, making them more vulnerable to corruption. Nominal salaries as well as their value in real terms have plummeted following deregulation, liberalization, the imposition of Value Added Tax in 1993 that would be increased from 15 percent to 18 percent in 1996 as well as other taxes, and worse still, the 50 percent devaluation of the CFA franc in January 1994. In order to avoid paying for the prohibitive tuition fees in the private sector, parents are all too eager to give bribes to school principals for their children to be enrolled (GNR-DHD, 2003).

The government has introduced an insidious semi-privatization of public education. On top of drastically reducing its financial support to public education, eliminating state appropriations to schools, and canceling nearly all scholarships for needy or deserving students (Diabré, 1998), it has introduced a de facto dual-track system. School principals are instructed to recruit students who are not entitled to government places by virtue of their grades. In public secondary schools, more than two-thirds of the students have made their way into the system using their financial clout and other connections. These students pay an official sum of money toward the day- to-day operation of the schools. Of the money thus collected, 25 percent is forwarded to the Ministry of Secondary and Higher Education to complement its operating budget. Many principals have become private for-profit providers in their own right in public schools by literally selling school places. In many instances, the shameful 'sticker price' is known. The Lycée Zinda, in the capital city, the Lycée Ouezzin Coulibaly of Bobo-Dioulasso, and the Lycée Provincial de Koudougou have several times been the epicenters of such scandals, although they are far from being the only cases. "Each student recruited that way 'brings in' 45,000 FCFA ($90.00) to 50,000 francs CFA ($100.00) and up to 100,000 francs CFA ($200.00) in the technical fields depending upon the prestige of the school." (GNR-DHD, 2003, p. 92).

The GNR-DHD thinks that the permission granted to principals to recruit in order to complement enrollments is the one to blame (GNR-DHD, 2003, p. 93.). Expanding access to school is, however, the buzzword in the official discourse and this policy is supported by the international community. To this basically flawed assistance, we now turn.

THE ASSISTANCE OF INTERNATIONAL DONORS: A BEAUTIFUL TYRANNY MISNAMED PARTNERSHIP (BROCK-UTNE, 2000)[2]

Several donors from the international community support Burkina Faso, contributing to 80 percent of the education budget. The World Bank, which has provided around $72 million in the last twelve years under the form of loans to the government, is the premier donor of the last decade (MAE des Pays Bas, 2003). The European Union as for her, has disbursed $18 million. The World Food Program (WFP) is also contributing tremendously to the development of basic education by providing food assistance to schools. Several other donors assisting Burkina Faso in the field of education are UNICEF, the African Development Bank (ADB), Switzerland, Norway, Belgium, and France. Nevertheless, the top three bilateral partners in basic education are the Netherlands, Japan, and Canada. They contributed respectively to the tune of $36.8 million, $14.4 million, and $13.9 million in the same period of time. Strong recriminations are leveled against the policies of international assistance. These policies are often lacking in "legitimacy" as they are most often developed without the actual input of the national stakeholders. Donors will do well to hearken to Norbeck Johan's advice to work with the beneficiaries of the projects, not only the political elite (Sunden, 2002).

With the tendency of external partners to develop projects where the participation of the government or other national stakeholders in crucial positions of decision making is absent, or tokenish at best, there is the risk of national disassociation with the project. Some donors will only fund projects, subscribing to priorities developed in their countries, and will not look at other donors' projects in order to balance the geographical distribution.

A case study of the education sector in Bolivia, Burkina Faso, and Tanzania highlights the lack of interaction of donors with the civil society that would enhance the support for the projects. Unfortunately, civil society

(NGOs, trade unions, and parents' associations) and the beneficiaries have not seriously been involved in the project (Zoungrana, 2001).

This form of technical assistance is not likely to foster the building of national capacities and does not serve the best interests of the populations. Faure et al. (2003) take to task the government for its readiness to accept conditionalities set up by donors. The reduction of teachers' pay is one of them.

The reduction of teachers' salaries has also always been part of the avowed plan of the World Bank and is one of the main aspects of the 10-Year Development Plan of Basic Education, the PDDEB (2000–2009), adopted in June 1999 and mainly funded by the World Bank. The World Bank is shocked at the fact that nearly 90 percent of the basic education budget is used to pay teachers' salaries. The General Reform of the Public Administration (RGAP) essentially aims to reduce wages, much to the indignation of workers. All new employees are no longer permanent workers. This subtle maneuver will make workers liable to be fired at will in an effort to keep down the wage bill, or at least this is its spirit.

While the status of teachers is being assaulted by PDDEB—unusual graft, corruption, and malpractices (in a nutshell, a mafia management of the public good)—are rife in the PDDEB headquarters. The Minister of Basic Education, Mathieu R. Ouedraogo was fired from the government in September 2005 for poor management, most probably on the insistence of donors. The audit carried out on PDDEB revealed $8 million unjustified expenditure.

SNEAB and SNESS, two education unions in close partnership, have always seen the PDDEB as undermining the educational system because it does not take into account the other levels of education. As an example, out of 80,000 students who passed the primary school certificate in 2005, only 26,000 will access grade 7 in the public secondary schools. The great majority, the 67.5% will have to repeat their classes, thus, cramming them, or will get into private institutions because of limited places in the public school system.

The minister has publicly instructed school heads to recruit all children, causing overpopulated classes. This has led some observers to see quantity as an end in itself (Some, 2006). To support their argument, the unions mention the reduction of time for teacher training, which has been cut from 24 months to 6 months in the national primary teachers' training institutions (ENEPs), the primary teacher education institutions, the multiplication of the multigrade classes, and double shifts without matching resources or fair teacher pay. Culture and language, crucial elements of the curriculum, have not been seriously integrated in the donors' strategy.

NATIONAL CULTURE, LANGUAGE OF INSTRUCTION, AND THE CULTURAL CONDITIONALITIES

The continued use of French as a medium of instruction fosters a kind of education that undermines endogenous knowledge. Thiong'o (1986) captures the importance of language in the colonial project in this fashion: Language was the continuation of the subjugation of the African mind through other means than the brutal ones of the bullet and the sword. In Burkina Faso, 85 percent of the population does not speak French and relies only on national languages. Brock-Utne (2002) would term it sheer denial of justice for the masses and a threat to the concept of democracy. The good news is that some alternatives are showing up. They have the potential to challenge the neoliberal and global order.

RESISTANCE TO THE NEOLIBERAL AND GLOBAL PROJECT

Resistance to the neoliberal and global project takes on different forms, all of which contribute to cushion the adverse effects of this apparently grinding machine.

Creative Alternatives from Below: Community versus Capital

Viable, albeit tentative alternatives rooted in the community are shaping up and indicate a more sustainable direction education can take. Communities are increasingly involved in basic issues of their children's education, perhaps out of the sense that they have been shortchanged by the too cheerful and glib pronouncement of education as a universal right. A provision that clearly puts responsibility on the community in a bottom up approach is the Satellite School Initiative (SSI). Started in 1995 with a UNICEF funding, SSI provides outreach educational services for primary school students—seven to nine years of age. These schools are located in mostly poor, rural villages without elementary schools. They are required to have a class enrollment of at least 50 percent girls (Tankano, 2000). Satellite schools (SSIs) help keep girls and boys close to their homes and culture. They are often obliged to "travel" some eight miles to school on foot. The local language is used during the first year, French being introduced to facilitate the communication in classic schools after the three years. SSIs are reported to have 94.9 percent continuation.

Equipped with double closet, gender separated latrines, they immensely contribute to the increase of girls' schooling in the country. At the end of the three years, the students are transferred to larger schools where they are credited with doing at least as well as their peers in the public school system. Most important, satellite schools aim to integrate the school and the community responsible for its management, and bridge the gender disparities.

Searching for alternative forms to the current educational system, l'Entraide Ouvrière Suisse (OSEO), alongside its partners, has also embarked upon an innovation that is worthy of consideration: bilingual education. This innovation is receiving support from several sources. The Embassy of the Netherlands, the Catholic Church, Intermon-Oxfam, the Swiss Cooperation, and Voisins Mondiaux are instrumental in this experimentation phase, in unison with the students' parents. In order to minimize resistance to change, the institutional strategy is based on a greater role of the civil society that steers the implementation in partnership with the government. Parents are involved all along the process of elaborating the curriculum and building the infrastructure. They shape the curriculum through symbolic practices: cultural productions such as tales, proverbs, traditional music, or in kind. "Thus, parents are empowered to take on an active role in the education of their children, the bilingual school being their school." (ADEA, 2003, p. 57) It brings them a sense of belonging as they own this environment friendly form of education. "Le village entre en classe et la classe va au village, c'est un va-et-vient mutuellement enrichissant."[3] (ADEA, 2003, p. 57)

This notion of horizontal community control rather than vertical imposition by the state that " . . . privatize[s] knowledge; reduce[s] wisdom into knowledge stock, a commodity sold and bought by those capable of paying for it," as Prakash and Esteva (1998, p. 55) vividly put it. They urge for a pedagogy of localization for "[t]o cherish the wisdom of their elders, the people must remain dropouts or refuseniks of the [current] educational system." (1998, p. 54)

This pedagogy of the grassroots steeped in learning in freedom "comes from belonging; from a sense of place—to which they belong and nurture; and which belongs to them, nurtures them."(p. 55) Education is little adapted to the " . . . demands of economic, technological, social, and cultural evolution." (MESSRS & MEBA, 1996, p. 6) The general improvement of the material and moral conditions of teachers and teacher trainers is crucial in this quest.

THE RESPONSE OF THE EDUCATION LABOR UNIONS

On December 1991, trade unions signed a Protocol of Understanding with the government. But as the government did not show any enthusiasm to rise up to its commitment, the Confédération Générale des Travailleurs Burkinabé (CGTB) launched several strikes. In 1993, the government organized la Commission Tripartite de Concertation (a Tripartite Bargaining Commission) that further bipolarized the trade unions. The Group of 13 comprised of 5 confederations and 8 independent unions sided with the government, limiting their militant action to a "dialogue" with the government, whereas the CGTB was more close to the opposition parties, demanding nothing less than the end of SAPs. The teachers' unions express their concerns about the disengagement of the government from secondary education and its management of the primary education that is lacking in transparence. They are also bent on improving the living conditions of teachers. If it is true that teachers in the primary, for example, consume 90 percent of the educational budget, in real terms, they are living very miserably on what is best seen as "per diems"[4] rather than real salaries. Burkina Faso has been the only country to accept an increase of just 10 percent in civil servants' salaries, including the teachers in the public sector, against an average increase of 25 percent in the subregion following the depreciation of its currency in 1994. The fact that the government is being congratulated by the World Bank as a model pupil of the Bank's should be apparent by now (Somda, 2005). Reducing the bill is the order of the day. Teachers are promoted just on paper without any corresponding change on their paycheck (SNESS, 2003).

The unions are fighting to rehabilitate the teaching profession, although the government has no rest playing up their differences. A schism appeared early on within the teachers' labor unions in the 1980s. Now, all in all, at least ten unions are operating at the basic education level comprising the middle school and the primary school as well as the secondary and higher education level; several labor unions polarize teachers' struggles for better conditions. This propensity to fragmentation erodes the bargaining power of their platform of demands. They rarely agree on a common strategy to deploy. The most visible teacher trade unions are the SNESS and the SYNTER in secondary and higher education, and the SNEAB and the SYNATEB in basic education. However, in 1995, these two unions at the secondary and higher education level pooled together in an effort to restore the teachers' housing allowance that was slashed to the bone from 50,000cfa (around U.S. $94) to 25, 000cfa (U.S. $47) in the mid-'80s. As Diabré (1998) maintains,

> [t]o attack the structural causes of the wage bill increase, the government decided to change the general rules governing the civil service in Burkina Faso, . . . [thus] automatic promotion was eliminated; labor productivity and incentives attached to performance were introduced; career civil service was limited to only a few ministries. (p. 88)

In fact, the teachers, disappointed at the government's insensitivity to their concerns, had adopted a very original form of protest in 1995. Classes were taught as usual, but students were not tested. Students in Garango in the Bulgu Province decided to protest in solidarity with their teachers. During a march where the police station and the Gendarmerie were pelted with stones, two students, Sidiani and Zigani, were killed by a trigger-happy gendarme (Amnesty International, 1997; L'Indépendant, March 19, 2003). Finally, the movement collapsed. It is rumored that money changed hands. This is not unlikely. Some labor leaders have been strongly suspected of being on a collusion course with the government, which makes the outcome of struggles against the wild beast of the global capital acting through SAPs look uncertain.

On a more optimistic note, though, all the education unions seem to have realized now that their very survival rests on solidarity in action. That is why the ten unions or so in education, alongside other unions, collectively went on strike on October 26 and 27, 2005 to demand that the government meet their platform: increase of wages and pensions, the execution of judgments passed by the court in the case of workers laid off without proper compensation, the application in the private sector of the 4 percent increase of salaries, etc. The general movement against *l'impunité*, or unpunished crimes has rejuvenated the trade union movement in Burkina Faso with the decisive participation of educators and students.

The Murder of the Journalist Norbert Zongo: A Blessing in Disguise for Civil Disobedience and the Infusion of New Blood to Education Workers

On December 13, 1998, a famous journalist and undaunted human rights fighter, Norbert Zongo, was killed at a time when he was investigating the death of David Ouedraogo, the chauffeur of the junior brother of the president of the Republic. The people, exasperated by a pervasive background of unpunished crimes, joined forces to bring the government to book. The murder of the journalist brought education workers to resist the government's actions in an increasingly united framework within organizational structures. A few days after the murder of the journalist, political parties, unions, and NGOs formed the Collective of Democratic Mass Organisations and political parties. The CGTB is a confederation to which belong the SYNTER, the SYNATEB, and the largest student union in Burkina Faso, l'ANEB. The movement "enough is enough" against *l'impunité* has had as consequences among others, an unprecedented mobilization of the national and international opinion around the assassination of the journalist and other blood and economic crimes; unparalleled information and education about civic and human rights, the awakening of popular consciousness; and an irrefutable gain in combativeness with respect to the defense of workers' rights beyond the fear of repression. The Collective is formed by political parties and associations of the civil society, such as youth and women organizations, foundations, the unemployed, widows, and students.

In October 2000, when the government "voided" the academic year at the University of Ouagadougou following a strike launched by disgruntled students over their living conditions—a measure that would dismiss thousands of students from campus—a national protest day was organized by the Collective. Opposition parties; members of the Collective; and women from the CGTB, SYNATEB and other unions organized in Ouagadougou a protest march against the liquidation of the educational system on Saturday 21, October 2000. It was deemed a tremendous success. This instance of solidarity in action forced the government to back down. It repealed the decision to throw students out as the result of the "voided" year, maintained the tuition fees at their previous level, and increased student aid, all of these laced with a long list of promises. However, as the force of the Collective wore out with time—several political parties having joined the 'protocol government' in February 2001 to share the national cake[5]—education workers lost some of their support. Yet they do not cave in to the government. All seems to indicate that workers have learned the lessons from their past inadequacies and have made up their minds to challenge the government with the struggle against expensive living cost, *viim yaa kanga*. Yet it might be too early to say for sure how effective the new coalition of trade unions is or whether the trade unions are going to surmount their ideological or personal differences and their propensity, for many of them, to hunt with the hound and run with the hare as broached earlier.

The struggle against *l'impunité* that was waged by the CGTB alone in the past thus found a favorable echo in the public eye. Already at its inception in 1987, the CGTB launched multiple actions in order to bring the government to book concerning several people killed or missing in the wake of political violence and to punish people responsible for torture, to end privatizations, and to audit past privatizations. On April 1997, the CGTB and the SYNATEB aided by the National Association of Free Unions/Workers' Force, the National Union of Information Workers (SYNATIC) and the National Union of Social Workers (SYNTAS) held a national protest day against *l'impunité* and the antisocial reforms, the contentious General Reform of the Public Administration (RGAP). The RGAP bids farewell to the open civil service and hires workers on a temporary basis. In February 1997, the same unions organized a rally at la Bourse du Travail, the trade unions' center, to castigate the repression against students, the revision of Article 37 of the Constitution that establishes an unlimited number of terms for the president, and the infamous General Reform of the Public Administration.

CONCLUSION

Education workers have been hard hit by the effects of SAPs. Yet, their reaction to SAPs has mainly been geared toward rooting out the effects of this policy rather than providing an alternative to the present educational system that has failed the populations. Stopping the privatization of schools, improving the poor material conditions of teachers rank high in the platform of demands. So far, the participation of the unions to the concertations with the government is just symbolic and insignificant, as only a few unionists are invited to these fora. The extreme fragmentation of the unions, the lack of internal democracy, and the politicization of their leadership do not bode well for long term gains. Most of the education union struggles are limited to fighting back their gains that have been eroded by SAPs. Likewise, the best the education unions can do is to unite, ignoring their differences that are minor when compared to the major, primary, contradictions that pit them against the government that has sided with the international capital to the detriment of the basic social needs of the populations. A more sustainable strategy would be to knit alliances with the civil society and international workers to allow struggles to actually shake the base of the government. As long as the actions are sporadic, a yielding launched by fits and starts, engaging only a portion of the education workers, and motivated by corporative issues, it will be difficult to fight out globalization and structural adjustments.

NOTES

1. National Reflection Group for Sustainable Development.
2. A poem by Hassen Kaynan, 1995, entitled, 'A beautiful tyranny misnamed partnership,' cited in Birgit Brock-Utne, 2000.
3. The village enters the classroom and the classroom goes to the village. It is a mutually enriching interaction (my translation).
4. A per diem is the money served on a daily basis to workers who are on a special mission beside their regular salaries. President Bongo Omar Odimba from the Republic of Gabon, replying to a journalist who wanted to know why salaries were constantly paid in poor Burkina Faso while the natural resource rich Gabon found it hard to pay its civil servants, sarcastically put in that one cannot rightly use the term salaries in the case of Burkina Faso, but per diems with regard to the insignificance of salaries.
5. Several political parties were content with some ministry positions in the government and became ruthless in the repression of the militants of the Collective fighting against *l'impunité*, the impunity. This is the case for the then ADF-RDA of opposition leader Hermann Yaméogo in the province of Bulkiemdé province, Koudougou whose militants aggressed and expelled local leaders of the Coalition.

REFERENCES

ADEA. (2003) *Etude de cas nationale, Burkina Faso: Améliorer la qualité del'éducation de base au Burkina-Faso*. Institut International de Planification de l'Éducation, Paris. [National case study, Burkina Faso: Improving the quality of basic education in Burkina Faso. International Institute of Education Planning, Paris]

Ajayi, J. F. A., Goma, L. K. H, & Johnson, G. A. (1996) *The African experience with higher education*. The Association of African Universities: Accra.

Amnesty International. (1997) *AI Report 1997: Burkina Faso*. Retrieved November 15, 2006 from http://www.Amnesty.org/ailib/aireport/ar97/AFR60.htm

AngolaPress. (2005) *Le Burkina Faso veut conjurer les fraudes aux examens scolaires*. Retrieved November 15, 2006 from http://www.angolapress-angop.ao/noticia-f.asp ?ID=330526. [Burkina Faso bent on averting cheating in exams]

ANN NEWS. (2005) *Burkina Faso: New plan for basic education*. Retrieved October 26, 2006 from http://www.africahome.com/annews/categories/burkina/EpFklkyVuuuyszGrrrrxIo.shtml

Bonal, X. (2002) Plus ça change . . . The World Bank global education policy and the post-Washington consensus." *International Studies in Sociology of Education*, 12 (1), pp. 3–21.

Brock-Utne, B. (2000) *Whose education for all? The recolonization of the African mind*. New York: Falmer Press.

———. (2002) *Language, democracy and education in Africa*. Uppsala: Nordiska Afrikainstitutet.

Carnoy, M. & Rhoten, D. (2002) What does globalization mean for educational change? A comparative approach. *Comparative Education*, 46 (1).

CNPS. (2001) *Etude retrospective sociale du Burkina Faso*. Etude Nationale Prospective "Burkina 2025." Ouagadougou:

Daboué, J. (2001) Burkina Faso : Une dette allégée de moitié, mieux gérée [A debt reduced by half, and better managed]. Retrieved August 10, 2008 from http://www.adeanet.org/newsletter/fr_latest/05-html.

Direction Générale de l'Economie et de la Planification. [National Council for Strategic Planning. (2001) Retrospective social study of Burkina Faso. National Prospective study "Burkina 2025". The General Management of the Economy and Planning]

Diabré, Z. (1998) The political economy of adjustment in Burkina Faso. The CAER II Working Papers. *The Harvard Institute for International Development*.

Dipama, B. (2003) Première Conférence sur l'enseignement Secondaire en Afrique. Ouagadougou, June 9–13, 2003. Subsaharienne [First Conference on Secondary Education in Sub- Saharan Africa]

Faure, S. D.& Freeman, T. (2003). *Local solutions to global challenges: Towards effective partnership in basic education*. Country Report: Burkina Faso. The Netherlands: Ministry of Foreign Affairs.

GNR-DHD. (2003) Perception de la corruption au Burkina Faso. Rapport sur le développement Humain-Burkina Faso—2003, Ouagadougou. [Perception of corruption in Burkina Faso, Human Development Report—Burkina Faso—2003.]

Guenda, W. (2003) Burkina Faso. In D. Teferra & P. G. Altbach (Eds.), *African higher education*. Indianapolis: Indiana University Press.

Guissou, B. (2003) Langues africaines et production intellectuelle pour la democratie et le developpement. Retrieved March 31, 2006 http://www.nu.ac.za/CCS/files/guissou.bf.

Hagberg, S. (2002) Learning to live or to leave? Education and identity in Burkina Faso. *African Sociological Review*, 6 (2).

Hill, D. (2004) Global and neo-liberalism, the deformation of education and resistance. *Journal of Critical Education Policy Studies*, 1 (1). Retrieved November 16, 2006 from http://www.jceps.com

Hursh, D. & Martina, C. A. (2003) Neoliberalism and schooling in the U. S.: How state and federal government education policies perpetuate inequality. *Journal of Critical Education Policy Studies*, 1 (2). Retrieved November 16, 2006 from http: //www. jceps.com.

Ki-Zerbo, J. (1978) *Histoire de l'Afrique noire* [History of Black Africa]. PARIS: Hatier.

———. (1992) Le developpement clés en tête. [The turnkey development in our minds] In J. Ki-Zerbo (Ed.), *La natte des autres: Pour un développement endogène en Afrique* [Sleeping on other people's bed : Toward an endogenous development of Africa] Karthala : Paris.

La CONFEMEN au Quotidien. (February 21, 1997) [The CONFEMEN day by day]. Editorial

Lefaso.net. (2005) Economie: Ces privations désastreuses. [Economy; These disastrous privatizations] Retrieved Sept. 07, 2005 from http://www.lefaso.net/article.php3?id_article

————. (2005) Liquidation de Faso Fani: Les syndicats crient à la magouille. http:// www.lefaso.ent/artile.php3?id_article [The selling off of Faso Fani :The labor unions proclaim there is some dirty business]

Les Ogres. (2005) Discours sur la "Dette Africaine" pronouncé par le Capitaine Isidore Dieudonné Thomas Sankara (Burkina) à Addis-Abeba. [Speech about the "African Debt" by Captain Isidore Dieudonne Thomas Sankara (Burkina), Addis- Abeba]. Retrieved, June 21, 2005 from http://lesogres.org/article. php3?id_article=423

L'Indépendant. (2003) Affaire Nébié: Disparition d'un accusé [The Nebie Case: A defendant reported missing]. *L'Indépendant*. Retrieved March 19, 2003 from www.fasonews.net/?opt= 14 &newsid=419.

MESSRS & MEBA. (1996) Loi d' Orientation de l' Education. Ouagadougou. http://www.meba.gov.bf/SiteMeba/documents/textes/loi-orientation-educa-tion-decembre96.pdf

Ministère des Affaires Étrangères des Pays-Bas (MAE). (2003) Solutions locales à des défi s mondiaux: Vers un partenariat efficace en éducation de base, Burkina Faso. Retrieved November 15, 2005 from http://www.euforic.org/iob. Ministry of Foreign Affairs of the Netherlands.

————. (2003) Local solutions to global challenges. Toward an effective partner-ship in basic education in Burkina Faso]. Ministère de la Fonction Publique et du Développement Institutionnel

MFPDI (Ministry of Public Civil Service and Institutional Development). (1998) Loi N0013/98/AN portant régime juridique applicable aux emplois et aux agents de la fonction publique. Ouagadougou:

————. (1998) Law N0013/98/AN stipulating the judicial regime applicable to the civil servants.

Nama, G. (2004) L'éducation au Burkina Faso: Des faits et des chiffres. In *Eduquer aux droits de l'homme: Des repères pour l'action* [Education in Burkina Faso: Facts and figures. In Educating for human rights: A benchmark for action]. Ouagadougou: Commission Nationale burkinabé pour l'UNESCO.

Nkrumah, K. (1965) *Neo-colonialism: the last stage of imperialism*. Lagos: Thomas Nelson and Sons.

Ouattara, V. (2006) L'ère Compaoré: Crimes, politique et gestion du pouvoir. [The Compaoré era: Crimes, politics and power management] Paris: Klanba Editions.

SNESS. (2003) Xe Journée mondiale des enseignants: Déclaration Conjointe SNEA-B et du SNESS [10th International Teachers' Day: A joint declaration]. Retrieved April 25, 2004 from http://www.bf.resafad.org/2003/sness/declas-neasness.htm

Somda, S. (2005) Rapport Général du Burkina-Faso: Forum syndical sur l'économie internationale, l'intégration régionale et l'économie politique. Confédération Nationale des Travailleurs du Burkina (CNTB). [General Report of Burkina Faso: Forum of unions on the international economy, the regional integration and the political economy]

Some, T. H. (2005) When private forces go poaching in the public orchard: Whither the "public" in education in Burkina and the USA? 3 (2). Retrieved, August 10, 2008 from http://www. jceps.com

————. (2006) Gender bias in Burkina Faso: Who pays the fifer? Who calls the tune? A case for homegrown policies. Journal of Contemporary Issues in Educa-tion, 1(1), 3–19.

Sundén, R. (2002) "Adult education in Tanzania." in A. Folke, N. Johan, & Rolf, S. (Eds.), *Development education and democracy: A development per-spective: Personal accounts and reflections*. Stockholm: Education Division at SIDA.

Tankono, M. (2000) Projets ecoles satellites et centres d'education de base non formelle [Satellite schools and centers for non formal basic education Projects]. Retrieved August 10, 2008 from http://portaileip.org/SNC/eipafrique/burkina2. html.

Thiog'o, N. W. (1986) *Decolonising the mind: The politics of language in African-Literature.* Nairobi: Heinemann.

TI. (2005) *Transparency International corruption perceptions index 2005.* Retrieved April 23, 2005 from http://www.transparency.org/cpi/2005/2005/.10.18.cpi. en.html#cpi

UNDP. (2002) *Human development indicators 2002: Burkina-Faso.* Retrieved, June 13, 2005 from http://hdr.undp.org/reports/global/2002

Université de Ouagadougou. (2002) *Annuaire statistique: Direction des affaires académiques et statistiques, 1994–95* [Statistics Directory: Academic and Statistics Office]. Ouagadougou: Université de Ouagadougou.

Unraveling the Washington Consensus . (April 2000) An Interview with Joseph Stiglitz, 21(4).

Zongo, M. (October 15, 2007) Enseignement supérieur: Arnaques et publicités mensongères [Higher education: Swindling and deceptive publicity]. Retrieved http://www.evenementbf.net/pages/dossier_2_125.htm

Zoungrana, C. (2001) *Burkina Faso Country Report: Increasing the effectiveness of donor co-ordination, a case study of the education sector in Bolivia,* Burkina Faso and Tanzania: Action Aid Alliance.

11 From "Abjectivity" to Subjectivity

Education Research and Resistance in South Africa

Salim Vally, Enver Motala, and Brian Ramadiro

INTRODUCTION

Over the last few years, socially engaged researchers and activists in South Africa have participated in a range of research projects in education and other areas of social policy. They have deliberately conceptualized and conducted research in and through communities where the challenges of poverty, oppressive conditions, and social exclusion are pervasive. In doing so, they have explicitly set out to stimulate discussion about these conditions and their underlying causes, to mobilize responses to these, and to raise public consciousness about the issues confronting such communities. This has also led to the emergence of stronger links between socially committed researchers based in academic institutions and community activists. It has stimulated the development and uses of research in communities, having direct effects on the accountability of public representatives about the use of public resources, and by implication, on how academic scholarship is viewed.

A number of reasoned arguments have been advanced to support such a perspective about the development of research. Perhaps the most important of these is the realization that often social research "objectifies" communities and reduces complex theoretical and practical issues to data gathering, and often produces outcomes that are patronizing and even offensive to such communities. This is largely because, especially in regard to communities that are bedeviled by egregious poverty and its social effects, research regards such communities as being in "deficit," devoid of history, knowledge, thinking and struggle. The solutions to "their problems" lie, in the perspective of such research, in some external intervention based on the advice of researchers and consultants. The latter's expertise is relied upon to make "recommendations" about the "problem." Often this means the intervention of researchers and consultants with little or no orientation to the deeper social characteristics of such communities, their class compositions, histories, languages, cultures, traditions, and experiences of resistance, and even less to their reservoir of knowledge, experience, and social consciousness.

These arguments are not to be conflated with arguments about local approaches to knowledge, as we argue later, but point to the critical importance of historical and contextual approaches to social analysis and for a better understanding of the character of such communities. They argue the importance of transcending the limitations inherent in superficial survey data and the case for richer and complex qualitative data which moreover recognizes the categories of gender, social class, "race," and identity necessary for meaningful social analysis.

While the surveys referred to in this article do not pretend to resolve the complexities of research, they are nevertheless important illustrations of the attributes of such research and its importance to historical and contextual analysis. They demonstrate both the context within which particular social questions arise and assert the importance of adducing qualitative information as *complementary* to the value of data adduced through surveys and their associated methods. Such a complementary approach is important for the production of evidentiary data that has both qualitative and quantitative attributes having value both to social analysis and practice. Not only is such analysis important to enhance theory and the explanation of social phenomena, but it is also instructive for developing resistance to the effects of social policy and practice which perpetuate poverty, exploitative and oppressive social conditions. Such approaches to social enquiry based on solidly grounded information and knowledge can also have value for engaging with the policy and decision making agencies of the state and with public representatives. Primarily though, the research relies on the assumption that it has value for the mobilization of strategies and for planning and organizing of local education and other campaigns to both inform local action and democratize issues relevant to educational struggles in communities.

A further assumption of such research is that, in order to resist the power of dominant discourses and the practices based on these, communities would need to form autonomous organizations representative of their interests and seek greater public accountability from state agencies and decision makers. In South Africa, despite the promise of postapartheid reform and some positive gains made through it, democratic accountability through open engagement about how public choices are made remains a serious problem. At this time, the almost continuous cycle of sometimes violent public protest action taking place across the country, arising from issues of "service delivery" is, despite the denials of some bureaucrats and politicians, a concrete expression of the failure of such accountability and democratic engagement.

The lack of service delivery around education, housing, health (particularly the HIV/AIDS pandemic), electricity, sanitation, and water has once again made townships and informal settlements into "hotbeds of activism;"

the Minister of Safety and Security recorded 10763 citizen's protests in the period of 2005 to 2006 (National Assembly, 2007). Out of these sustained protests, mass organizations such as the Landless People's Movement, the Anti-Privatisation Forum, Anti-Eviction Campaign, the Treatment Action Campaign, and the Abahlali Base Mjondolo (Shack-dwellers movement) have been given impetus. These new social movements have increasingly allied themselves with local education resistance. The praxis of South Africa's Education Rights Project, discussed later in this chapter, is based on the struggles of these community organizations as well as on teacher unions, student organizations, and working class parent bodies.

THE PROMISE OF 'TRANSFORMATION'— THE HISTORICAL CONTEXT

1994 was indeed an important year for the people of South Africa. It signaled the demise of the hated apartheid system and the commencement of a process for the establishment of a democratic state which was to be secured through the development of a Constitution in which basic civil and socioeconomic rights would be entrenched. The South African Schools Act (DoE, 1996), following the Constitutional right to basic education, defined basic education as ten years of compulsory schooling for all learners. This was an important beginning and signaled the intention to make education a key social goal. A number of other reforms were also signaled, both through the raft of policies that were passed to "transform" the education system and a series of practical administrative and other arrangements affecting many aspects of the educational system. For instance, the racist and fragmentary system of apartheid administration was supplanted by a system of provincial departments of education in the expectation that these would not only produce a unified nonracial system, but also improve the character of the system as a whole and lend itself to the "national effort."

The last thirteen years has seen a steady stream of reforms and a host of policies and strategies intended to institutionalize an education system of high quality. Yet these gains were hardly adequate since the challenges facing the avowed project of social "transformation" heralded by the African National Congress (ANC) in government were, in the first place, hedged in by the intractably severe structural inequality that characterized South African society through centuries of practice. This was compounded by the self-imposed limits of the ANC's agenda of "national democratic" revolution (Alexander, 2002).

Moreover, the possibilities for systemic change in education were dependent on how the constraining conditions for reform arising from outside the education system impacted on it. Such analysis required both an understanding of the broader historically engendered social pathology, and by the limitations of the very process of political settlement preceding 1994.

Without such analysis, the possibility for targeted and purposeful *social* interventions needed for genuine transformation were, as we have come to realize, truncated.

Beyond the Promise

Over the last few years there has been an abundance of data pointing to the high—even rising—levels of social inequality, income poverty, and unemployment. According to Statistics South Africa (2002), a statutory body, 27 percent of adults are unemployed. This is a narrow definition of unemployment and excludes those who have given up looking for work. Survival strategies such as employment in precarious and poorly paid work in the informal sector are not considered in these unemployment statistics. The addition of such categories would increase the unemployment figures to catastrophic levels. The quality of jobs is also declining as permanent secure employment is replaced by precarious and vulnerable forms of intermittent employment at low pay and without benefits. Many prefer using the more accurate expanded definition of unemployment in South Africa which is 41 percent (COSATU, 2006). Unemployment is highly racialized, gendered, and unevenly distributed by region. Of the unemployed, over 70 percent are under the age of 35 (Ibid). Black women and those in rural areas fare worse in comparison to men and urban areas.

Equally disturbing statistics exist in respect of income poverty and many other human development indices, including health, sanitation, and mortality. HIV/AIDS has ravaged many working class communities as pharmaceutical companies block the use of generic medicine and the state drags its feet in rolling out antiretroviral drug treatment.

The pervasiveness of this reality inspired from about 1998 the need for the reinsertion of the voice of those who felt most marginalized by the inability of the new state to address its pressing needs. This included the reemergence of community based initiatives to confront the problem of disempowerment. Examples of these attempts are described only briefly here as space and time do not permit us to come to grips with the details of what was done to conceptualize, plan, design, and conduct a community based enquiry and to critically examine its purposes and outcomes. The few examples we refer to constitute an approach to social enquiry based on the premises argued above. We regard these studies as formative and developmental rather than exhaustive explorations. A recent publication about community based struggles for social change speaks more fully about the many and accumulating struggles of researchers and social activists engaged in and with communities in issues beyond educational struggles (Ballard, et al, 2006).

The initial impetus for this activity was provided by the Poverty and Inequality Hearings organized by the South African Non-Governmental Organization Coalition (SANGOCO). Between March 31 and June 19,

1998, over 10,000 people took to the streets, participated in public hearings, and made submissions about their experiences of continued poverty and inequality in postapartheid South Africa.

The hearings were organized thematically and held in all nine provinces of the country. They dealt with employment, education, housing, health, the environment, social security, and rural development. These hearings were supplemented by background papers compiled by NGOs and research organizations involved in the different fields. The research focused on the legacy of poverty and inequality in each sector and its impact on people's lives; the extent to which current practices and policies contributed to improve conditions and recommendations on the measures required to assist groups to access their socioeconomic rights. In addition to the verbal testimonies, the Education Theme co-coordinators received scores of written submissions from parents, teachers, school governing body members, Early Childhood Development and adult education providers and learners, student and youth organizations, trade unions, NGOs, and church groups. These ranged from the carefully worded arguments of research organizations to the poignant testimonies of some of the most marginalized such as child workers and prisoners.

The hearings provided concrete evidence that the inability to afford school fees and other costs such as uniforms, shoes, books, stationery, and transport were some of the major obstacles blocking access to education. In some cases, parents or even the pupils themselves discontinued schooling as costs imposed too heavy a burden on the family. The lack of electricity, desks, and adequate water and toilet facilities in schools were also referred to in a number of submissions. Overcrowded classrooms continued to be a standard feature in poor communities. Frustrated by unfulfilled promises, many poor communities, particularly women in these communities, scraped together their meager resources in order to provide rudimentary education facilities in their communities.

The hearings brought public attention to these issues nationally and exerted pressure on government officials and politicians to reexamine and reverse contested strategies such as the government's neoliberal macroeconomic strategy (GEAR-Growth, Employment and Redistribution Strategy) and its negative effects on the promise of providing for basic needs and services. In the absence of grass roots community organizations to take forward the demands of the people, the hearings had only a limited impact. In fact even three years after the hearings, the Department of Education's School Register of Needs Survey (Department of Education, 2001), which quantifies the provision of physical infrastructure for South Africa's schools, continued to show that adverse conditions persist and in some cases have increased.[1]

A consequence of the macroeconomic strategy of the government, in which fiscal austerity was the key, saw the emergence of privatization of public services in a range of areas including education, health, housing, and even the supply of water. This was simultaneously a concrete expression of the increasing grip of human capital theory conceptions of development applied to the public schooling system and the extension of these through stringent budgetary constraints and fiscal austerity allied to marketization, 'public-private partnerships,' cost recovery and cuts to education, and other social services. These strategies were pursued simultaneously with rhetorical support for redistribution and redress, (Samson and Vally, 1996) and expressed the contradictory impact of the politically "negotiated settlement" between the ANC (and its allies), the nationalist apartheid regime and most importantly, national and multinational corporate interests. This denouement ensured the continued and extended interests of old and new national elites, albeit through new configurations of power sharing with the new elites. Alexander (2006) writes:

> Ardent as well as "reluctant" racists of yesteryear have all become convinced "non-racialists" bound to all South Africans under the "united colors of capitalism" in an egregious atmosphere of Rainbow nationalism. The same class of people, often the very same individuals, who funded Verwoerd, Vorster and Botha are funding the present regime. The latter has facilitated the expansion of South African capital into the African hinterland in ways the likes of Cecil John Rhodes or Ernest Oppenheimer could only dream . . . In this connection, it is pertinent to point out that the strategy of Black Economic Empowerment—broad-based or narrow is immaterial—is no more than smoke and mirrors, political theatre on the stage of the national economy. The only way that erstwhile Marxist revolutionaries in the liberation movement can justify their support and even enthusiastic promotion of these developments is by chanting the no longer convincing mantra: *There is no alternative*! Hence, we need to examine this particular mystification and abdication of intellectual responsibility.

Over the past few years, a new layer of cadre are insistent that there must be alternatives to neoliberalism and resistance against the *status quo* in South Africa is growing. New independent grass roots social movements have formed and are establishing continuity with past movements. They are beginning to expose the hollowness of electoral promises around social delivery and corruption. They have also taken the lead in resisting neoliberalism in all spheres of life.

Subsequent to the poverty and inequality hearings of 1998, the staff from the Education Policy Unit together with activists from various social movements formed the Education Rights Project (ERP) in 2002. An important difference with the period of the Poverty and Inequality Hearings was the presence of nascent but increasingly expanding social movements. The ERP worked closely with these movements in its five campaign areas, namely, the cost of education, infrastructure and facilities, sexual harassment and violence, farm schooling and adult basic education.

Like the earlier People's Education Movement (See Motala and Vally, 2002), the ERP's participatory research initiatives with the various emerging social movements and community organizations, is a form of social accountability. It asserted the need for civil society to have access to collective self-knowledge, independent of government, in order to hold the state to account for its policies. It is used as a social check on the state's "numbers" and "statistics," which are forwarded by state functionaries as "official justification" for its policies, and in this instance, the right to education. This critical research according to Kincheloe and McLaren (1998: 264) "becomes a transformative endeavor unembarrassed by the label 'political' and unafraid to consummate a relationship with an emancipatory consciousness." Those in the ERP initiative see their research as "the first step towards forms of political action that can address the injustices found in the field site or constructed in the very act of research itself" (Ibid).

The troubles and struggles of individuals and communities to educate their young in very trying conditions, to make the hard-won right to education in South Africa's constitution a reality, are vividly portrayed in these testimonies. In addition to collecting personal testimonies, a number of communities across the country have worked with the ERP to design tools and collect local quantitative data about the cost of schooling (e.g., school fees, books, school uniforms), violations of education rights, and basic household and community data.

The importance of such a research process is that it promotes democratic and cooperative practices in the production and the designation of what constitutes knowledge; it demystifies the research and facilitates a social and active response to complex policy issues. The outcomes of the research inform the design of a campaign aimed at improving local education. This will ultimately contribute to democratizing the debate on, for instance, the impact of government budgets on local education as communities themselves will have the data to challenge or support assertions made by the state or other organizations about provisioning for education.

The ERP deliberately chose to structure its research through a process of direct collaboration and work with community based organizations in the areas in which the research was to be conducted. Guided by this principle, initial collaborative work was carried out in two sites in the province of Gauteng. The sites were Durban Roodepoort Deep (DRD) and Rondebult. Both communities have relatively strong social movements affiliated to the Anti-Privatization Forum (APF). The research endeavor in these communities was used as a model in subsequent work with communities throughout the country.

The research was conducted over the period 2003–2005.[2] In brief, the research consisted of house-to-house surveys in the case of one site—Durban Roodepoort Deep, where in-depth interviews were conducted by local youth activists with community members. In Rondebult, interviews, focus groups, and a short questionnaire were used to gather data. Members of the community were engaged throughout the development of the research process, its methodology and design, and in carrying it out. With the assistance of the ERP, the data (in both these case studies and with other communities) was analyzed and then presented at mass community meetings where a discussion was held regarding actions to be taken to deal with the problems identified. This led, in the first instance, to the realization that democratic discussion and debate was critical to influence social policy and practice and the choices made by government. It also reinforced the view that communities themselves required the data necessary to challenge or support assertions made by the state or other organizations about provisioning for education. In the case of DRD, this led to important concessions by the state regarding the costs of scholar transport. What was realized moreover was that, until communities are able to act autonomously, powerful interests opposed to the interest of working class communities will continue to be dominant in the making of social choices and its underlying values.

Durban Roodepoort Deep (DRD), also known as Sol Plaatjie, is a community living in what previously was a hostel or compound[3] for mine workers of the Durban Roodepoort Deep Mines. The hostel is approximately a kilometer from a relatively new settlement known as Bramfisherville in Soweto. These residents had come to DRD in about January 2002 when almost 2,500 families were evicted by the Johannesburg Metropolitan Council from an informal settlement known as Mandelaville in Soweto. Mandelaville has its genesis in the Soweto Uprising of 1976. The site on which the original Mandelaville settlement was built, long before the eruption of shacks, was a municipal building razed to the ground by students in 1976. From about 1977, a handful of homeless families and individuals began occupying the burned down building. By the time of the forced eviction, in 2002, some people had lived in Mandelaville for twenty-five years.

The residents had moved from Mandelaville on the assurance that DRD would be a temporary stop on the way to more permanent and properly serviced arrangements, including housing through the government's Reconstruction and Development Programme (directed especially at poorer communities). In the first few weeks of the settlement, nearly as many people were moving out as were moving into the settlement owing to dire conditions like the absence of basic amenities—shops, schools, clinics, and transport—and rampant violent crime. Approximately eight hundred families stayed, in the hope that while they waited for the promised houses, school transport would be provided and a temporary clinic would be built. From the preliminary data gathered through a door-to-door census of 763 households in the area, the community was fairly typical of similar communities around the country, and evinced some clear characteristics such as that:

- The average household income was R894 ($1 equaled 7 South African rand at the time of going to press) per month. Fifty-five percent of households reported to have at least one member of the household in formal employment. Only 5 percent of households reported to have at least two people in formal employment. Twenty-one percent of the sampled households reported to have a member who was employed on part-time basis. This category comprised almost exclusively of part-time and casual workers—domestic workers and gardeners in and around the nearby suburbs. One hundred and twenty-six households reported that, apart from income earned through employment, they did not receive any other income.

- Just less than fifty percent of households reported to be paying for child school transport. These households paid an average of R115 per month for scholar transport. A hundred and thirty-one households reported to have a second child at school that they also needed to pay scholar transport for. The mean for transport fares for the second child is very close to that of the first child—R118 for the first child compared to R116 for the second. In other words, more than fifty percent of households paid up to R230 per month in transport fares.
- The average school fees in DRD were R201 per month. There is large variation in the amount of school fees households pay reflecting the number of children of school going age in each household; variations in school fee charges in different schools, and the fact that some households were unable to pay school fees. Seventy-one households had at least two children at school and paid an additional average of R87 per month in school fees for the second child. Households with at least two children at school paid an average of R288 on school fees per month. The foremost cited reasons for not attending school were the cost of school fees and transport.

In February 2004, the Education Rights Project, the Anti-Privatization Forum, and an education subcommittee formed by the community of DRD cohosted a workshop for caregivers with children of school going age. The workshop sought to stimulate discussion about the right to basic education, to gain insight into the community's view of the relation between education and imaginations for community development, to identify key barriers to the right to basic education, and to develop plans around local action. Most importantly, the workshop was also used to consider the methodology for community participation and the nature of the data required to investigate issues relating to the right to basic education.

The group identified several barriers to basic education. Firstly, the existence of undemocratic and unrepresentative school governing bodies was noted by many. It was reported that members of a school board of governors tended to be drawn from caregivers who could afford to pay school fees. The consequence of this is that the views and interests of very poor parents were marginalized. Secondly, the cost of schooling was seen as particularly onerous. For this group, the burdensome costs were, in the following order: scholar transport, school uniforms, and school fees. Thirdly, the use of corporal punishment in schools was pervasive. Despite the prohibition against corporal punishment, the participants believed that this practice was still common, especially in primary schools. Finally, internal community migration and forced removals exerted a negative effect on schooling. Many participants reported that their children had lost school years as a result of poverty induced internal migration from city to city and of forced municipal removal of shack dwellers by the state.

Community members also reflected on the conditions which could improve the quality of schooling. Their proposals included the construction of a school within a reasonable walking distance from where children lived, state provision of at least one meal a day for school children, and free stationery and textbooks for all grade levels. Suggestions about how to confront and deal with these barriers included the need for all adults in the community to inform themselves of the education rights enshrined in the constitution and other legislation. A call was made for a public meeting with local education officials where the community could raise its concerns, suggestions, and demands. The media was identified as a potentially useful partner both showing the poor conditions under which people lived and as a means of increasing pressure on the government to act. The group emphasized the importance of independent self-organization, mobilization, and public protest by the community itself. In their reflections in the middle of 2005, after much struggle and protest, members of the community said:

> We do not have free and quality education in this community. Whatever gains we have made for our children around school transport and the erection of the primary school is what we have fought for ourselves.[4]

> We are concerned about the safety of our children. I cannot say that we are happy about the school that has been recently erected near DRD because the fact is our children have to walk some distance to this school. They [i.e., government] must not pretend that they brought this school because they wanted to; they are responding to the pressure of our children. The reason why I do not approve of the school being outside this camp is that this is not a safe place and children can get murdered or raped on their way school. Even more important, if this school was inside this camp we could meet and talk to the people that are teaching our children—at the moment they are strangers to us. I am an old man now and I do not have any children at school. But I am still a concerned citizen and it pains me to see children not at school. Because here, in this camp, we are expected to produce doctors, lawyers, ministers . . . you name any top position . . . presidents, who can understand the situation of the poor.[5]

> I really do not think that the right to education applies to my community—because children that need to be at school are not at school

because they cannot pay school fees. It really does not matter that there is a law about school fees exemptions because schools are unwilling to implement it.[6]

I am not sure why some children do not go to school. It may be because the parents do not have money for food and therefore cannot concentrate in class because they are hungry. With regard to adults I know that many of them, just like me, would like to go to school but there is no opportunity, however, to do so in this community[7]

I think that a reason for why some children are not at school has to do with the eviction from Diepkloof. People lost birth certificates and report cards. These are difficult to get back when you do not have money to make endless trips to the Department of Home Affairs.[8]

These views of members of the community should be contrasted to the "deficit" view of a state official who typically responds in a way many community activists have labeled as callous, aloof, and indifferent:

I do not know why children are not at school. I think you should ask their parents they might be in a position to answer your question. There are buses and there is a school nearby—what more do you want from government? If they do not want to take a bath and go to school, how am I supposed to answer that question? I do not know whether or not buses will be provided for the children next year; if they are not provided I would have little influence on that issue because it does not fall under my department.[9]

Rondebult was established in 1998 as part of the government's Reconstruction and Development Programme (RDP). It is about five kilometers from Leondale/Spruitview to the east of Johannesburg. The people were resettled from an old and well-established township with schools, clinics, and shopping centers. Similar to other resettled communities, the people of Rondebult were adversely affected by the effects of the relocation. These include the impact on their livelihoods and the breakup of social networks and family relations built over many years, as well as the absence of any health care services and schools in the area. Children have to travel long distances to access schooling. The majority of people in the community are unemployed. A large number of those who are employed work as domestic servants and casual workers in nearby suburbs and industrial areas.

As in DRD, there were no schools. Also like DRD, the choice was to allow their children to walk the long and dangerous distances to school, pay the expensive scholar transport, or keep the children out of school. Here, too, engagements between the ERP and the community soon revealed that barriers to education in the area were not just limited to the issue of transport.

The other factors which militated against the right to basic education were school fees, the cost of textbooks and stationery, and child hunger.

Seventy-five percent in a random sample of caregivers reported to be out of work. Only in a single instance were both caregivers reported to be in full-time employment, and even in this case, they could afford neither the school fees nor the school bus fares. For the rest of the caregivers who reported to have had some kind of productive employment, most reported that they were involved in informal trading, or worked on part-time or casual terms for anything ranging from once to three times a week. Informal trading and domestic service work generates very little income, typically an income of between R50–R100 per day.

Ninety-seven percent of the respondents paid R400 per year on school fees. Transport fares were reported to be R40 per month for each child. Average school uniform costs per child were R200 per year. The average household had 2.5 school going age children, translating to average school uniforms spending of R500 per year. Added to this were the costs of textbooks, depending on the school and grade level, of R90 to R150 per annum. Based on this data, an average Rondebult household spent a massive 33 percent of its total earnings on schooling.

These case studies have assisted the ERP and social movements to pressure the state into reviewing the formula for fee exemptions and have strengthened the capacity of communities to organize around violations of education rights. As a consequence of massive campaigning and lobbying by social movements[10] and an intense press campaign against the school fees policy, in September 2002 a review of the Financing, Resourcing and the Costs of Education was announced. The government set up a reference group of 27 members, consisting of a core team from the DoE, and "prominent economists and managers from inside and outside government" (DoE, 2003: 8) as well as the World Bank.

Although the ostensible purpose of the review was to "stimulate and inform constructive discussion" on how government schools are resourced, the Review Report was formulated amid numerous complaints by labor and community based organizations, who charged that there was no participation by any representatives of education unions, school educators, governing bodies, or community organizations (APF submission, April 2003). In addition to the lack of participation by key groups, critics argued that the Review was not adequately publicized to encourage wide ranging responses, and the time frames for submissions did not allow for democratic processes to run their course.

EDUCATION, POVERTY AND SOCIAL MARGINALIZATION

These enquiries provide evidentiary proof about the effects of the policy choices of government—especially through its orientation to the costs of education. There is clear evidence that school fees constitute a real barrier to the right to education for poor working-class communities. Until recently, government remained steadfast about a fee policy which inevitably led to the exclusion of many children from schools. The reason for this seems to be the unbending resolve of policy makers to pursue conservative macroeconomic policies in which the choice of austerity measures outweigh the imprimatur of the rights enshrined in the Constitution. These measures, whose inspiration lies largely in the monetarist discourses, policy advice, and practices of agencies like the World Bank, trump all other considerations regardless of history and context.

The implication of this is that the right to education will remain largely unrealized for the rural poor and working class children and systemic inequalities and disparities will continue to exist for both girls and boys not only because of factors endogenous to the educational system itself, but also because of the larger and external constraints on the exercise of the right to education. Despite the greater educational access attained in South Africa, compared to most of the African continent, education inequity continues to be a fundamental and systemic characteristic of the system.

These case studies are consistent with the results of other studies and confirm the reality that poverty and poor public services provision in poor communities are inextricably linked. It implies also that reforms that are directed at the educational system alone are not adequate. The structural character of poverty and inequality cannot be resolved alone through education policy reform, including the equalization of educational finance across the system, because of the externalities which constrain the conditions for educational access, and most importantly, educational quality.

Educational interventions remain important, but are partial in relation to the social outcomes of education and the goal of social transformation—i.e., the transformation of South African society from among the most unequal societies to a more equal society and ultimately a challenge to capitalism itself. Transitionally, a broader and more purposeful approach to social reform and redistributive strategies is required, a clearer orientation to the underlying values of society, to issues of wealth and income distribution and social empowerment, and the relationship between a purposeful state and civil society.

ENGAGED RESEARCH AND COMMUNITY ACTIVISM

More important perhaps is the suggestion implied in these studies that a large part of the problem confronting such communities is the inability of decision makers to construct a proper dialogue about the complex relationship between the delivery of services and the persistence of poverty. The approaches adopted in these studies speak to their public purposes in relation to communities in which poverty and oppressive conditions are pervasive.

The second relates to how social reform policies are conceptualized. They highlight the importance of community participation through independent social movements in campaigning for access to quality education and other social goods. They constitute a critique of more conventional approaches to reality, in which the certainties of academic approaches appear to be taken uncritically, and debilitate the communities of the poor and oppressed.

In criticizing the dissonance between much research and action, Jean Dreze (2002, p. 20), a long-time collaborator with Amartya Sen on works dealing with public action by community groups in India, has this to say:

> Social scientists are chiefly engaged in arguing with each other about issues and theories that often bear little relation to the world. . . . The proliferation of fanciful theories and artificial controversies in academia arises partly from the fact that social scientists thrive on this confusion (nothing like an esoteric thesis to keep them busy and set them apart from lesser mortals). . . . To illustrate, an article in defense of rationality (vis-à-vis, say, postmodern critiques) would fit well in a distinguished academic journal, but it is of little use to people for whom rational thinking is a self-evident necessity—indeed a matter of survival. . . . It is no wonder that 'academic' has become a bit of a synonym for 'irrelevant' (as in 'this point is purely academic').

Dreze is at pains to show that he is not dismissing the importance of academic rigour but that scientific pursuit can be enhanced even further if it is grounded in "real-world involvement and action" (Ibid, p. 21).

Academic research is largely disdainful of the importance of the voices of marginalized communities and their rich and valuable experience is equated with 'anti-science,' its traditions, history, and culture are effaced from public view, and all of it is regarded as irrelevant to policy analysis.

> In effect, removing the experience of those most affected by the direct consequences of the dominant "solutions" for the problems of developing societies means a reliance on conceptions based largely on poor conceptions of issues such as poverty and inequality,[11] a-contextual theorizations and political and economic agendas to manipulate the outcomes of development in the interests of particular ideological interests.

A critique of such analyses, paraded as "innovative knowledge," raises questions about the power and relevance of particular knowledges based on such conceptualizations and about their effects on the countries of the "South" and the conditions for their democratic development. It also raises questions about the need for reexamining such knowledges with a view to postulating alternative approaches to the development of ideas through an examination of the deeper and directly relevant sources of knowledge. Such a deeper and socially informed approach would have to burrow beyond the epistemological dependencies written into South African history and search for new modes of thinking respecting "other" and contextually relevant viewpoints and concepts.

In discussions about the context of changing societies in the developing world, very little attention, if any, is paid to the importance of the experiences and knowledge that lie deep in the reservoirs of the lived reality and reflection of these societies. Even less attention is paid to the constitutive struggles they undertake to protect their communities. Yet the history of ignoring such knowledges is replete with the skeletons of failed "development" and other projects based on the conceptions, theories, and practices that are totally inappropriate for the possibilities of genuine development. The failed discourses of modernization continue, despite this reality, to be purveyed as salient to the conditions prevalent in structurally underdeveloped social formations and strong global institutions continue to put huge resources into these failed modes of "development."

Our intention here is neither to romanticize the value of local, traditionally based, indigenous or other epistemologies nor to argue the case for a postmodern discourse. Nor are we attempting to argue from a "communitarian" viewpoint which Mamdani defines as an "Africanist" perspective based on the "defense of culture" in which the "solution is to put Africa's age old communities at the center of African politics"—communities that have been "marginalized from public life as so many 'tribes.'" (Mamdani, 1996, p.3) We are also mindful of and agree with Hobsbawm's (2004, p. 5) view that:

> The major immediate political danger to historiography today is "antiuniversalism" or "my truth is as valid as yours, whatever the evidence." This naturally appeals to various forms of identity group history, for which the central issue of history is not what happened, but how it concerns the members of a particular group. What is important to this kind of history is not rational explanation but "meaning," not what happened but what members of a collective group defining itself as outsiders—religious, ethnic, national, by gender, lifestyle or in some other way—feel about it. This is the appeal of relativism to identity-group history.

We agree also with his argument that against this "endless claptrap and further trivia" of "in-group histories" it was necessary to reassert a belief in history as necessary to an enquiry about "the course of human transformations" and to deal with the problems of distortion "for political purposes" as also to deal with the claims of the "relativists and postmodernists who deny this possibility." (Ibid, p. 5)

We would add, however, that for such reasoned enquiry about "what happened" to take place, it was necessary in the first place to seek a restitution and recognition for the heritages, normative value systems, legacies, and experiential knowledges of communities which have hitherto been ignored in the construction of their destinies. It was, as Amilcar Cabral (1973) said, necessary to "return to the source" even while we acknowledge that such sources too must invariably contain the paradoxes of local and regional histories, the markings of its own internal struggles, and of its engagement with other knowledges, both the richness and the poverty of some of its expositions, the claims of social hierarchies, and the diversity of its voices. Yet this experience and knowledge, too, has an insistent right and a claim to relevance and legitimacy because of the directness and testable authenticity of the basis of its experiences.

Rarely is it understood that these voices, too, could make a real contribution to the discourse of democratic development, to finding solutions, through engaging in participatory research about the nature of the issues confronted by communities. The role of these voices as potential agents for social change is wholly ignored and this has consequences for how research is conceptualized and practiced.

Yet a number of new social movements have used the democratic space available today to increasingly create a groundswell of support for resistance around education. The praxis of these organizations is based on an understanding of democratic citizenship that speaks to people's lived experiences. Increasingly silent apathy and hopeless resignation is giving way to creative initiative and courageous attempts by young people and their parents to continue the long South African traditions of democratic participation from below as well as research that has a dialogical relationship with this resistance.

NOTES

1. Of the 27,000 schools in South Africa, the study estimated that 27 percent of schools had no running water, 43 percent were without electricity, 80 percent were without libraries, and 78 percent of schools had no computers. 12,300 schools used pit latrines and 2,500 schools had no toilets at all. In schools that did have toilets, 15.5 percent were not in working order. Schools requiring additional classrooms numbered over 10,700. According to the Survey, the number of state paid educators decreased dramatically by 23,642 while School Governing Body-paid educators, almost exclusively in the schools for middle- and upper-class communities, increased by 19,000 signaling, a decline in state funding while creating a labor market in the supply and distribution of teachers.
2. The details of the methodological approaches, research design, a detailed report of the data collected, and its limitations are not dealt with in this paper and are available by reference to the Report done for the purpose. See Vally and Ramadiro, 2007.
3. These constituted dormitory bed spaces for migratory male workers under the apartheid system and ensured direct controls over the lives of these workers.
4. Percy Khoza, community leader and school bus organizer 10/12/2005 (translated from isiZulu)

5. Tata Rabbi, elderly community and religious leader, 09/12/2005 (partially translated from isiXhosa and isiZulu)
6. Daniel Dabula, Deputy Chairperson Mandelaville Crisis Committee, 07/11/2005 (translated from isiZulu)
7. Dudu Dube, leader of a women's forum, 09/12/2005 (translated from isiZulu)
8. Percy Khoza, community leader and school bus organizer 10/12/2005 (translated from isiZulu)
9. Councillor Paulos Mahlabi, ward 17, 07/11/2005
10. The demands for a review of funding came from a variety of civic and social organizations—chief among them were civil society groups, student and community organizations, who were key in boycotting school fees; the Anti-Privatisation Forum; the Anti-Eviction Campaign; the Global Campaign for Education; the Education Rights Project; and the South African Democratic Teachers Union. It is worth underscoring the role that social movements played in pressurizing the government for a comprehensive review, particularly because their absence from the Review Committee and its deliberations is striking.
11. See du Toit A (2005, p. 1) which argues that in relation to the measurement of poverty "econometric approaches to chronic poverty are dependent upon mystifying narratives about the nature of poverty . . . they direct attention away from the underlying structural dimensions of persistent poverty."

REFERENCES

Alexander, N. (2002) *An ordinary country.* Pietermaritzburg: University of Kwa-Zulu-Natal Press.
———. (2006) South Africa Today. The Moral Responsibility of Intellectuals." Lecture delivered at the 10th Anniversary celebration of the Foundation for Human Rights in Pretoria, 29 November 2006.
Anti-Privatisation Forum (APF). (2003) *Response submission to Ministerial Review of Financing, Resourcing and the Costs of Education.* Unpublished submission, April.
Ballard, R.; Habib, A.; & Valodia, I. (eds) (2006) *Voices of protest: social movements and post-apartheid South Africa.* Pietermaritzburg: University of Kwa-Zulu-Natal Press.
Cabral, A. (1973) *Return to the source: selected speeches by Amilcar Cabral.* New York: Monthly Review Press.
COSATU. (2006) Possibilities for fundamental social change. Political Discussion Document, unpublished, June.
Department of Education (DoE). (1996) *South African schools act.* Pretoria: Government Printers.
———. (2001) *Report on the school register of needs survey.* Pretoria: Government Printers.
———. (2003) *Review of financing, resourcing and costs of education in public schools,* Pretoria: Government Printers.
Dreze, J. (2002) On research and action. *Economic and Political Weekly,* XXXII, no. 9.
Du Toit, A. (2005) *Poverty measurement blues: some reflections on the space for understanding "chronic" and "structural" poverty in south Africa.* Paper prepared for the first international Congress on Qualitative Enquiry, University of Illinois at Urban Champaign, 5–7 May. Paper ID 1–295.

Hobsbawm, E. (2004) *Asking the big why questions*. Speech to the British Academy colloquium on Marxist Historiography, December.

Kincheloe, J. L. & McLaren, P. (1998) Rethinking critical theory and qualitative research. In N. Denzin and S. Lincoln (eds.) *The landscape of qualitative research theories and issues*. Thousand Oaks: Sage.

Mamdani, M. (1996) *Citizen and subject*. Princeton: Princeton University Press.

Motala, S. & Vally, S. (2002) From people's education to Tirisano. In Kallaway, P. (ed.) *The history of education under apartheid*. London: Peter Lang.

National Assembly. (2007) Written Reply to Question No 1834, 36/1/4/1/200700232, Reply submitted, 22 November, 2007.

Samson, M. & Vally, S. (1996) Snakes and ladders: the promise and potential pitfalls of the national qualification framework. *South African Labour Bulletin*, 2(4).

Statistics South Africa. (2002) *Income and expenditure of households in South Africa, statistical release poll*. Pretoria: Government Printers.

Vally, S. & Ramadiro, B. (2007) *The social movements and the right to education in South Africa:Selected case studies from the Education Rights Project (ERP)*. Report for the Centre for Civil Society, University of KwaZulu-Natal.

12 Mozambique

Neocolonialism and the Remasculinization of Democracy

João M. Paraskeva

INTRODUCTION

In this chapter we will unfold one of the most intricate problematics in what I call Mozambique's neocolonial times—the masculinization of the democratic cannon imposed by the west. An accurate way to start such analysis is to contextualize Mozambique's current neocolonial era in the intricate neo-rightist contemporary predatory insights and practices. In so doing, we will unveil how Mozambique's neocolonial times are deeply propelled by gender segregation, within the very marrow of unionism and how adult education and higher education are struggling to win the battle for a more just democracy. We will end this analysis claiming that democracy is bypassing the poor, arguing for the need to transform the state as a new social movement, and as an alternative, to build a new just democracy.

NEO-RADICAL CENTRISM

The current New Right political, economic, and cultural framework did not come 'out of the blue.' A truthful analysis of their emergence and the effects of the New Right policies throughout the world in general, and especially in contexts such as Southern Africa in this particular case, requires examining the emergence of Reaganism-Bushism and Thatcherism-Majorism in the United States and England, considered by many scholars as the high point of the 'right turn.'

As House (1998, pp., 14–15) argues, "the Reagan administration pursued economic policies that reduced taxes and greatly increased expenditures on the military, thus incurring the largest national debt in history [let alone the undeniable evidence that] inequality of income and wealth among Americans increased dramatically." House (1998, p. 19) argues that "four Regan policies accounted for much of the shift in income distribution [namely], tax rate reduction, federal budget management, deregulation, and monetary and debt policy." This economic policy framework would dramatically affect, for example, the educational sphere. Whereas Liberals were seeking to "increase educational spending" (House, 1998, p. 19) because they thought (and defended) that "improved education leads to improved job skills, employment, and a wealthy economy, including international competitiveness," (House, 1998, p. 19) the conservatives maintained that "inadequate education [meaning Liberal education] led to poor job skills, which led to unemployability and unemployment, which led to low wages and poverty, which led to welfare, family dissolution, and crime, and to a declining national economy" (House, 1998, p. 19)—a reality overtly palpable in Mozambique's neocolonial times.

Among the political conservative strategies to 'rescue' the public societal apparatuses is privatization, or as the neoliberals like to say, the end of the state monopoly—something that characterized Mozambique neocolonial epoch, as well.

Crossing the Atlantic, Hall's (1988) analyses shows that Thatcherism aligned itself with the same economic views and political steps that undergirded Reaganism. Characterizing the political context in England before the rise of the conservative 'right turn' during the 1980s, Hall (1988) describes that both the Right and the Left were able to adopt a particular consensus over specific issues that assured a kind of social stability. However as Hall (1988, p. 37) reiterates straightforwardly "the underlying conditions for this stabilization did not exist" since, as he argues,

> the British economy and the whole industrial structure were too weak, too tied to a traditional worldwide imperial financial role, too undermodernized, 'backward' and undercapitalized to generate the huge surplus required both to sustain the capital accumulation and profitability process and cream off enough to finance the welfare state, high wages, and improved conditions for the less well-off—the only terms on which the historic compromise could operate.

Thus, in the economic sphere of "wages, production, strikes, industrial conflict, union militancy, and so on" (Hall, 1988, p. 37), and in the emergent areas of social life including "crime, permissiveness, race, moral and social values, traditional social roles and mores" (Hall, 1988, p. 37), the society fell into a crisis that inaugurated a complex phase of conflicts "that frequently accompany the struggles for the formation of a new hegemonic stage." According to Hall (1988), this was the key moment for the conservative 'right turn,' led by Thatcher. In fact, according to Hall (1988, pp. 35–36), it was a particular political conjuncture in Britain that marked the emergence of the New Right, an emergence that occurred first within the "Conservative party, and then in two successive governments of Mrs. Thatcher and the political philosophy (Thatcherism) that she represents."

As Hall (1988, p. 39) argues, the mission of Thatcherism was to reconstruct not only "an alternative ideological bloc of a distinctively neoliberal, free market, possessive individualist kind [and] to transform the underpinning ideologies of the Keynesian state and thus disorganize the power bloc," but also "to break the incremental curve of the working class power and bargaining strength, reversing the balance of power and restoring the prerogatives of management, capital, and control." (Hall, 1988, p. 39) Based on a belief in a free market and a strong state, Thatcherism conceived its strategy anchored in a narrow economic view, and the real aim was "to reconstruct social life as a whole around a return to the old values— the philosophies of tradition, Englishness, respectability, patriarchalism, family, and nation." (Hall, 1988, p. 39) In so doing, Thatcherism ended up rebuilding the common sense, but changing the meanings of particular central social concepts that underpin a just society (Paraskeva, 2003; 2007; 2008). Hall (1988, p. 40) reminds us that Thatcherism "succeeded in reversing or putting into reverse gear many post-war historic trends [by changing] the currency of political thought and argument."

As one can clearly see from House's (1998) and Hall's (1988) scrutiny, the similarities between Reaganism and Thatcherism are quite palpable and unmistakable. In both political and economic approaches, we can identify a symbiosis between neoliberal and neoconservative drives and arguments.

Understanding such 'right turn' requires being aware of a particular political context that created the favorable and 'flattering' political conditions for this powerful emergence. The 'rightist turn,' is not dissociated from the crises that the social democratic accord achieved after World War II, and "right-wing resurgence is not simply a reflection of the current crises; [rather], it is itself a response to that crises." Apple (2000, p. 23) The 'cultural center' was transformed, and quite naturally, key concepts such as 'family,' 'community,' and 'nation' was profoundly altered. Not surprisingly, we witnessed the re-creation of a new 'cultural mainstream,' one that fractured the common good and saw traditional social democratic state policies—say within education and health care—as part of the problem and not the solution to the social crises (Apple, 2000; Paraskeva, 2003; 2008).

However, both Fairclough (2000) and Mouffe (2000) provide us with another powerful analysis that describes the complexity of the most current New Right forms.

In trying to analyze the very latest metamorphosis of New Rightist policies, which push the very meaning of democracy to one of paradox because they give the dangerous idea that there is no alternative, Mouffe (2000, p. 108) stresses that both Blair and Clinton were able to 'construct' a "radical centre." Unlike the "traditional centre, which lies in the middle of the spectrum between right and left" (Mouffe, 2000, p. 108), the 'radical centre' is the new coalition that "transcends the traditional left/right division by articulating themes and values from both sides in a new synthesis" (Mouffe, 2000, p. 108). This current coalition, as Mouffe (2000, p. 109) reminds us, stresses that "the alternative to state action is a 'generative' politics that provides a framework for the life-political decisions of the individual and allows people to make things happen themselves." Thus, "democracy should become 'dialogic,' and far from being limited to the political sphere, it has to reach the various areas of personal life." (Mouffe, 2000, p. 109) In so doing, as we had the opportunity to claim, they pave the way for the market mechanisms. So, based on Mouffe's (2000) accurate analysis, one would be profoundly naïve to dissociate the impact of the attempt to erase historical political agendas such as those from the left and the right, led by the so-called 'radical center,' from the redefinition and reconfiguration of the common sense. Both are anchored in and an integral part of a strategy of (de)(re)meaning a re-semantic set of processes. Likewise, Fairclough (2000) maintains, "the 'third way' is a political discourse built out of the elements from other political discourses, of the left and right." However, unlike Mouffe (2000), Fairclough (2000, p. 44) stresses that the 'radical center' strategy does not consist only in "bringing together elements from these [left and right] political discourses." As he (2000, p. 45) argues, this 'radical center' was really able not only to "reconcile[e] themes which have been seen as irreconcilable [but also to go] beyond such contrary themes, transcending them."

On another issue, and also unlike Mouffe (2000), Fairclough (2000) argues that this strategy is not based on a dialogic stance. That is to say, the 'radical center' achieved consent within the governed sphere "not through political [democratical] dialogue, but through managerial methods of promotion and forms of consultation with the public; [that is to say] the government tends to act like a corporation treating the public as its consumers rather then citizens." (Fairclough, 2000, p. 129) Notwithstanding the seeming differences between Fairclough (2000) and Mouffe's (2000) approaches, one becomes deeply aware of the main source that is driving the current complex reconfiguration of specific key social meanings. This process aims to interfere dynamically and efficiently within the reconfiguration of the common sense, a common sense that is under, as Laclau and Mouffe (1985, p. 105) highlighted, a complex process of articulation. In other words, the practice establishes "a relation among elements such that their identity is modified [precisely] as a result of the articulatory practice" (Laclau and Mouffe, 1985, p. 105). Nowadays, following Agamben's (2005) approach, such radical centrism is showing a much more complex posture. What is at stake now is the edification of a state of exception one were the forces overcomes the law, thus naturalizaing, among other issues, genocidal policies and practices We are actually intensely facing a neoradical centrism (which is precisely the case of Mozambique nowadays—cf. Paraskeva 2003) a new form of totalism that—to use Brosio's (2008, p. 1) Marxist analysis tenaciously annihilate or demolish any kind of collective agency quite needed to "rescue society its schools from the latest, namely neo-liberal, capitalist attack on working people and the possibilities for our achieving deep and inclusive democracy" (Brosio, 2008, p. 1).

The current New Right trend, Apple (2000, pp. xxiv–xxv) argues, should be understood as a non-monolithic bloc, able to build an intricate and powerful coalition incorporating antagonistic groups, namely, neoliberals, neoconservatives, authoritarian populists, and a specific fraction of a new middle class. According to the New Right agenda, the only way to address 'properly' the crisis in a myriad of societal spheres is to expand the market dynamics to those spheres and consequently reduce state intervention. Public institutions are portrayed as failures. Although Apple's (2000) reading and interpretation over the hegemonic neo-radical centrism raise some concerns, especially when one pays close attention to realities such as Mozambique—something that we had the opportunity to analyze elsewhere (Paraskeva, 2008)—it helps one understand that neoliberal policies rely on a powerful attack on egalitarian norms and values, and the dangerous fallacy that "too much democracy—culturally and politically [is] the major cause of 'our' declining economy and culture," (Apple, 2000: 91) which is of utter importance to understand neoliberal lethal effects in secularly devastating realities like Mozambique.

Hill (2003) pushes the debate to quite different platform, however. According to him, the relation between neoliberalism and weak state is not so linear. According to him (2003), neoliberalism needs a strong state to promote its own interests. Actually, if one pays a close attention to Southern African realities, one specifically notes how accurate Hill's analysis is. Capital, Hill (2003) claims, needs a strong dynamic State, especially in areas such as education and training—fields which are deeply related with the formation of an ideological sub-missed labor force. What we do have in fact here, as we and others were able to claim (Somers, 2001; Hursh, 2006; Paraskeva, 2003; 2008) is that it is actually the State that is paving the way for market mechanisms. In essence, as we had the opportunity to dig elsewhere (Paraskeva, 2008), neoliberal imprimatur is a result of a nonstop tension, not only within the neoliberal platform, but also between the State and the market forces, and our claim is that it is precisely that intricate tension that is pumping the oxygen for the neoliberal intellectual engines.

Up to here, we have been able to unfold the neoliberal cartography, a powerful non-monolithical bloc, what we ended up coining 'neo-radical centrism.' In so doing, we were able to unveil, not only how such neo-radical centrism is deeply rooted in both Reaganism and Thatcherism, and how such a hegemonic bloc wisely imposes a set of polices which highlight a market driven society, backed up by the State, including the promotion of wider social inequality. This also the case in Mozambique today and it is deeply connected with the decline of what Trinidade (2003: 109–125) felicitously coined as the decline of the socialist experiment. However, notwithstanding its disastrous impact on less advantaged members of the population, the neo-radical centrism managed to achieve support from that majority on the social perimeter with a mammoth impact in Southern African countries like Mozambique. One of those lethal stamps is the upgrade of gender segregation. A very brief historical review seems to be important.

MOZAMBIQUE AND THE
REMASCULINIZATION OF DEMOCRACY

After some 500 years of various forms of resistance to western imperial colonization, primarily colonization wearing a Portuguese face, Mozambique was about to achieve its sovereignty on June 25, 1974. Or so the people of Mozambique thought. The events preceding and following this anticipated and monumental change in history of the country has been detailed and analyzed elsewhere (Paraskeva, 2006; 2008). Independence turned out to be a mere image because Mozambicans could not have expected that very day to be an indisputable benchmark in the beginning of the next step of the imperial colonial formula—a predatory neocolonial era that did not think twice about helping to push the country to a bloody civil war. Mozambique never was and is still not in the hands of the people of Mozambique, even though a nationalistic indigenous new middle class—with no substantive economic power and eager to copy and paste past colonial practices—seized power since independence (Fannon, 1963). As Cabral argues, despite substantive differences from colonialism, neocolonialism should be perceived as a continuity of the capitalist usurping of freedoms.

> With regard to the effects of imperialist domination over the social structure and historical process of our people, we should first of all examine the general forms of imperialist domination. There are at least two forms: the first is direct domination by means of a power made up of people foreign to the dominated people (armed forces police, administrative agents and settlers). This is generally called classical colonialism or colonialism. Indirect domination by a political power made up in part or entirely of native agents is referred to as neo-colonialism (Cabral, 1966: 10).

Thus, as Cabral demystifies, "both in colonialism and in neo-colonialism the essential characteristic of imperialist domination remains the same: the negation of the historical process of the dominated people by means of violent usurpation of the freedom of development of the national productive forces." (Cabral, 1966: 10) Nkrumah saw neocolonialism representing "imperialism in its final and perhaps its most dangerous stage" (Nkrumah, 1965: 1) as well. As he argues (1995: 1) "in place of colonialism as the main instrument of imperialism we have today neocolonialism. The essence of neocolonialism is that the State which is subject to it is, in theory, independent and has all the outward trappings of international sovereignty. In reality its economic system and thus its political policy is directed from outside." (Nkrumah, 1965: 1)

Moreover, neocolonialism, like colonialism, Nkrumah argues, "is an attempt to export the social conflicts of the capitalist countries [and] the temporary success of this policy can be seen in the ever widening gap between the richer and the poorer nations of the world." (Nkrumah, 1965: 3–5) This is actually one of the core leitmotivs of neocolonialism. That is, it "increases the rivalry between the great powers which was provoked by the old-style colonialism." (Nkrumah, 1965: 3–5) Hill (2003) accurately did not minimize the impact of national and global inequality as part of the capitalist neoliberal invoice. As he argues, "inequality between States and within each State raised dramatically during global neoliberalism [which] multiplies class inequity (influenced by race and gender dynamics) within each State developing class inequity between States (influenced by race and gender dynamics)" (Hill, 2003: 28) as well. Summing up, in both colonialism and neocolonialism, "the question is one of power [and] a State in the grip of neocolonialism is not master of its own destiny. It is this factor which makes neocolonialism such a serious threat to world peace." (Nkrumah, 1965: 3).

Since the beginning of the 1980s, Mozambique was incapable of avoiding an imperialistic New Right turn. In other words, from a Marxist-Leninist society in crescendo (following independence in 1974), the country capitulated to a neoliberal framework with all its lethal implications. It was the end of what Osório (2003) calls a "welfare state towered by a revolutionary ideology of collective nature" (Osório, 2003: 349), or what Boaventura Sousa Santos (2006) calls "the collapse of the revolutionary model and its abrupt replacement under external pressure, by the neo-liberal capitalist model, which introduced both structural adjustment and the transition to democracy" (Sousa Santos, 2006: 47). Incidentally, Nyerere (1998) claims "the world changed indeed! The withering of the State used to be the ultimate objective of good Marxists. Today the weakening of the State is the immediate objective of free-marketeers." (Nyerere, 1998: 3)

One of the implications of such abrupt replacement—among too many others—is what we called the (re)masculinization of Mozambican society. Although gender segregation has been vividly palpable over the last 500 years of crude western colonization and should be understood as an integral part of a hierarchal class and of racial western imperial colonization strategies, it has achieved a superior level of complexity during the neocolonial times. An accurate way to understand such complexity is to analyze gender discourse and practices within the very marrow of one of the most powerful examples of resistance against neoliberal policies in Mozambique's current neocolonial times—unionism, unionism leadership, and woman's access to political power. We will also unveil how education, especially both adult education and higher education in Mozambique are struggling to challenge such (re)masculinization. In so doing, we will be able to document how the Mozambican neocolonial era is (re)founding refined gender segregation. Before we do that it will be wise to highlight quite briefly Mozambique's historical developments over the last thirty years.

As Sousa Santos (2006) argues, "in the past thirty years Mozambican society has experienced a series of radical political transformations, many of them traumatic, which have followed each other with dizzying speed." What is quite important, Sousa Santos argues, is that "all these transformations occurred as ruptures, as processes, which, instead of capitalizing on the positive features of previous transformations, aimed to sweep away all traces of them and make new beginning, unable or unwilling to accommodate the immediate past." (Sousa Santos, 2006: 48) While the positive features were varnished, the negative—such as gender iniquity—continued to propel Mozambican society.

According to Osório (2003), women's struggle for power in Mozambique should be framed within two different yet related intricate historical phases. The first stage deals with the first fifteen years of independence. It was the beginning of what we call the first neocolonial era, one in which the country was completely subjugated to an unexpected imperial neocolonial wave from the Eastern and particular Asian countries (Paraskeva, 2006; Paraskeva, 2008). It was an era marked by a FRELIMO's one party Marxist-Leninist regime and a revolutionary state in which women had a subordinate position, although 'some rights were granted by the party' through the Mozambican's Women's Organization (hereafter OMM) based on women's crucial role during the armed struggle against western colonialism. The one party state blocked any attempt to promote a just democratic society (Slovo, 1989). Thus women's access to and "power occupation was oriented by fidelities and solidarities built during the armed struggle [that is] women's public visibility emerged in a context of countries liberation from imperial and colonial domination." (Osório, 2003: 354—355) Whereas the OMM congregated women's emancipatory aspirations—challenging a colonial traditionally gendered framework—and clearly had a substantive impact in society claiming for equal rights between men and women, its subordination to the party pushed dramatically OMM to a position of ambivalence. That is while rhetorically, OMM was in the front line, not only in the struggle against colonial and traditional postures, but also participating dynamically in building a new society, the fact is that, by and large, "women were cultural animators in political rallies controlled by man." (Osório, 2003: 355) Actually, the struggle developed by OMM, Osório (2003) argues, was only possible through (and within) the Party, a Party that was massively dominated by men, both in its composition and leadership, thus overtly showed gendered totalitarian practices, allowing no space at all for difference. Basically, OMM was quite far from a social movement sensible to desires and aspirations of Mozambican women. Instead, it was an organization politically and culturally submitted to the Party.

With the advent of a multiparty system in 1992—that marks the second phase of women's struggle for power in Mozambique's neocolonial period—such tensions and conflicts reached an irreparably fractured point. It was the beginning of the second neocolonial era as well, creating an abrupt divorce with the previous one in which, as mentioned before, the country was profoundly subjugated to Eastern, and in particular, Asian nations' imperial colonial interests. The country surrendered to worldwide neoliberal conjunctures, thus reducing the state intervention. From a revolutionary state to a weak state (in some cases, virtually no state at all[2] the country was experiencing new problems, new issues that were raised, new forms, mechanisms, and solutions for women's participation in society (Osório, 2003). While we are clearly facing a new set of social dynamics—OMM split from FRELIMO in 1992 and rejoined the Party two years later—the fact is that powerful parties such as, say, FRELIMO and RENAMO, blatantly expressed a "politically correct discourse while maintaining a paternalistic position towards woman's role in society." (Osório, 2003: 357) Like in the recent past, Osório (2003) argues, women's political participation not only follows the male model of power, but also women's access to political power is profoundly dependent on a particular male familiar background. Thus, women's access to power only occurs through a male position—something that brings to the fore unacceptable issues of oppression, exploitation, submission, inferiority, and inequality, not without powerful forms of resistance, though.

In fact, the emergence of a liberalized economy and its lethal impact on society fuelled powerful forms of resistance in the Mozambican society. One of those forms of resistance was the emergence of multifarious unionist cartography—completely destroyed during the very fifteen years of independence. At the very marrow of such cartography, as Arthur (2004) highlights, gender intestine clashes were impossible to hide, despite the fact that Mozambique was the only member of the Coordinator Council of Southern African Unions (STUCC) that did not have in 1993 any female representative structures within any Mozambican union. However, more oppression, more exploitation, more unemployment, more starvation, was the crude price of the new free economy imposed by the International Monetary Fund (hereafter IMF) and the World Bank (hereafter WB) to readjust countries' economies—a reality which targeted women in such a way that it was impossible for the unions to ignore and to exclude women from any serious public debate.

As Nkrumah highlights, the "result of neocolonialism is that foreign capital is used for the exploitation, rather than for the development of the less developed parts of the world." (Nkrumah, 1965: 7) Neoliberal politics, Shivji (2003) discloses, "thrust down the throats of African people, is a corollary of the economic policies of the Structural Adjustment Programs based on the Washington Consensus, mindlessly propagated and imposed by the World Bank and IMF." (Shivji, 2003: 7) As Hill accurately reminds us, "the major principle of capitalism is the sanctification of private profit mechanisms which is based on the exploitation of the working class." (Hill, 2003: 26) It is, Hill argues, "an assumption and a crude practice of class exploitation quite influenced by race and gender dynamics as well" (Hill, 2003: 26). Actually, the way the IMF maps the world, "industrial vs. underdeveloped countries" leaves no little doubt over the sanguinary link between neoliberalism and neocolonialism (Shivji, 2003: 7).

It was in the context of the emergence of the neoliberal policies and the consequent resistance to those policies that in 1992 Mozambique saw the emergence of the Woman Workers Committee (WWC), a women's union that distanced itself from FRELIMO's OMM, and that was able to gain a substantive position within a myriad of other unions, namely FRELIMO's Mozambican Workers Organization (hereafter OTM), and the Independent and Free Unions (hereafter SLIM). By 1994, both FRELIMO's OTM and SLIM were already integrated in its higher union structured women's workers committees, respectively the National Woman Workers Committee (CONMUT) and Woman Workers Committee (COMUTRA). Despite such representativity, the contradiction between discourses and practices toward a more equal and just society were quite crystal. Undeniably, Mozambique's new unionism cartography was incapable of dealing with gender eugenicist practices (Osório, 2003; Arthur, 2004), in which, obviously, class dynamics were quite towering.

As Arthur (2004) analyzes overtly, this shows that union discourses did function in two different tones. That is, while rhetorically no one dares to publicly challenge women's emancipation as an incontrovertible civic right, and rhetorically the vast majority of the unions acknowledge that women have been oppressed by the traditional societal values that considered them as inferior to men, that women's emancipation is not a utopia, and that neoliberal discourses and practices are hunting down more women than men, the fact is that mainstream union policies and practices are rapped, as Arthur (2004) explicitly desiccates, by and within FRELIMO's social theory, a theory which claimed that women's freedom (not actually women's access to power) was deeply anchored in the revolutionary fight against women's alienation. That is, whereas the multiplicity of unions and the integration of woman workers' committees in such unions should be understood, not only as a monumental break with the one party doctrinal society, but also as a form of resistance to neoliberal rapacious practices, and a stage in which difference and the struggle over equality and cultural and economic justice was (re) founded, the fact is that such discourses and practices were profoundly contaminated by, as Williams (1989) would put it, a performative contradiction or as Freire (2003: 63) would put it a gendered self-deprecation. That is, for a long time "women were oppressed and humiliated [and oddly as it might be] they assume such position and reproduce it." (Arthur, 2004: 304).

More than three decades after independence, women's access to power is only possible through male mechanisms, a reality that highlights the total absence of autonomy from Mozambican women's organizations. However, as Arthur highlights, such lack of autonomy represents a fear "which hides a panic of the emergence of new dynamics of an independent struggle for women's rights, a struggle that puts in danger a male establishment." (Arthur, 2004: 308) A very clear example of such panic can be seen by the way, for example, mainstream discourses perceptively and distortedly deal with issues related to feminist struggles and female agency toward a more equal and just society as foreign influences, foreign manipulation, a bourgeois project thus derogating feminism, a set of intricate processes, the basis of which was founded long before independence in 1973 with the emergence of FRELIMO's OMM. As Machel emphasizes, such

> ideological offensive, concealed in the struggle for women's liberation, in reality aims to divide men and women. This ideological offensive is an offensive of the capitalist society to confuse women and divert their attention from the primary objective of women's economic independence, freedom and equality in all areas of social, community, political and economic life (Machel, 1974: 63).

While this statement should not be taken out of context, it is undeniable that even after independence, women's access to and power occupation in Mozambique is still a mirage. While it is not at all easy to eradicate convoluted gender conceptions and practices fuelled over the last 500 years of colonial and neocolonial subjugation, (un)expectedly, as we were able to demonstrate, such gender segregation achieved a superior level of complexity during the current neocolonial times, thus creating another mirage—the very idea, let alone the practices of everyday life—of a more just and democratic society.

We are not claiming here that gender segregation occurred in the same way both in colonial and neocolonial times. In fact, part of that is deeply related with the very differences between colonialism and neocolonialism. Cabral helps us understand such intricate disparities. While, as we had the opportunity to see before, they both have common imperialist domination characteristics, "in the neo-colonial situation—conversely to colonialism—the more or less vertical structure of the native society and the existence of a political power composed of native elements-national state-already worsen the contradictions within that society and make difficult if not impossible the creation of as wide a front as in the colonial situation." (Cabral, 1966: 13)

What we are claiming, along with Osório (2003) and Arthur (2004), is that clearly both colonialism and neocolonialism in Mozambique should be perceived as producers of foundational mechanisms of regendered inequality, thus contributing to an unjust society. Such mechanisms help conceptualize and upgrade an androcentric class racial ethnic model of society quite important within the colonial and neocolonial strategy. Unsurprisingly, this androcentric class model of society not only intervenes decisively in women's access to power, but also determines and directs the legitimate way in which women do politics. In fact, instead of a more just and equal society, what we have is a more masculine democracy which (re)creates gender segregation on a daily basis. In fact in Mozambique neocolonial times, democracy is bypassing and avoiding the oppressed.

That education does have a key role in the struggle against gender segregation in Southern African regions such as Mozambique is undeniable as the Dakar Declaration (2000) overtly testifies. It is unacceptable, the document

(2000) claims, that in the beginning of the new millennium more then 113 million children remain unschooled, that 880 million adults remain illiterate and that gender discrimination continues to permeate the educational systems. In fact both adult education and Higher Education in Mozambique represent a credibility check to the above argument. In Mozambique colonial times the Portuguese Empire did not see Mozambicans as needing education, but rather needing to be domesticated and assimilated (Lima Vieira, 2006, p. 34) with the precious help of the Catholic church that instigated massively class, gender, race, and tribal eugenic social practices, in neocolonial times such segregation remains incontestably the towering issue. As the United Nations Development Programme 2003 (hereafter PNUD) vividly shows close to 80% of the population remains illiterate, among those close to 86% are women (cf. PNUD, 2003; Lima Vieira, 2006). Such disquieting figures are also confirmed by Action Plan For The Reduction of Absolute Poverty I (hereafter PARPA, 2001–2005) launched by the Mozambican Minister of Finance and Planning linking illiteracy with poverty. According to PARPA I, (2001–2005) the very best way to fight poverty is to challenge illiteracy by reducing it by 10% in 4 years. As Lima Vieira (2006) accurately remind us PARPA I (2001–2005) is clearly aiming quite high since we are talking about 6.5 million people in country of 17 million. As several scholars overtly argue (Ferrão, 2002; Gómes, 1999; Mário and Nandja, 2005; Lima Vieira, 2006) the interface between illiteracy and poverty (the very best invoice of neo-colonialism) directly affects more women then man. What is interesting to notice is how the vey concept of adult is profoundly gendered as well in Mozambique colonial and neo-colonial times. As Lima Vieira (2006) claims a woman's rise to an adult stage is extremely gradual, not as fast as a man's. In a nation considered amongst the poorest in the world with high rates of male emigration, where woman assume a key role in the family structure such reality is a silenced holocaust. While it is quite true that illiteracy was considered a top priority in FRELIMO's III Congress (the very first one after independence) it also true that illiteracy figures remain shamefully high, undeniably affecting more women than men. Poverty is gendered, raced, tribed, and classed. Illiteracy figures in Mozambique today are still critical (Sugishita, 2001).

This reality is perfectly evident in the filed of Higher Education as well. In fact Higher Education is another political arena where the ways in which Mozambican society is struggling to address gender equality is visibly evident, thus helping to fight the (re)masculinisation of the societal weave. In a case study conducted by Mário, Fry, Levey and Chilundo (2003) one unambiguously notice not only the herculean political task facing the Public Higher Education system in Mozambique in the struggle against poverty and enormous social inequalities, but also the frustrated tension between socialist desires and the mission of a utilitarian public university (Mário, Fry, Levey and Chilundo, 2003). While it is undeniable that Mozambique is probably the southern African country that experienced the most dramatic changes over the last 30 years, it is also irrefutable that the country has been incapable of building a more just class, gender and race Higher Educational system, one which fosters a more democratic society. One need not discuss how Mozambique's neo-colonial nightmare is deeply fuelled by a world imperial(ism) strata which continues to push the nation to a kind of dead end. With the advent of the socialist desire in the 1970's the public university to justify its existence "adopt a utilitarian stance, training human resources for what were considered to be the pressing needs of the new socialist economy" (Mário, Fry, Levey and Chilundo, 2003, p. 8). However, such aim failed to recognize how classed, gendered, raced, and tribed the Mozambican societal weave were and the role that Higher Education should have had in fighting such sagas. With the crumbling of the socialist dream and the expected emergence of the market fundamentalism mastered by the IMF and the World Bank—with the consequent abruption of private Higher Education institutions, societal aims became more and more economically driven. As the Mário, Fry, Levey and Chilundo (2003) report claims gender segregation is brutally explicit throughout the entire educational system showing a shocking figure in Higher Education. It is both interesting and puzzling to notice how The Strategic Plan of Higher Education is quite insipid with regards to gender policies. While the document covers critical aspects and addressed noteworthy aims (for instance, massification is one of the main areas of concern) the parallels with particular neoliberal claims (Mário, Fry, Levey and Chilundo, 2003) are both accurate and visible while little or no attention at all has been paid to the role of women in the new Mozambican society. Actually, in Mozambique "schools in general are not girl friendly or even safe" (UNICEF, 2008). In Mozambique's neo-colonial times the battle is one of access. Such a social saga affects more women than men. The crude reality of the numbers is quite clear: less than 1% of the population reaches Higher Education and over 1 million do not go to school.

DEMOCRATIZING DEMOCRACY—FINAL THOUGHTS

During one of our trips to Angola last year to work with central and local government and community representatives building what we conceptualized and coined as a Public Community University in the province of Lunda Sul, a campesina[3] approached us and bluntly asked a simple question: when is this thing that you guys call democracy going to end? One need not analyze deeply to understand such a question to the overall Mozambican reality as well. While it seemed that after independence the country would start a set of processes to achieve laudable benchmarks of modernity such as freedom, equity, peace, and solidarity, in fact, those points of reference became a mere fantasy for the vast majority of the population of Mozambique. It is actually quite possible, Sousa Santos argues, to characterize Mozambique's neocolonial era "as an era with modern problems without modern solutions" (Sousa Santos, 2003: 26). That is why the Portuguese left, the radical critical intellectuals claim the need to reinvent social emancipation and to fight for a State as a new social movement, and in doing so, improve a new democratic model of society (Sousa Santos, 1998). Such a prominent desire could not be confined to Mozambique alone. In fact, as Sousa Santos claims, "democratic struggles cannot be confined just to a national space and time [they are heavy dependent] of an international coordination and cooperation between States." (Sousa Santos, 1998: 68)

One of the biggest challenges facing Mozambique today—and southern African countries in general—is to democratize democracy since, as Vavi (2004) suggests, democracy has bypassed the poor. As the African intellectual (2004) posits, there is a common denominator in [southern Africa]: poverty and high unemployment. In order to democratize democracy, Sousa Santos (2003) highlights, we need to reinvent social emancipation because traditional modern social emancipation was pushed into a kind of dead end by neoliberal globalization.

It is precisely the case of Mozambique's neocolonial times. In Mozambique's neocolonial times, the neoliberal invoice exhibits, as in the UK-recalling Dave Hill's analysis—"loss of equity, social justice and economic justice, loss of democracy and democratic responsibility and loss of critical thinking" (Hill, 2003: 28). Such losses are painfully visible in Mozambique today. The traffic of human organs and babies in Mozambique's neocolonial times leaves little doubt about the lethal implications of neoliberal neocolonial effects in the country (Paraskeva, 2006).

However, a different form of globalization, a counter hegemonic globalization that has propelled a myriad of social movements and transformations, has challenged such globalization—however hegemonic as it may be. In reality, the emergence of a myriad of unions and women's struggle to access and share power in Mozambique neocolonial times is a clear evidence that some gains in the struggle against neoliberal neocolonialism should not be minimized. It is exactly within the very marrow of such counter hegemonic forms of globalization and in its clashes with the neoliberal hegemonic globalization that new itineraries of social have been woven. Such clashes, such economic, political and cultural quarrels, were metaphorically coined by Sousa Santos as the "clash between North and South" (Sousa Santos, 2003: 26), which would bring to the fore—in some realities is already overtly visible— "the wrangle between representative and participatory democracy" (Sousa Santos, 2003: 26). It is undeniable that the dawn of (an unjust) democracy in Mozambique's neocolonial epoch was something imposed by the neoliberal agenda.

We are not claiming here that the struggle for democracy in southern African contexts like Mozambique emerges only before the need to react to the invasion of neoliberalism. As Shivji (2003: 1) argues, "neither formal independence nor the victory of armed liberation movements marked the end of democratic struggles. They continued, albeit in different forms" (Shivji, 2003: 1).

As Shivji claims, the struggle for democracy "is primarily a political struggle on the form of governance, thus involving the reconstitution of the state and creating conditions for the emancipatory project." (Shivji, 2003: 1) This is important to emphasize in the light of the hegemony of neoliberal discourse, which tends to emasculate democracy of its social and historical dimensions and "present it as an ultimate nirvana." (Shivji, 2003: 1)

Undeniably, the fight for reinventing social emancipation needs a strong state. That is why the late Tanzanian president and one of the most charismatic African leaders, Nyerere, who also was deeply implicated in the struggle against colonialism in Mozambique, (in some sense, the history of Tanzania is the history of Mozambique as well) claims that African countries should refuse unconditionally the very neoliberal idea of weakening the state (Nyerere, 1998). Nyerere warns us to avoid any kind of euphemisms between strong and totalitarian state, as he argues "in advocating a strong State, I am not advocating an overburdened State (. . .) so a call for a strong State is not a call for (a) dictatorship." (Nyerere, 1998: 3)

Somehow we are clearly before what Sousa Santos (1998) coined as a State that should be seen as a spotless new social movement. That is, "a more vast political organization in which the democratic forces will struggle for a distributive democracy, thus transforming the state in a new—yet powerful— social and political entity." (Sousa Santos, 1998: 60) Such a State is "even much more directly involved in redistribution criteria, and profoundly committed with economic and cultural inclusive policies." (Sousa Santos, 1998: 60) It is actually such a State—as a spotless new social movement—Sousa Santos argues, "that will reawaken the tension between capitalism and [real] democracy, and this can only be achieved if democracy is conceived and plasticized as redistributive democracy." (Sousa Santos, 1998: 61)

Such a perspective will challenge western neocolonial lethal and xenophobic prescriptions for undeveloped countries such as good governance, which was deeply criticized by Nyerere, when he attended a 1998 meeting of the Global Coalition for Africa (hereafter GCA) in Harare, Zimbabwe, chaired by the former president of Botswana, Ketumile Masire. According to Nyerere (1998), good vs. bad governance should be recognized as a political ideological construction that propels unacceptable concepts and practices such as "the deserving poor," something that cleverly attempts to hide, not only an absence of international welfare from the most powerful nations, but also the connection between good governance and neoliberalism. That is to say that good governance is a conceptual imperial construction created and promoted by "the industrialized market economy countries of the North" (Nyerere, 1998: 2), tied to frameworks such as economies based "on the principle of private ownership and of international free trade and a good record of human rights." (Nyerere, 1998: 2) In other words, Shivji claims, good governance "is constructed primarily on the terrain of power" (Shivji, 2003: 5), despite the fact that the good governance pastoral, "does not admit of the relationships of power." (Shivji, 2003: 5)

As Rodney (1973) highlights, underdevelopment has been wisely interwoven with economic equations. However, Rodney argues, "if underdevelopment were related to anything other than comparing economies, then the most underdeveloped country in the world would be the U.S.A, which practices external oppression on a massive scale, while internally there is a blend of exploitation, brutality, and psychiatric disorder." (Rodney (1973: 12)

In brief, "good governance [sounds] like a tool of neocolonialism" (Nyerere, 1998: 2), Nyerere (1998) challenges imperial colonial and neocolonial powers before what he calls "the ignored truth." According to Nyerere, "all the institutions and processes of democracy and democratic administration cost a great deal of money to establish, to maintain, and to operate." (Nyerere, 1998: 5) It is the only way for African countries, providing that they accepted that "democracy means much more than voting on the basis of adult suffrage every few years; it means (among other things) attitudes of toleration, and willingness to cooperate with others on terms of equality." (Nyerere, 1998: 5)

Thus, democratizing democracy implies challenging notions and practices labelled in the trapped dichotomy of good vs. bad government, and in so doing fighting for the very idea of a new democracy. This dichotomy turns out "to be profoundly a discourse of domination rather than that of liberation and democracy." (Shivji, 2003: 9) Such new democracy, Shivji stresses, exhibits three crucial elements: popular livelihoods, popular power, and popular participation (Shivji, 2000).

At the very core of Mozambique's sovereignty is the struggle for a more just and democratic society in which class, gender, racial and ethnic justice, and equality are structural. As argued by Shivji,

> the great democratic struggles of the African people expressed in their independence and national liberation movements remain incomplete. A so-called democracy constructed on ahistorical and asocial paradigms of neo-liberalism are an expression of renewed imperial onslaught, which is profoundly anti-democratic. It may as well proclaim: Democracy is dead. Long live democracy. (Shivji, 2003: 10)

Such new democracy implies "new democratic struggles for a redistributive democracy, which are in fact anti-fascist struggles, [since unfortunately] fascism is not a threat, but a burden, a reality" (Sousa Santos, 1998: 63), [a reality] that becomes irreversibly poisonous, when in particular contexts, like Mozambique, it breathes and wears the mask of democracy. Thus, the struggle for a redistributive democracy is the very first crucial step to reinforce the State's role in a more just society—converting the state into a spotless new social movement. It is, actually in this sense, that along with Sousa Santos (1998), we claim socialism as an endless democracy, and as the very best alternative for Mozambique as well. The task of committed intellectuals, Shivji argues, is "to recognize the new imperialism called globalization and articulate the ideologies of resistance expressed in popular struggles." (Shivji, 2003: 10) Perhaps in so doing we will be able to rescue the most substantive arguments of one of the most crucial southern African political moments—the Arusha Declaration—namely, "that all human beings are equal; that in order to ensure economic justice, the state must have effective control over the principal means of production, and that it is the responsibility of the state to intervene actively in the economic life of the nation so as to ensure the well-being of all citizens, and so as to prevent the exploitation of one person by another or one group by another, and so as to prevent the accumulation of wealth to an extent which is inconsistent with the existence of a classless society." (Nyerere, 1967: 2)

This declaration created the foundation for a set of policies that established the principles of socialism—not only for Tanzania, but for southern Africa—based on an absence of exploitation, the major means of production and exchange under the control of the peasants and workers, the existence of democracy and having socialism as a belief.

The task is to reinvent daily how to democratize democracy. Probably a new struggle has, in fact, to begin. Lumumba's vision maintains its relevance: "Together, my brothers, my sisters, we are going to begin a new struggle, a sublime struggle, which will lead our country to peace, prosperity, and greatness." (Lumumba, 1960: 1) This is the best way, as the Mozambican writer Couto claims, that we have to challenge a past that was wrongly wrapped and portrayed in a deformed way, a present dressed with borrowed clothes and a future ordered already by foreign interests." (Couto, 2005: 10) Wisely, one should not choose money as 'the' weapon, because, as Nyerere argues, "the development of a country is brought about by people, not by money." (Nyerere, 1967: 129)

NOTES

1. I am indebted to Donaldo Macedo, Jurjo Torres Santomé, David Hursh, and Zainul Sajan Virgi for some of their critical insight over some of the arguments portrayed here.
2. As an example, customs, in Mozambique's neocolonial times, is in the hands of a British private company that paradoxically owns a trading company which import and exports goods.
3. A peasant.

REFERENCES

Action Plan for the Reduction of Absolute Poverty I (PARPA) (2001—2005). *Plano de Acção para a Redução da Pobreza Absoluta (2000–2004)*, Ministério do Plano e Finanças. Maputo: Quarto Press.

Agamben, G. (2005) *The State of Exception*. Chicago: The University of Chicago Press.

Apple, M. (2000) *Official knowledge: Democratic education in a conservative age*. New York: Routledge.

Arthur, M. (2004) Fantasmas que Assombram os Sindicatos. Mulheres Sindical-izadase as Lutas pela Afi rmação dos seus Direitos, Moçambique, 1993–200. In Boaventura Sousa Santos (org.) *Reconhecer para Libertar. Os Caminhos do Cosmopolitismo Multicultural*. Porto: Edições Afrontamento, pp., 295–326.

Brosio, R.(2008) *Marxist Thought: Still Primus Inter Pares for Understanding and Opposing the Capitalist System*. Journal for Critical Education Policy Studies Volume 6, Number 1, Retrieved August 2008 http://www.jceps.com/?pageID=article&articleID=113.

Cabral, A. (1966) *The weapon of theory. Marxism and Anti-imperialism in Africa* Retrieved December 2006 from www.marxists.org.

Couto, M. (2005) *Pensatempos*. Lisboa: Caminho.

Declaração de Dakar (2000). *Declaração de Dakar Texto Adoptado pela Cúpula Mundial de Educação* Dakar, Senegal. Dakar: Senegal, 26—28 April. Retrieved July 2008 http://www.interlegis.gov.br/processo_legislativo/copy_of_20020319 150524/20030620161930/20030623111415/view.

Fairclough, N. (2000) *New labor, new language?* London: Routledge.

Fannon, F. (1963) *The wretched of the Earth*. London: Penguin.

Ferrão, V. (2002) *Compreender Moçambique: política, economia e factos básicos*. Maputo, Moçambique: Editora Escolar.

Freire, P. (2003) *Pedagogy of the oppressed*. New York: Continuum.

Gómes, M. B.(1999) *Educação Moçambicana: Historia de um Processo: 1962–1984*. Maputo, Moçambique: Livraria Universitária. Universidade Eduardo Mondlane.

Hall, S. (1988) The toad in the garden: Thatcherism among theorists. In. C. Nelson and L. Grossberg (eds.) *Marxism and the interpretation of culture*. Urbana: University of Illinois Press, pp., 35–57.

Hill, D. (2003) O neo-liberalismo global, a resistência e a deformação da educação. *Revista Currículo sem Fronteiras*, 3(2), pp., 24–59. Retrieved in December 2006 from www.curriculosemfronteiras.org.

House, E. (1998) *Schools for $ale: Why free markets won't improve America's schools, and what will*. New York: Teachers College Columbia University.

Hursh, D. (2006) Democracia sitiada. Capitalismo global, neoliberalismo e educação. In J. Paraskeva, W. Ross e D. Hursh (orgs) *Marxismo e educação* Volume 1, Porto: Profedições, pp., 155–192.

Laclau, E. & Mouffe, C. (1985) *Hegemony and socialist strategy: Toward a radical democratic politics*. London: Verso.

Lima Vieira, M. A. (2006) *Educação de Adultos, Analfabetismo e Pobreza em Moçambique*. Piracicaba: Universidade Metodista de Piracicaba.

Lumumba, P. (1960) *Independence day. Marxism and anti-imperialism in Africa*. Retrieved December 2006 from www.marxists.org.

Machel, S. (1974) *A Libertação da Mulher é uma Necessidade da Revolução, Garantia da sua Continuidade, Condição do seu Triunfo*. Maputo: Edições da Frelimo.

Mário, M. Fry, P. Levey, L. and Chilundo, A. (2003) *Higher Education in Mozambique. A Case Study*. Maputo: Imprensa e Livraria Universitária: Universidade Eduardo Mondlane.

Mário, M. and Nandja, D. (2005) A alfabetização em Moçambique: desafios da educação para todos. Background paper prepared for the education for all global monitoring report 2006. Literacy for life. UNESCO.

Mouffe, C. (2000) *The democratic paradox*. London: Verso.

Nkrumah, K. (1965) *Neo-colonialism, the last stage of imperialism. Marxism and anti-imperialism in Africa*. Retrieved December 2006 from www.marxists.org

Nyerere, J. (1967) *The Arusha declaration. Marxism and anti-imperialism in Africa*. Retrieved December 2006 www.marxists.org.

————. (1998) *Good governance for Africa. Marxism and anti-imperialism in Africa.* Retrieved December 2006 from www.marxists.org.

Osório, C. (2003) Poder Político e Protagonismo Feminino em Moçambique. In Boaventura de Sousa Santos (org.) *Democarizar a Democracia—Os caminhos da Democracia Participativa.* Porto: Edições Afrontamento, pp., 349–372.

Paraskeva, J. (2003) [Des]escolarização: Genotexto e Fenotexto das Políticas Curriculares Neo-liberais. In Jurjo Torres Santomé, João Paraskeva e Michael Apple. *Ventos de Desescolarização. A Nova Ameaça à Escolarização Pública.* Lisboa: Edições Plátano, pp., 57–115.

————. (2006) Portugal will always be an African nation: a Calibanian prosperity or a prospering Caliban? In Donaldo Macedo and Panayota Gounari (eds.) *The globalization of racism.* Boulder: Paradigm Publishers.

————. (2007) Kidnapping public schooling: perversion and normalization of the discursive bases within the epicenter of New Right educational policies. *Policy Futures in Education,* 5(2), pp. 137–159.

————. (2008) *Here I stand a long [r]evolution.* Rotterdam: Sense Publishers.

Rodney, W. (1973) *How Europe undeveloped Africa. Marxism and anti-imperialism in Africa.* Retrieved December 2006 from www.marxists.org

Shivji, I. (2000) Critical elements of a new democratic consensus in Africa. In O. Othman & M. Halfani (eds.) *Reflections on leadership in Africa Forty years after independence.* Brussels: VYB University Press.

————. (2003) *The struggle for democracy. Marxism and anti-imperialism in Africa.* Retrieved December 2006 from www.marxists.org

Slovo, J. (1989) *Has socialism failed? Marxism and anti-imperialism in Africa.* Retrieved December 2006 from www.marxists.org

Somers, M. (2001) *Romancing the market, reviling the state: the politics and knowledge of civil society and the public sphere. From political economy to neoliberalism.* A.E. Havens Center for the Study of Social Structure and Social Change. Madison: University of Wisconsin—Madison.

Sousa Santos, B. (1998) *Reinventar a democracia.* Lisboa: Gradiva.

————. (2003) Prefácio. In Boaventura de Sousa Santos (org.). *Democarizar a Democracia—Os caminhos da Democracia Participativa.* Porto: Edições Afrontamento, pp., 25–33.

————. (2006) Legal pluralism in Mozambique. *Law & Society Review,* 40(1), pp., 39–75.

Sugishita, K. (2001) Avaliação de Programas de Educação de Adultos e Não Formal em Moçambique. Operations Evalutaion Department. The World Bank. Retrieved, July 2008. http://www1.worldbank.org/education/adultoutreach

Trindade, J. C. (2003) Rupturas e Continuidades nos Processos Políticos e Jurídicos. In Boaventura de Sousa Santos e João Carlos Trindade (orgs.) *Conflito e Transformação Social: Uma Paisagem das justiças em Moçambique.* Porto: Edições Afrontamento. pp., 97—127.

UNICEF (2008) Mozambique. Education. The picture. UNICEF Retrieved July 2008 http://www.unicef.org/mozambique/education_2043.html.

United Nations Development Programme (PNUD) (2003). Retrieved July 2008 www.undp.org.

Vavi, Z. (2004) *Democracy has by-passed the poor. Marxism and anti-imperialism in Africa.* Retrieved December 2006 from www.marxists.org.

Williams, R. (1989) *Resources of hope.* London: Verso.

13 From the State to the Market?

China's Education at a Crossroads

Ka Ho Mok and Yat Wai Lo

INTRODUCTION

In the last two decades, China has experienced significant economic transformations and social changes. The economic reforms which started in the late 1970s have unquestionably enabled some social groups to become wealthy, but the same processes have also widened the gap between the rich and the poor, as well as intensified regional disparities in China (Keng, 2006; Weil, 2006). Most significant of all, embracing the market economy has led to the growing prominence of ideas and strategies along the lines of neoliberalism in reforming not only the economic sector, but also public sector management and social policy delivery (Wong & Flynn, 2001; So, 2006). Having been influenced by the global trends of privatization, marketization, and commodification of education, China has appropriated neoliberal policies, and far more pro-competition policy instruments have been adopted to reform and restructure its education (Min, 2004). As depending upon state financing and provision alone will never satisfy the growing demands for higher education, China has therefore increasingly looked to the market/private sector and other non-state sectors to venture into education provision, hence diversifying education services and proliferating education providers.

It is against such a wider socioeconomic background that the private/ *minban* education sector has paid for much of the education expansion, leading to revolutionary changes and imparting a growing "privateness" to China's education system (Mok, 2008). Obviously, the adoption of pro-competition policy instruments along the lines of privatization, marketization, and commodification in transforming the social service delivery, together with the adherence to the neoliberal ideas of governance, have further intensified social inequality and deepened the crises of regional disparities (UNDP, 2005). This chapter sets out in the wider policy context outlined above to examine how China's education has been transformed, especially when far more pro-competition and market oriented reform measures are adopted. With particular reference to the intensified inequalities in education, this chapter will also examine how the Chinese government has made attempts to address the problems that have resulted from the marketization of education in the last two decades.

PART ONE: EMBRACING NEOLIBERALISM: EDUCATIONAL RESTRUCTURING IN POST-MAO CHINA

The Changing State Role in Education and the Growth of Individual Contributions

Since the late 1970s, the open-door policy and economic reforms have transformed the highly centralized planning economy into a market oriented and more dynamic economy. By then, Chinese economy has had significant and consistent growth with an average rate of 9–10 percent annually. Nonetheless, the total allocation of government fund on education has been repeatedly reported low. In 1995, only 2.41 percent of GDP was allocated to education, it was slightly improved by increasing to 2.79 percent and 3.22 percent in 1999 and 2002 respectively. But state education financing declined again in 2005 with only around 2.79 percent of GDP being allocated to education (see Table 13.1). Most recently, even the State Council of the People's Republic of China has openly recognized insufficient government funding being allocated to education. In this connection, the 11th Five-Year Plan (2006–2010) calls on governments at all levels to make the development of education a strategic priority and "to commit to a public education system that can be accessed by all" (cited in Li, 2007, p.8).

Table 13.1 Public Education Expenditure as a Percent of GDP

Year	Goss Domestic Product	Government Appropriation for Education	Percentage (%)
1992	2,663.8	72.9	2.74
1995	5,847.8	141.2	2.41
1999	8,206.8	228.7	2.79
2000	8,946.8	256.3	2.86
2001	9,731.5	305.7	3.14
2002	10,517.2	349.1	3.32
2003	11,739.0	385.1	3.28
2004	15,987.8	446.6	2.79

unit: billion *yuan*
Sources: NBSC, 2005
Note: Government appropriation for education includes the expenditure of central and local governments on education.

With reductions in state financing in education, local governments and individual education institutions have attempted to increase the student intakes and tuition fees in order to generate additional revenues for financing educational developments and improving teachers' incomes. Some local education ministries and individual schools/higher education institutions have charged unreasonable fees from students in recent years. According to Yang Dongping, one of the leading education policy analysts in mainland China, the fee charging situation at the basic education level has become worse since the students and parents have been asked to pay more for education. Comparing the total fees being contributed by parents among 50 counties in 2002 with that of the previous year, it recorded about 7.8 percent increase. The same study also reports that among these 50 counties, 45 of them were blamed for overcharging students and parents for education related fees (Yang, 2004).

Given that similar problems can be easily found in other places in the mainland, what really worries us is that many more concrete live cases have been reported that suggest Chinese citizens have to bear higher school and university fees. Despite the fact that free education at the elementary level is regarded as a constitutional right for Chinese citizens, it has been widely reported that public schools charge different kinds of fees and hence create an additional financial burden on parents. The press recently reported that many students in Beijing could not afford to pay the excessive fees charged by the public school. It was reported that public schools generally charge 300 *yuan* to 500 *yuan* for one semester, and parents are requested to pay a miscellaneous fee, ranging from the amount of 600 to 1,000 *yuan* (*China Daily*, 26 August 2006, p.5). Similarly, with the continual decline in the central government's allocations, the higher education sector relies heavily upon the financial support from local governments and individual contributions. Coinciding with "multiple channels" in financing, the state describes the use of a mixed economy of welfare as a "multiple-channel" (*duoqudao*) and "multi-method" (*duofangfa*) approach to the provision of educational services during the "primary state of socialism" (*shehui zhuyi chuji jieduan*), indicating a diffusion of responsibility from the state to society (Mok, 1996; Cheng, 1990). The introduction of a "fee-paying" principle has significantly affected higher education financing in China. Before the 1990s, the number of fee paying students was only a very tiny group, but now all university students have to pay tuition fees and the user pays principle has been made the foundation of Chinese education. According to Wang (2007), China now faces a new equity issue in education, especially when students have to pay at least 7,000 yuan annually for higher education. Paying for such an amount would cost thirty-five years of income of ordinary peasants in rural China. Hence, the most recent yearbook compiled by the Chinese Academy of Social Sciences reports that spending on education was ranked sixth on a list of serious public concerns by Chinese citizens in 2006, with school bills gobbling up more than 10 percent of the average household budget on Mainland China (*Bluebook of Chinese Society*, 2007). Not surprisingly, the above reported cases have only shown the tip of the iceberg of the problems of overcharging school fees. There are many more stories suggesting that public schools in China have charged excessive fees, hence we can make sense of why Chinese residents have recently regarded education expenditures as one of the big "mountains" (heavy financial burden) to them (Zhu, 2005; Yang, 2005).

In addition, there is a strong belief that getting degrees in western universities can bring their children a brighter future. Hence, a growing number of families in urban China have tried very hard to send their children to study abroad. According to the Chinese Service Centre for Scholarly Exchange of the Ministry of Education, more than 100,000 students have chosen to study overseas since 2002 although they have to pay high tuition and living expenses. With the massification of higher education since the late 1990s, university graduates in China have found difficulties in getting employment. Therefore, pursuing higher degrees overseas has become increasingly popular with intentions to differentiate themselves in the highly competitive labor market. As statistics released by the Chinese Service Centre for Scholarly Exchange has shown, 71.3 percent of graduates returning from study overseas have found jobs within six months, and 32.7 percent of them have secured employment in foreign companies. Noticing these positive figures, many Chinese parents are becoming eager to send their children to study abroad. Nonetheless, the choice to send their children to study overseas would mean parents have to endure hardship in securing sufficient money to pay for their children's education (*China Daily*, 28 February 2007, p.20).

As Cummings (1996) suggests, education under the influence of traditional Asian values is a matter not for the individual but for the family. The reason behind this is that a tertiary student in China is obligated to carry the hopes of an entire family. This is a deeply rooted traditional value, which has formulated a strong mindset favoring learning and education commonly shared among Chinese people no matter where they live in rural or urban areas. Nonetheless, Yin Jianli, a researcher with Beijing-based NGO Western Sunshine Action, recently pointed out that "the initial elation of a university offer quickly turns into frustration for many rural families because supporting a college student can plunge them into dire straits." (quoted from Li, 2007, p. 8) According to recent reports, for those students coming from lower socioeconomic backgrounds, even though they have got excellent results in the national college entrance examinations, they are deprived of the opportunity to receive higher education simply because their families are not able to pay for the education expenses. A recent news reporting a very sad story that the father of Chen Yi, one of the top students in class in Shanxi, committed suicide out of shame in June 2006 because he was financially unable to send his son to university despite the fact that his son had passed in the national college entrance examinations (Li, 2007). Putting the above observations together, it is clear that pursuing education has caused tremendous financial and psychological pressures on many families (in both urban and rural China) today (Mok, Wong and Walker, 2008).

Proliferating Education Providers and the Rise of Private/*Minban* Sectors

Another prominent change resulting from the adoption of the neoliberalist approach in education is the growing prominence of the "privateness" in China's higher education. In 1998, there were around 50,000 private/*minban* education institutions at various levels, approximately recruiting around 10.66 million students. Under the support of government initiatives, the number of private/*minban* education institutions has reached over 70,000, which recruit 17.69 million students in 2004 (*China Education Yearbook*, 1999; 2005).

The rise of private/*minban* sectors in China's education has developed a hybrid of public and private. In addition to those schools run by non-state sectors and actors, public schools in China have undergone a process of privatization and marketization, by which these public education institutions are no longer entirely public in nature but are classified as *gouyou minban* (state owned and people run), which means that schools remain under government ownership, but the proportion of finance from the private/nonstate sector is increased mainly through charging tuition fees (Mok, 2005). This policy of transformation (*zhuanzhi*) has provided a higher degree of autonomy regarding school management, especially in terms of personnel and finance. Under the new management framework, school teachers no longer enjoy an "iron rice bowl" and they may be dismissed because of underperformance in these privatized public schools. Nonetheless, these schools can offer financial incentives to reward the teaching staff with good performance (Shanghai Research Institute of Educational Sciences, 2005). In the higher education sector, *gouyou minban* institutions are named second tier colleges, which refer to the extension arms of public (national) universities. Similarly, these colleges are run as "self-financing" entities and operated in terms of "market" principles. Considering conventional *minban* schools and colleges lacking "self-discipline" and posing difficulties for management, these kinds of publicly owned but privately run institutions are established as alternatives for achieving the policy objectives of expanding enrollment rates of education (Mok & Ngok, 2008). Despite queries about the legitimacy of the rising for-profit nature of the *gouyou minban* institutions in the society, *minban* education has become an inevitable trend in China, particularly with the increase in the number of "quasi *minban*" institutions. Recent statistics show that over 1,000 public schools have applied this "privatized" running mechanism by 2004 (Lin & Chen, 2004, p. 46). In 2005, there were 344 second tier colleges throughout China, enrolling 540,000 undergraduate students (Chen & Yu, 2005, p. 167).

Putting the above discussions together, it is clear that China's higher education has become far more diversified, especially when the sector has been going through the processes of proliferation of providers, diversification of financing, and marketization of education against the decentralization policy environment. Despite the fact that the growing prominence of privateness in higher education has created more learning opportunities for Chinese citizens, such transformations along the lines of a neoliberalist approach have also resulted in educational inequality, regional disparity and social injustice in post-Mao China.

CULTURAL EXPECTATIONS AND THE COMMERCIALIZATION OF EDUCATION

Another major impact of neoliberalism on China's education is the growing trend of the commercialization of education. It is beyond doubt that economic reforms started since the late 1970s have created favorable conditions for the commercialization of education in China. Today, parents in urban China have an obsession of giving their children the best education despite the overwhelming financial burdens. Parents' obsession with children's education has facilitated the emergence of after school education, which has become an important indicator of the commercialization of China's education. In order to prepare their children for the competitive globalizing world, Chinese parents consider that learning English is very important for the future of their children. It is particularly true when most urban families are allowed to have a single child under the one child population policy. Believing that the mastery of English could enable their children to have a brighter career future, a growing number of parents have tried to send their children for private tutoring classes or private English schools to learn the language. In addition to academic performance, Chinese parents are increasingly concerned about whether their children could master a wide variety of skills. Equipping their children with special skills has become a popular trend in China, especially when these artistic or athletic skills can count as part of their entrance exam scores, thereby giving them a better chance of getting into prestigious universities. Xiao Di, a grade two pupil in a primary school in Beijing, is scheduled to have after school classes in music, mathematics, English, piano and dance from Friday evening to Sunday, which obviously occupies her whole weekend. Indeed, a success story in the neighborhood can push many parents to become more eager to send their children to after school classes. As a consequence, many parents in China are prepared to pay additional costs in order to send their children to after school classes as well as to hire the best high school teachers to give private tutoring to their children, especially when it comes to the final run-up to the university entrance examinations (*China Daily*, 27 March, 2004; 5 June, 2007).

In response to this phenomenon of overloading children, the Chinese governments have made attempts to reduce the pressures for drilling students for examinations and tests as well as extracurricular activities. The Ministry of Education, for example, requests parents to stop enrolling their children in extracurricular courses and requesting schools to limit daily homework to one hour (*China Daily*, 5 June, 2007). Despite the good intentions of the new policies, there is ongoing debate about the proposed changes among parents. Without changing their mentality and mindsets, students who have more time after school are sent to study in various training classes and with private teachers outside school to improve their performance in a wide range of subjects. Fearing that their children would lag behind, many parents have tried very hard to pay for private tutoring in order to make their children more competitive (*China Daily*, 23 March 2007, p.5). After analyzing the above social phenomenon, Hong Chengwen, a pedagogy specialist at Beijing Normal University, argues that such a phenomenon is closely associated with the Confucian emphasis on education and traditional family values. Indeed, after school education is not only popular in China, but also in other countries within the "Confucian cultural sphere" (*China Daily*, 27 March, 2004). In short, the deeply rooted cultural belief in providing good education to children has undoubtedly fostered the commercialization of education in China.

PART TWO: WHEN NEOLIBERALIST EFFICIENCY CLASHES WITH SOCIALIST IDEALS—UNEQUAL ACCESS AND INEQUALITY IN EDUCATION

Education Inequalities and Overcharging Students Within Chinese Cities

The social structural characteristics of communist China are important factors affecting the access and equal opportunities to education attainment. In the era of the planned economy, the Chinese institution *hukou* (household registration system) was the key determinant of the opportunity for receiving education, and even affected life chances of Chinese citizens. The *hukou* system was established in 1958 and it determined where one could live and what benefits one was entitled to enjoy. As a means to control population mobility, the *hukou* system had determined the different life chances between the people living in urban and rural areas of China (Liang, 2001). Because China has been ruled by a duality between urban and rural areas, people living in urban areas have enjoyed better social services and welfare provision provided by their urban work units systems, while citizens in rural China had enjoyed less privilege when compared to their urban counterparts. In addition, since major universities, particularly top tiered national universities, have long been concentrated in major Chinese cities; urban dwellers have enjoyed far more opportunities for higher education than their rural counterparts. Thus, the household registration has significantly limited the opportunities for rural residents to enjoy same access to education since the establishment of the People's Republic of China.

Even in the post-Mao era, the *hukou* system has still imposed institutional constraints for rural migrants to enjoy equal schooling/higher education opportunities despite the fact that many of them have stayed in urban China for work and residence because rural urban migration has become increasingly common throughout the country in the post-Mao era. Being regarded as temporary immigrants or 'floating population,' these new urban immigrants cannot obtain the similar social status as their urban counterparts because they are still classified as rural citizens without an urban *hukou* registration. Given that local governments are responsible for the financing of schools in their jurisdiction, if temporary migrant children were allowed to be admitted to local schools, it would still mean that they had to bear the financial burden (Liu, et al., 1998). Based upon the two student admissions criteria for schools in urban China, first, students must have residence within the local school district in the city; second, students must be registered in the school district as well, children of these rural migrants would encounter difficulties in getting their school places. Even though some local schools in cities accept these temporary migrant children, their parents have to pay the education endorsement fee (*jiaoyu zanzhu fei*), which is considerably high (Cao, 1997). Furthermore, many local governments and schools would overcharge children of the migrant workers when they were admitted, according to a report released by the *New York Times* regarding migrant scavengers in the Shanghai municipal dump, one of whom was working to pay 10,000 yuan for secondary education and 1,000 yuan for primary education (*New York Times*, 3 April 2006). Obviously, such an institutional barrier has disadvantaged the temporary migrant children in terms of educational opportunities because they are less likely to be enrolled in school than their urban and even rural counterparts (Wang & Zuo, 1999). Hence, it is clear that the household registration has built in institutional barriers for promoting equal access to education between urban and rural citizens in China.

As for the higher education sector, although admission is not restricted, *hukou* and students are free to apply for admissions to universities nationwide, charging excessive fees from students is also a problem. This is because since university financing has taken far more decentralized, privatized, and marketized modes to generate additional funding in support of the massification of higher education, the central government tends to shift its financial burdens to local governments, while local governments attempt to devolve the responsibilities to students, parents, private enterprises, local communities, and the society (Ngok & Kwong, 2003). In 2005, more than 20 percent of the total concurrent budgets of Chinese higher education institutions came from tuition fees. Unlike 'the good old days' when higher education was nearly free of charge, no student would be deprived of rights to receive higher education because of poverty. Such a public dominated mode of higher education system could provide more opportunities for social mobility (Levin & Xu, 2005, p. 53). It is clear that with the adoption of the neoliberal approach in running higher education, the sector has significantly transformed along privatizing and marketizing trends, thus changing the nature of higher education from public goods to private commodity in the post-Mao era (Chou, 2006; Wan, 2006).

Realizing the intensified financial difficulties for students to pay for their higher education, the government introduced the national student loan scheme in eight major cities, including Beijing and Shanghai in 1999 and then extended to the rest of the country in 2004 (*People's Daily*, 5 March 2007). The loan scheme, with a maximum annual loan of 6,000 yuan per person, mainly offers financial help to students being admitted by public universities. In addition, the government also provides various grants to students with financial difficulties. For example, the National Scholarship grants an annual amount of 4,000 yuan to support outstanding students, while the National Grant Scheme provides a monthly subsidy of 150 yuan to students from poor families. The government launched a "Green Path System," which guarantees that students would not lose their offers of admission because of financial difficulties (China Higher Education Student Information, 2007). Most recently, Premier Wen Jiabao announced to further increase government expenditure on grants and loans for university students from 1.8 billion yuan in 2006 to 20 billion yuan in 2008. Showing the government's determination to provide education to students coming from poorer families, Wen announced to waive the tuition fees of all normal universities and colleges (teaching training) under the Ministry of Education in order to attract more students to enroll in education training in order to provide more trained and qualified teachers for the less developed parts of China (*Mingpao*, 5 March 2007).

Despite the government's efforts to help students for resolving their financial difficulties in paying for higher education, the financial assistance from government is far from adequate. The loan schemes mainly offer help to those students who are admitted to public universities, especially those studying in national universities. Nonetheless, those studying in the *minban* institutions, regardless of whether they are normal *minban* or *gouyou minban*, have received limited or even no financial support. As a result, the rise of "privateness" in China's education with topping up tuition fees implies denying students from poor families access to quality education. Furthermore, the popularity of private tutoring or other supplementary education has inevitably resulted in social stratification as Bray (2007) rightly suggests. Although the government has made attempts to resolve the problems related to educational inequality, the foremost importance attached to education has resulted in more expenses imposed on families and parents. Hence, it is easier for those who are willing and financially able to pay for better education. But the same processes have still worsened the education inequalities within Chinese cities.

In short, the growing prominence of the "privateness" in educational finance and provision has indeed intensified the problems of education inequalities in China. As Yang (2007) argues, the education system in China has never been inclusive because of the *hukou* system, which has long been creating the institutional barriers for promoting equal access to education for both urban and rural residents. Our above discussions have clearly shown how the adherence to the neoliberal approach has further widened the urban rural divide, especially when those who can afford could enjoy far more educational opportunities. Although the government has attempted to address the issues by developing the student loan scheme as discussed earlier, such measures are insufficient to address the core of the problems—differential treatments between the urban and the rural residents, which favour the former but socially exclude the latter (Mok and Lo, 2007).

The Widening Regional and Urban Rural Divide

Educational inequality also exists in forms of urban rural disparity and regional disparity. This is because the government undertook a polarized policy of development between coastal and inland provinces as well as between the cities and the countryside. For instance, the government expenditure on education in China is highly uneven. According to official statistics, 214,913 million yuan were allocated to the coastal region,[1] constituting 55.8 percent of the educational budget. Regarding nongovernmental financial resources,[2] 36,361 million yuan were generated in the region, representing about 67.2 percent of the total. However, the population of the coastal region constitutes only 41.4 percent of the total population (MOE, 2004). When comparing the financing situation between these places, the total non-governmental financial resources of three selected wealthy regions grew to 3.45 billion yuan in 2004, but it recorded only 800 million yuan in the three poor regions (see Table 13.2) (MOE, 2004). Such a comparison has clearly shown the educational disparities between the rich and the poor regions in China. Putting the current developments of private/*minban* education into perspective, it is clear that the people living in the eastern coastal areas of China have disproportionately experienced the success of economic growth in the last two decades, and many of them are willing and have the financial ability to pay for these overseas programs.

Table 13.2 Non-state Educational Grant in Selected Regions in 2003

Region	Social Organizations and Individual	Donation and Fund-Raising	Total
National	25,901	10,459	36,360
Beijing	624	522	1,146
Tianjin	477	21	498
Shanghai	1,315	491	1,806
Gansu	186	57	243
Guangxi	251	97	348
Guizhou	150	58	208

unit: million *yuan*
Sources: MOE, 2004

With reference to the above educational funding figures (Table 13.2), it is obvious that the economic reform and development in the last thirty years has significantly improved the livelihood of those living in the coastal areas. Nonetheless, the same social and economic transformations have also intensified the coastal inland disparity. This has resulted in a concentration of education opportunities in the socioeconomically prosperous regions at the eastern coastal area. Regarding urban rural disparity, the most recent *China Human Development Report 2005* indicates that the gap between the rich and poor in China has been widening, while the richest 10 percent of urban dwellers controlled 34percent of urban wealth, but the poorest 10 percent held a mere 0.2 percent. When extending to compare the richest 20 percent of the urban population with the poorest 20 percent, their respective shares in 2002 were 51 percent and 3.2 percent. Commenting on this urban rural income gap, the United Nations commented that China has perhaps the highest income disparity in the world (UNDP, 2005). Regarding educational inequalities, recent studies have suggested that educational inequalities are larger the higher the level of schooling (Qian & Smyth, 2005; Rong & Shi, 2001).

Against a similar socioeconomic context, Yang sets out to examine educational opportunities between urban and rural China. He argues that the disparities in educational funding and provision between urban and rural hinterland has been a persistent problem since the foundation of the People's Republic of China (Yang, 2007). Like other developing countries being influenced by the global trends of privatization, marketization, and commodification of education, China has been appropriating the neoliberal policies, but the issues of social access and economic justice have emerged on the table, especially when the Chinese society is experiencing the growth of social class disparities (Luke & Ismail, 2007; Cheng, 2006).

Obviously, China now confronts the intensification of educational inequality. Although the country has experienced economic growth and educational expansion, the implementation of the education reforms with the neoliberal approach has inevitably led to "differential impacts upon different groups," as Mak (2007) described in other Asian societies. The economic reforms since the late 1970s have undoubtedly given rise to the new rich or new middle class in China (Lui, 2005; So, 2005), recent consumption studies have confirmed that as incomes rise, spending patterns change. It is projected that urban spending on recreation and education will grow by 9.5 percent annually during the next two decades, holding its place as one of the largest consumption categories in urban areas and making China one of the fastest growing recreation and education markets in the world (Farrell, et al., 2006, pp. 66–67). Our above discussions regarding the growing popularity of the commercialization of education and the increasing financial contributions from parents for children's education have clearly demonstrated the intensification of educational inequalities and disparities between the urban and the rural areas. Despite the fact that some of the urban families are eager to pay additional costs for enriching their children's education, many of them have raised the concerns of increasing financial burdens for education. For those living in urban China whose financial abilities might be better than people living in rural China, there are intense financial pressures for children's education. It is not difficult to imagine how citizens in rural China respond to the growing educational disparities. Obviously, inequalities in education are becoming unacceptable, especially when more people living in rural China have found themselves being socially and economically marginalized (Khan & Riskin, 2005; Keng, 2006), and many of them still face the problems of having no education opportunities or receiving only poor schooling (Murphy, 2004).

Bringing the 'Welfare' back in? Strategies in Promoting Education Equality

Realizing that educational inequalities have become intensified, the central government recognizes the importance of providing basic education to the citizens, hence, the school education sector has attracted relatively more state funding than that of higher education. With a continual increase in state funding to elementary education in recent years, the net enrollment rate of primary school children grew to 99 percent in 2005, while the gross enrollment rate of junior secondary schools reached 95 percent (China Education and Research Network, 2006). Since the promulgation of the Compulsory Education Law in 1986, nine-year compulsory education has been implemented and the universal senior secondary education has been in progress in economically developed areas. Nevertheless, compulsory education has not been implemented evenly across the country, particularly when educational development in many rural areas is far behind those urban areas. In response to this uneven educational development, the Chinese authorities have allocated extra resources to create more educational opportunities in rural areas during the 10th Five-Year Plan (2001–2005). For instance, in late 2005, the State Council decided to further reform the funding system of school education in rural areas, with the nine-year compulsory education funded by the general public finances (China Education and Research Network, 2006). Furthermore, during the Fifth Plenary Session of the 16th Central Committee of the CCP, the Chinese government further promulgated a strengthening and rejuvenating strategy through science and education, which clearly gives a higher priority to education when compared to other policy areas in the 11th Five-Year Plan (2006–2010). Among the various tasks, the consolidation of nine-year compulsory education in rural areas has been given high priority with the implementation of the "Two Basics" project to universalize nine-year compulsory education and to eradicate illiteracy among the middle and young aged groups in the western part of China. Regarding educational finances, the government decided to waive all the tuition and miscellaneous fees of students from rural areas of western China in 2006 in order to release parents from the heavy burden of educational expenses. The same policy was introduced to the central and eastern parts of the country in 2007 (China Education and Research Network, 2006). Most recently, Premier Wen Jiabao announced a hefty educational investment plan in his latest government report. A total of 85.85 billion yuan was allocated on education from central budget in 2007, showing a 41.7 percent increase over the previous year. In order to uphold the principles of educational equality and equity, part of the funding has been specifically used to support children from poor families to enhance them to get access to education. In addition, the government continues to provide free textbooks for students from lower socioeconomic backgrounds and living allowances for those studying in boarding schools. If these proposed policies are successfully implemented, about 150 million households with school-age children in rural areas would benefit (*People's Daily*, 5 March 2007).

In the last two decades, the central government has adopted a policy of decentralization in education. While the central ministry is only responsible for macro-management, the local governments, or, more specifically, the county and township governments, have to take up major responsibilities (including financing, personnel, and curriculum design) for achieving the policy goals of compulsory education. However, the revision of the Compulsory Education Law in mid-2006 has strengthened the role of provincial governments in governing education. The newly amended law requests provincial governments to play a coordinating role in assuring local governments' investment on compulsory education (MOE, 2006). According to Yang (2005), the revision probably is a way to tackle the problems related to corruption commonly found among local schools and education departments for charging excessive fees having given more operational autonomy and financial flexibility. (3)

CONCLUSION: SHIFTING POLICY PARADIGM FOR A HARMONIOUS SOCIETY

Our above observations have clearly shown that the Chinese authorities have been struggling for a balance between rapid economic growth, which would possibly further intensify urban rural divide and inequalities, and more balanced social developments, which would promote the socialist ideals for upholding social equality and equity. The attempted reversal from the market driven approach to a more welfare based paradigm is not without problems. The success of the policy paradigm shift depends very much on the state's political will during the course of the postcommunist transition characterized by the processes of reinventing capitalism or inventing a new kind of socialism.

Analyzing the present case study from a comparative perspective, will China move toward the attraction of capital flows to cities and the amelioration of the unequal distribution of knowledge, power, language, and material resources to growing populations, as Luke and Ismail (2007) project for the future developments for urban education in the Asia Pacific? Will China be developed into a society of fundamental social divisions between the poor and the rich in terms of education opportunities with the emergence of binary provision in education? Will the urban rural divide be further widened, with an education system receiving only marginal state support for the unemployed and working poor and a selective, private system operating on a user pays basis? If the above scenarios happen, the Chinese government will face immense pressures and tensions, especially as the present regime has to honor its longstanding stated focus on social equality. Therefore, the Chinese government has to revisit the policy orientations with emphasis on the extension of neoliberal market economics to education, with forces of marketization, privatization, and commodification of education. If the Chinese government fails to properly balance the tensions between economic efficiency and social inequality, these social problems could accumulate to create significant political pressures, which would result in political crisis, particularly when Chinese society has been divided by the diversity of economic and social interests. In order to strike a balance between a rapid economic growth and a balanced and healthy social development, the present government has called for developing a harmonious society.

Nowadays, "people-oriented development" and "harmonious society" have become increasingly popular jargon shaping the political discourse in China. According to Ngok (2005), under the new political discourse of "people-oriented development," the present political regime is more aware of the importance of the well-being of the people, especially devising new policy measures in helping those socially disadvantaged groups. When choosing policy instruments, more attention has been given to address the fundamental interests of the overwhelming majority of the country's people and minimize the gap between the rich and the poor. However, while the state is intensifying the funding for poverty relief and helping those less advantaged social groups, a "self-dependent spirit" is emphasized by the Chinese leaders (*People's Daily*, 12 February 2005). With a recognition that leaving the whole sector to be driven and guided by market forces because such market oriented strategies may fail to address the "social justice" and "social equality" by the Chinese leadership, a new social policy paradigm is in formation with emphasis on developing "people-oriented" social policy and social protection strategies in order to rectify the market failure in social/public policy provision. The government headed by Hu Jintao and Wen Jiabao has made attempts to address the inequality and overcharging issues in education. In 2006, both Hu and Wen chaired meetings over high-level meetings in the Communist Party's Politburo to stress the importance of education and call for a shift from the market driven approach to a more welfare based education system. In these meetings, senior leaders called on governments at all levels to make the development of education a strategic priority and to commit a public education system that can be accessed by all. In order to achieve such policy objectives, the Ministry of Education has started to develop a new mechanism to calculate college costs and cap university tuition fees. In addition, students from underdeveloped central and western regions have begun to receive cheap bank loans or allowances to enable them to attend schools or colleges (Li, 2007). In this regard, the Chinese authorities probably are making attempts to balance between "market efficiency" and "social equality," but we still need to examine how effective policies are implemented in different localities. The best scenario is that the Chinese government would succeed in developing appropriate regulatory frameworks in governing the market in social policy without slowing down its economic growth. Given that this could be the biggest challenge to the CCP in the future, the development of whether the new notion of "people-oriented" approach can promote better social policy and social protection for the Chinese people when China's economy is becoming increasingly globalized would be worthy of attention.

NOTES

1. Coastal region here includes Beijing, Tianjin, Hebei, Liaoning, Shanghai, Jiangsu, Zhejiang, Zhejiang, Fujian, Shandong, Guangdong, Guangxi, Hainan.
2. Non-government financial resources here refer to input from social organizations and individuals and donation.

3. Since the completion of the 17th National Congress of the Communist Party of China, children of migrant workers (peasant workers) have been provided with free education in China. The principal author of this chapter, Ka Ho Mok, went to the Zhejiang area in China to examine how education is delivered and found that these children can now enjoy free education in some economically prosperous areas in the eastern coastal area (Fieldwork, October 2007, Ningbo and Hangzhou, China). The authors want to thank the Chiang Ching-Kuo foundation in supporting the research project 'A Comparative Study of Changing University Governance in China and Taiwan.' Part of the field observations reported on this chapter are based upon the fieldwork funded by the foundation.

REFERENCES

Bluebook of Chinese Society 2007. (2007) Beijing: Social Sciences Academic Press.

Cao, H. (1997) Where to put their school desks?, *China New Digest, 315*, pp. 3–6.

Chen, C.G & Yu, Q.Y. (2005) *Zoujin Dazhonghua: 21 Shijichu Guangzhou Shi Gaodeng Jiaoyu Fazhan Yanjiu (Towards Massification: Research on Guangzhou's Higher Education Development in Early 21st Century).* Guangzhou: Jinan daxue chubanshe.

Cheng, E. (2006) China: Capitalist restoration worsens inequality. *Green Left Weekly*, 12 April, pp. 1–4.

Cheng, K.M. (1990) Financing education in mainland China: What are the real problems? *Issues and Studies*, 3, pp. 54–75.

China Daily (Hong Kong Edition). Various issues in 2004, 2006, and 2007.

China Education and Research Network. (2006) *The educational development during the 10th 5-year plan.* Retrieved June 18, 2006 from http://www.edu.cn/news.

China Education Yearbook 1998. (1999). Beijing: People's Press.

China Education Yearbook 2004. (2005). Beijing: People's Press.

China Higher Education Student Information. (2007) Retrieved June 18, 2006 from http://www.chsi.com.cn

Chou, P. (2006) *Taiwan higher education on the crossroad: Its implication for China.* Paper presented at the Senior Seminar of Education 2020 Program. 6–11 September, East-West Center, Hawaii.

Cummings, W. (1996) Asian values, education and development. *Compare*, 26 (3), pp. 287–304.

Farrell, D., Gersch, U.A., & Stephenson, E. (2006) The value of China's emerging middle class. *The McKinsey Quarterly*, Special Edition.

Keng, C.W. (2006) China's unbalanced economic growth. *Journal of Contemporary China*, 15 (46), pp. 183–214.

Khan, A.R. & Riskin, C. (2005) China's household income and its distribution, 1995 and 2002. *The China Quarterly*, 182, pp. 356–384.

Levin, H.M. & Xu, Z.Y. (2005) Issues in the expansion of higher education in the People's Republic of China. *The China Review*, 5(1), pp. 33–59.

Li, R. (2007) Casualties of the rush to profit from schooling. *South China Morning Post*, January 27, 2007.

Liang, Z. (2001) The age of migration in China. *Population and Development Review*, 27, pp. 499–524.

Lin, T. & Chen, Y. (2004) "The plights and outlets of public primary school and middle school in the course of institution changing." *Forum on contemporary education*, 5, pp. 45–49.

Liu, C., Taibin, L., & Jun, L. (1998) A case study of migrant sponsored schools in western Shanghai. In S. Zhang, W. Le, C. Xu, and C. Song (Eds.) *The floating population in Shanghai:Current situation and future prospects*. Shanghai: East China Normal University Press.

Lui, T.L. (2005) Bringing class back in. *Critical Asian Studies*, 37 (3), pp. 473–480.

Luke, A. & Ismail, M. (2007) Introduction: reframing urban education in the Asia Pacific. In A. Luke & M. Ismail, M. (Eds.) *Handbook of urban education*. London: Routledge.

Mak, G. (2007) Women in Asian education and society: Whose gains in whose perspectives? In A. Luke & M. Ismail, M. (Eds.) Handbook of urban education. London: Routledge.

Min, W.F. (2004) Chinese higher education: The legacy of the past and the context of the future. In P. Altbach and T. Umakoshi (Eds.) *Asian universities: Historical perspectives and contemporary challenges*. Baltimore: The John's Hopkins University Press.

Mingpao, March 5, 2007.

Ministry of Education [MOE]. (2004). *China educational finance statistical yearbook 2004*. Beijing: Zhongguo Tongji Chubanshe.

———. (2006) *China educational finance statistical yearbook 2006*. Beijing: Zhongguo Tongji Chubanshe.

Mok, K.H. (1996) Marketization and decentralization: development of education and paradigm shift in social policy. *Hong Kong Public Administration*, 5(1), pp. 35–56.

———. (2005) Riding over socialism and global capitalism: Changing education governance and social policy paradigms in post-Mao China. *Comparative Education*, 41(2), pp. 217–242.

———. (2007) Fieldwork and field interviews conducted in Ningbo and Hangzhan, China for the project 'A Comparative Study of Changing University Governance in China and Taiwan. Funded by Chiang Ching-Kuo Foundation.

———. (2008) The growing importance of the privateness in education: challenges for higher education governance in China. *Compare*, forthcoming.

Mok, K.H. and Lo, Y.W. (2007) The impacts of neo-liberalism on China's higher education. *Journal for Critical Education Policy Studies*, 5(1) May 2007. Available at http://www.jceps.com

Mok, K.H. & Ngok, K.L. (2008) One country, diverse systems: Politics of educational decentralization and challenges for regulatory state in post-Mao China. *China Review*, forthcoming.

Mok, K.H., Wang, Y.C. and Walker, R. (2008) Embracing the market: examining the consequences for education, housing and health in Chinese cities. Paper presented at the Symposium on *The Quest for Social Cohesion in Greater China: Challenges for Social Policy and Governance*. 20 June, 2008. Centre of Asian Studies, University at Hong Kong.

Murphy, R. (2004) Turning Chinese peasants into modern citizens: Population quality, demographic transition, and primary schools. *The China Quarterly*, 177, pp. 1–20.

National Bureau of Statistics of China (NBSC). (2005). *China statistical yearbook 2005*. Beijing: Zhongguo Tongji Chubanshe.

The New York Times, April 3, 2006.

Ngok, K.L. (2005) *Redefining development in China: Towards a new policy paradigm for the new century?* Paper presented at International Conference on Changing Governance and Public Policy paradigms: Asian Perspectives, Zhongshan University, November, Guangzhou.

Ngok, K.L. & Kwong, J. (2003) Globalization and educational restructuring in China. In K.H. Mok and A. Welch, A. (Eds.) *Globalization and educational restructuring in the Asia Pacific Region*. Basingstoke: Palgrave Macmillan.

People's Daily, February 12, 2005; 5 March 2007.

Qian, X.L. & Smyth, R. (2005) Measuring regional inequality of education in China: Widening cost-inland gap or widening rural-urban gap?" *ABERU Discussion Paper,* 12, pp. 1–12.

Rong, X.L. & Shi, T.J. (2001) Inequality in Chinese education. *Journal of Contemporary China,* 10(26), pp. 107–124.

Shanghai Research Institute of Educational Sciences. (2005) The causes, implications and trends of the policy of transformation in public schools. *Education Development and Research,* 8B, pp. 16–23.

So, A.Y.C. (2005) Beyond the logic of capital and the polarization model: The state, market reforms, and the plurality of class conflict in China. *Critical Asian Studies,* 37 (3), pp. 481–494.

So, W.Y. (2006) Privatisation. In Tubilewicz, C. (ed.) *Critical issues in contemporary China.* London: Routledge and Hong Kong: Open University of Hong Kong Press.

United Nations Development Programme (UNDP). (2005) *China's human development report 2005.* Washington, D.C: United Nations Development Programme.

Wan, Y.M. (2006) Expansion of Chinese higher education since 1998: Its causes and outcomes. *Asia Pacific Education Review,* 7 (1), pp. 19–31.

Wang, F. & Zuo, X. (1999) Inside China's cities: Institutional barriers and opportunities for urban migrants. *American Economic Review,* 89 (2), pp. 276–280.

Wang, Y.B. (2007) *China's higher education on a overpass of 4-fold transitions.* Paper presented to the Video seminar series of *Universities and Ideas.* April 30, 2007. Zhejiang University: Hangzhou China.

Wei, Y.T. & Zhang, G.C. (1995) *A historical perspective on non-governmental higher education in China.* Paper presented to the International Conference on Private Education in Asia and the Pacific Region. University of Xiamen, Xiamen.

Weil, R. (2006) Conditions of the working classes in China. *Monthly Review,* 58 (2). Retrieved June 18, 2006 from http://canadiandimension.com/articles/2006/07/29/596

Wong, L. & Flynn, N. (eds.) (2001) *The market in Chinese social policy.* Basingstoke: Palgrave.

Yang, D.P. (2004) The new development paradigm and China's education. In X. Yu, et al., (eds.), *Analysis and forecast on China's social development 2005.* Beijing: Social Sciences Academic Press.

———. (2005) Towards social justice:Education in 2005. In X. Yu et al., (Eds.) *Analysis and forecast on China's social development 2006.* Beijing: Social Sciences Academic Press.

Yang, R. (2007) Urban-rural disparities in educational equality: China's pressing challenge in a context of economic growth and political change. In A. Luke & M. Ismail, M. (Eds.) *Handbook of urban education.* London: Routledge.

Zhu, Q.F. (2005) Social and economic indicators: Analysis and assessment. In X. Yu et al., (Eds.) *Analysis and forecast on China's social development 2006.* Beijing: Social Sciences Academic Press.

Contributors

Dr. Gian Carlo Delgado-Ramos is an economist from the National Autonomous University of Mexico (UNAM) with doctoral studies at the Autonomous University of Barcelona, Spain. He is a researcher of the program "The World in the 21st Century" at the Interdisciplinary Research Centre on Sciences and Humanities, UNAM. His main research areas are "strategic natural resources and international security," as well as "social, economical and environmental aspects of high technology development". Author of several papers published in America and Europe. His latest book: *War for the Invisible: business, uncertainty and implications of nanotechnology* (Ceiich, UNAM. Mexico, 2008). Correspondence: giandelgado@unam.mx Blog: www.giandelgado.net

Adam Davidson-Harden (PhD Education, University of Western Ontario) is a Social Sciences and Humanities Research Council of Canada postdoctoral fellow at the Faculty of Education, Queen's University, Kingston, Ontario. His primary research interests are in the political economy of education and social policy in the context of neoliberalism. He also does work in the areas of peacebuilding and development.

Fuat Ercan is professor at the Department of Development Studies at Marmara University, Istanbul. He is the author of *Money and Capitalism* (in Turkish), *Capitalism and Education: Criticism of Neo-liberal Education Policies* (in Turkish), *Societies and Economies* (in Turkish), and several other books. He has published numerous articles on Marxist critical political economy both in Turkish and English. Correspondence: ercanfu@yahoo.com, ercanfu@marmara.edu.tr

Julián Gindin is completing his PhD in sociology at the University Research Institute of Rio de Janeiro (IUPERJ), with a scholarship from the National Council for Scientific and Technological Development (CNPq). He has worked on Argentinean and Latin American Unionism; specifically on Teacher Unionism in Latin America as a researcher within the Laboratory of Public Policy/State University of Rio de Janeiro (Brazil). Correspondence: jgindin@iuperj.br

Dave Hill is professor of education policy, University of Northampton, UK. For twenty years he was a local and regional political and labor union leader in England. He cofounded the Hillcole Group of Radical Left Educators in Britain in 1989 and, inter alia, coedited a trilogy on schooling and inequality for Cassell and Kogan Page. He is Routledge series editor for *Education and Neoliberalism* and also Routledge series editor for *Education and Marxism*. He is chief editor of the international refereed academic journal, the *Journal for Critical Education Policy Studies*. Correspondence: dave.hill35@btopenworld.com and dave.hill@ northampton.ac.uk

Ravi Kumar teaches at the Department of Sociology, Jamia Millia Islamia University, New Delhi. He has written over a dozen articles and papers on education, communalism, and politics. His publications include *The Politics of Imperialism and Counterstrategies* (coedited, Delhi: Aakar Books, 2004), *The Crisis of Elementary Education in India* (edited, Sage, 2006), *Global Neoliberalism and Education and its Consequences*, (Forthcoming, coedited, New York: Routledge). His specializations are social movements, identity politics, social theory, and sociology of knowledge. Correspondence: ravik05@gmail.com

Ka Ho Mok is Associate Dean of Faculty of Social Sciences and Professor in the Department of Social Work and Social Administration, University of Hong Kong. Previously he was Chair in East Asian Studies and Founding Director of the Centre for East Asian Studies. He has been researching and publishing extensively in comparative education policy in East Asia, contemporary social and political development studies in China and East Asia, and comparative governance and public policy in East Asia. In the last decade, he has published 12 books / monographs and numerous articles. He is founding editor of the *Journal of Asian Public Policy*. Correspondence: KH.Mok@bristol.ac.uk

Enver Motala was a lawyer for the independent trade union movement during the apartheid era and also played a significant role in the anti-apartheid education movement. After the first democratic elections, he was appointed the deputy director–general of education in the province of Gauteng. He is presently an associate of the Education Policy Consortium for whom he has coordinated research projects on democracy, human rights, and social justice in education in South Africa. He has also done similar work for the Nelson Mandela Foundation. Correspondence: emotala@lantic.net

Thomas Muhr holds a German teaching degree, two British master's degrees, and is currently completing his ESRC-funded PhD in the Centre for Globalisation, Education & Societies at the University of Bristol

(UK). Thomas works on different aspects of the Latin American revolutionary processes, with a particular focus on Venezuela's Bolivarian higher education, social justice, and human rights within the democratic socialist development model and its regionalization and globalization under the Bolivarian Alternative for the Americas (ALBA). Correspondence: Thomas.Muhr@bristol.ac.uk or t.muhr@gmx.de

Ahmad Mukhtar works as Commercial Secretary in the permanent mission of Pakistan to the WTO, Geneva, Switzerland. Apart from his work with the board of investment and Ministry of Commerce in Pakistan, he has worked with USAID and EU as independent consultant. His research interests in WTO are the Trade in Services (GATS), Intellectual Property (TRIPS), Biotechnology, and Agriculture. He has written various articles and research papers. He has taught various courses at the masters level in different universities as visiting professor. Correspondence: ahmadmukhtar@gmail.com

João M. Paraskeva was born in Mozambique. A former school teacher in Southern Africa, he is currently a professor at the Institute of Education and Psychology at the University of Minho, at Braga, Portugal, and visiting professor at the University of Coruña, Spain, and the Federal University of Pelotas, Brazil. He is founder and senior editor of *Revista Currículo sem Fronteiras—A Journal for a Critical and Emancipatory Education.* Among his more than 20 books published are *Marxismo e Educação—Volume 1, Ideologia, Cultura e Currículo* His research interests are anchored in critical neo-Marxist and post-structural approaches. Correspondence: paraskeva@iep.uminho.pt

Jill Pinkney Pastrana is associate professor at University of Wisconsin, Eau Claire, Foundations of Education. Her ethnographic research focuses on themes of educational policy within neoliberal contexts. Former director of research "Innovación Educacional" in the Programa de Innovación a la Formación de Profesores, de la Universidad de la Frontera y el Ministerio de Educación de Chile, 1998–1999. Her current research is on high school student activism and education policy in Chile. Her primary interests are critical pedagogy, education transformation, and popular participation within marginalized contexts. Correspondence: pastrajp@uwec.edu

Brian Ramadiro is an educational and political activist and the deputy director of the Nelson Mandela Institute for Education and Rural Development at the University of Fort Hare. His political tradition is pan-Africanist and socialist. His political work has been around youth issues, 'race' and culture, and education. His current projects include the promotion of bilingualism and multilingualism in education and rural development. Correspondence: bramadiro@ufh.ac.za

Ellen Rosskam is Southeast Europe Policy Scholar at the Woodrow Wilson International Center for Scholars conducting research on the liberalization of education in Turkey. She is also a Policy Scholar under the Division of International Security Studies at the Woodrow Wilson Center, as the Principal Investigator of a study in 200 countries of 800,000 civil aviation workers. She is visiting professor, University of Massachusetts, Lowell, USA, and visiting Senior Fellow, University of Surrey, England. Dr. Rosskam is a social protection specialist working internationally. She has led global, regional, and national level research projects, and has worked in over forty countries. Her latest books include *Excess Baggage: Leveling the Load and Changing the Workplace* (Baywood, NY), 2007, and *Winners or Losers? Liberalizing public services* (Ed. Rosskam), (ILO, Geneva), 2006. Correspondence: eerosskam@yahoo.com

Dr. John Saxe-Fernández teaches in the School of Political and Social Sciences of the National Autonomous University of Mexico (UNAM), where he leads "The World in the 21st century" research program of the Interdisciplinary Research Center on Sciences and Humanities (Ceiich). His latest book: *Terror and Empire* (Random House-Mondadori. Mexico, 2006). His next book: *State of Exception. Grijalbo.* Gian Carlo Delgado-Ramos and John Saxe-Fernández have published several books together such as *Imperialism and World Bank* (Centro Marinello. Cuba, 2004; Popular. España, 2004) and *Economic Imperialism in Mexico* (Arena. México, 2005). Correspondence: saxe@servidor.unam.mx Blog: www.jsaxef.blogspot.com

Daniel Schugurensky is associate professor at the Ontario Institute for Studies in Education of the University of Toronto (OISE/UT), and associate director of the Center for Urban and Community Studies at the University of Toronto. His current areas of teaching and research focus on the political economy of education, popular education, university community relationships, citizenship learning, and participatory democracy. Correspondence: dschugurensky@oise.utoronto.ca Website: http://fcis.oise.utoronto.ca/~daniel_schugurensky/

Touorouzou Hervé Somé is a former Fulbright scholar and teaches at D'Youville College, Buffalo, New York, where he teaches graduate courses in social and philosophical foundations of education, education research, and critical issues in education. He taught English as a foreign language in Burkina Faso, then became a teacher trainer at the English Inspection, in the Ministry of Secondary and Higher Education (MESSRS, Ouagadougou). His academic interests include economics of education, education finance, globalization and education, teacher development, cost sharing in higher education, equity pedagogy, and qualitative research methods. Correspondence: thsome63@yahoo.com.

Ferda Uzunyayla has a master's degree at the Department of Development Studies at Marmara University, Istanbul. Her dissertation is entitled "Changing Turkish Education Policies in the Integration Process to the Europe Union."

Salim Vally is a senior researcher/lecturer at the Education Policy Unit, School of Education, University of Witwatersrand. He was a regional executive member of the high school South African Students Movement until its banning in 1977. In 1979 he left South Africa as a result of fierce repression by the erstwhile apartheid regime. He returned to South Africa to teach in township schools, and spent eight years as a trade unionist in one of the newly formed independent trade unions. He is the spokesperson of the Anti-War Coalition and the Palestine Solidarity Committee. Correspondence: salim.vally@wits.ac.za

Antoni Verger was awarded a PhD from the Universitat Autònoma de Barcelona (UAB) for his work on WTO/GATS and Higher Education. Since 2003 he has been a member of the research group 'Analysis of Social Policies Seminar' that is part of the Department of Sociology of the UAB. Currently, he is a postdoctoral researcher of the AMIDSt (Amsterdam Institute for Metropolitan and International Development Studies) of the Universiteit van Amsterdam. His principal research topics are globalization and education politics, as well as education and international development. Correspondence: a.verger@uva.nl

Yat Wai Lo is Instructor at The Hong Kong Polytechnic University and PhD Candidate of Centre for East Asian Studies, University of Bristol, UK.

Index

UNIVERSITY OF WOLVERHAMPTON
LEARNING & INFORMATION SERVICES